R. Alastair Campbell is Tutor in New Testament at Spurgeon's College, London.

John Riches is Professor of Divinity and Biblical Criticism, University of Glasgow.

Studies of the New Testament
and Its World

EDITED BY JOHN RICHES

The Elders

The Elders:
Seniority within Earliest Christianity

R. ALASTAIR CAMPBELL

T&T CLARK
EDINBURGH

T&T CLARK LTD
59 GEORGE STREET
EDINBURGH EH2 2LQ
SCOTLAND

First published 1994

ISBN 0 567 09702 1

British Library Cataloguing-in-Publication Data
A catalogue record for this book is available from the British Library

Typeset by Trinity Typesetting, Edinburgh
Printed and bound in Great Britain by Bookcraft, Avon

for Elizabeth

Contents

CONTENTS

Preface

Questions of church order have always interested me since my student days when the Anglican-Methodist union scheme foundered on the rock of unwarranted claims for episcopacy and ordination. I subsequently joined a Baptist church, eventually becoming a Baptist minister, so that the problems of the Apostolic Succession came to seem rather remote, but the onset of charismatic renewal forced the Free Churches in turn to look again at their structures of organisation. Many Baptist churches in Great Britain began to appoint elders in addition to their traditional deacons, and believed that in doing so they were returning to the church order of the New Testament.

It will be clear to those who read to the end of this book that I do not endorse that belief, but I have not written this book in order to make that point. I set out on the road of doctoral research with no clear idea of where I was going, and when my studies in the Pastoral Epistles crystallized around the topic of the elders, I pursued it for its intrinsic interest, reaching the conclusion that if the development of church order in the New Testament was less variegated than some scholars have supposed, it is also less readily applicable today than many church people hope. For if the elders were an ever-present feature of the New Testament churches and their social world, they still offer no obvious precedent for any office of eldership that exists, or might be revived, in our churches today.

This book, then, is an edited version of my London doctoral thesis, written in the service neither of reform nor reaction, and with no intention of advancing the claims of any particular Christian denomination. Exegesis without presuppositions is impossible, of course, but disinterested research is not. If this study enables us to understand more clearly what the ancient writers mean when they speak to us of the elders, it will have accomplished its purpose.

We will understand better where we have come from — and why we cannot hope to return!

In offering this book for publication, I would like to acknowledge most especially the help I have received from my supervisor, Professor Graham Stanton, of King's College, London, and to thank him for his unfailing patience and encouragement.

In preparing my thesis for publication I have received many helpful comments from my examiners, Professor Leslie Houlden and Dr John Muddiman, and also from Dr Joel Marcus and Dr John Barclay, who read the script on behalf of the publishers and suggested many improvements without which the book would be more flawed than it now is.

I also wish to acknowledge gratefully the help I have received from Dr Bruce Winter and Tyndale House, Cambridge, who provided a grant in the early stages of my research and extended their hospitality to me on many occasions.

I would like to thank the Council of Spurgeon's College for encouraging me to undertake this work while in their employ, and for their generous provision of sabbatical leave in which to complete it, and my colleagues at the College of their stimulating discussions and supportive fellowship.

Finally, I wish to pay tribute to my wife, Elizabeth, without whose confidence and patience this study would never have been completed.

The abbreviations used for ancient sources and for journals and standard works of reference are those recommended in the *Handbook of the Society of Biblical Literature* (1991), pp. 201–10. Abbreviations which do not appear there are listed at the head of the list of Works Cited. Unless otherwise stated the text and translation of classical Greek authors is that printed in the relevant volumes of the *Loeb Classical Library* (LCL), and the abbreviations used are those of the *Oxford Classical Dictionary* (OCD).

Spurgeon's College
February 1994

Chapter One
Introduction

During the last century and a half, the organization of the earliest Christian churches and the origins of the Christian ministry, as they are revealed, and in part concealed, by the New Testament documents, have been the subject of many impressive studies. Indeed, the ground has been fought over so many times, that it must appear hardly possible at this time of day to contribute anything new to the discussion. Surely what can be known is well documented, and what has not been discovered is lost for ever? And surely the areas of disagreement are well enough marked out and the positions of the various disputants, being grounded in diverse Christian traditions and communions, are firmly entrenched? In his survey of the last twenty-five years of New Testament scholarship N. T. Wright identified four areas in which he felt that real progress had been made, but ecclesiology was not among them.[1]

Yet in all this debate the role of the elders in the New Testament churches has suffered neglect. They have rarely been the explicit subject of study, tending instead to be referred to in the course of studies that focus on other things.[2] 'Elders' appears regularly as an entry in Bible dictionaries and other works of reference, but these articles usually relay consensus opinions rather than present the

---

[1] Neill and Wright, *Interpretation*, pp. 360–450. The areas are: the religious background of the NT, the life of Jesus in its historical context, the meaning and message of Paul, and the study of the Fourth Gospel. He did not, however, rule out the possibility of further advance in the area of NT ecclesiology (p. 367).

[2] W. Michaelis published a short study entitled *Das Ältestenamt* in 1953, but this is more a synthesis of NT teaching than a socio-historical enquiry.

THE ELDERS

fruit of original research.[3] It is twenty years since A. E. Harvey challenged the still widely held view that eldership in the early church was an office derived from the synagogue.[4] The present study endorses his conclusions and seeks to build on them.

This comparative neglect of the elders is due to the way in which debate about the origins of the Christian ministry has been dominated by two questions: the relationship of elders to bishops, and the relationship of *charisma* to office. The first debate was in response to J. B. Lightfoot's influential demonstration that the words 'overseers' and 'elders' refer to the same people in the literature of the apostolic and sub-apostolic periods.[5] It was pursued mainly by English scholars,[6] and flourished in the first half of this century, but was to some extent kept alive by discussions within the ecumenical movement. The second debate goes back to R. Sohm's protest (in 1892) against a legal and institutional understanding of the church and its ministry, and has been given new life by the charismatic movement and by the renewed interest in Paul's teaching on spiritual gifts. Until recently it has tended to flourish in Germany.

In both these debates interest in the elders has been at a discount. In the first debate the focus has been on the bishops, and the question of when and how a single bishop emerged. The existence of the presbyterate, as an office derived from the synagogue, has simply been assumed. In the second debate the elders have been viewed negatively, as antithetical to the charismatic understanding of the church which it is supposed Paul held. In German Protestant scholarship, still heavily influenced by F. C. Baur's antithesis between Jewish and Pauline Christianity, the elders have been seen as holders of an office that was Jewish in origin, and legalistic in

---

[3] An exception is the article, πρεσβύς, contributed by Bornkamm to *TDNT*. This is the standard scholarly treatment of the subject, unsurpassed in its comprehensiveness and detail. It is hardly possible to add to Bornkamm's evidence when it comes to matters of fact, but his interpretation of that evidence is open to question, especially where it relates to the influence of the synagogue.

[4] Harvey, 'Elders', *JTS*, 25 (1974), pp. 318–32.

[5] Lightfoot, *Philippians*, pp. 93–7, 179–267. First edition in 1868.

[6] Lindsay, *Church*, Streeter, *Primitive*, Farrer, 'Ministry' and Dix, 'Ministry'.

character.[7] Its introduction into Pauline churches at a later stage is seen as a decline.

During the last twenty years there has been an explosion of interest in the social world of the first Christians, and especially in the Graeco-Roman household as the matrix of the early churches. This has already prompted reconsideration of local church leadership in the acknowledged letters of Paul,[8] in the post-Pauline churches,[9] and in the Apostolic Fathers.[10] However, there has been no full-length study that has concentrated on the elders as such, or that uses the fruits of recent study of the early Christian household to throw fresh light on the old questions of the nature and origin of the office of the elders in the Christian church, and its relationship to that of the overseers.

The present study will take as its starting point the influential work of Rudolf Sohm (1841–1917), and the way in which his views have influenced New Testament scholarship and helped to produce what may fairly be called a consensus view, chiefly among Protestant scholars. Sohm, of course, was only one of a number of scholars who in the nineteenth century helped to form this consensus, among whom may be mentioned Baur, Ritschl, Lightfoot and Hatch. While they differed from one another on many points, they converged in the opinion that the increase of the church's organization entailed the decrease in its spiritual power. The selection of Sohm as our point of reference is justified because of the way in which his views have remained influential in the century following the publication of *Kirchenrecht*.[11] From a representative sampling of the scholars who took up Sohm's legacy we shall see that while Sohm's

[7] One of the most influential exponents of this view this century has been H. von Campenhausen, *Ecclesiastical Authority and Spiritual Power in the Church of the First Three Centuries* (1953, E.T. 1969).

[8] Chapple, 'Local Leadership'.

[9] MacDonald, *Pauline Churches*.

[10] Maier, *Social Setting*.

[11] In an article entitled, 'R. Sohm nous interroge encore', (*RSPT* 57 (1973), pp. 288–94), Y. Congar lists 117 works dealing with Sohm's views.

understanding of *charisma* has been remembered, what he had to say about the elders has largely been ignored.[12]

We shall begin by examining the identity and role of the elders in a variety of Jewish contexts prior to the New Testament, including Ancient Israel and Jewish national life in the Second Temple period, as well as the first-century synagogue and the Qumran community. It will be shown that the term is exceedingly vague and flexible, connoting honour and leadership, but denoting no particular office that the churches might be thought to have 'taken over'. A survey of the history and literature of the Graeco-Roman world will show that while οἱ πρεσβύτεροι was not usually the title of an office, here too older people enjoyed a respect derived from the prominence of their family and their position within it. The findings of comparative anthropology will confirm this by suggesting that while the status of older people has always been eroded in urbanized societies, such as the Graeco-Roman empire increasingly was, this erosion is much less when people live in extended families, such as those in which the earliest churches were born.

Successive chapters follow on the letters of Paul, the Acts of the Apostles, and the Pastoral Epistles. In them it will be suggested that the household context is itself the best explanation of the non-appearance of the term 'the elders' in Paul's writings. We shall see that the household church is a neglected feature of the evidence of Acts. Recognition of the importance of the house-church in Acts will suggest that there is actually no gulf to be bridged between 'Pauline' and 'Jewish-Christian' church order. This in turn calls in question the view that the Pastorals witness to a merging of patterns of church order originally different. Instead we return to Sohm's view of the elders and see how it can be established on a better foundation. In this way, what the Pastorals say about church offices is located more exactly in the developing story of the churches' leadership. Finally, the development of the elders is traced into the second century to see how the Christian presbyter emerged as an

---

[12] A much fuller account of the debate than has been possible here can be found in Brockhaus, *Charisma*, pp. 7–94, and most recently in Burtchaell, *Synagogue*, pp. 60–179.

individual office-holder out of an institution that had always hitherto been corporate. Once again the household context of the
churches is shown to illuminate the situations that have prompted
both the letters of Clement and Ignatius.

This study is thus socio-historical in character. It proceeds on the
assumption that, since earliest Christianity was amongst other things
a social phenomenon, the study of the first churches will be illumi-
nated by a better understanding of their social context. In particular
it will be suggested that a better understanding of the role of 'the
elders', and the respect in which they were held, within patriarchal
societies very different from our own, is essential if we are not to
misunderstand the place of the elders in the church. Use will be
made of all three methods of study identified by G. Theissen,[13]
constructive, analytic and comparative, in order to understand the
Sitz im Leben of the New Testament documents and the role of the
elders within it. Theissen's own example of the use of constructive
methods is relevant to this study also, namely the list of leaders in
the church at Antioch (Acts 13:1–3). The same kind of procedure
can be applied to nearly contemporary Jewish material in order to
see how the term 'elders' functioned in first-century Jewish society.
Analytical methods will be applied to texts like the Pastorals, or the
letters of Clement and Ignatius, to suggest what is really going on,
in this case the concentration of power in the hands of one of the
elders with consequent loss of status by others. Comparative proce-
dures will involve looking at evidence both ancient and modern
that throws light on the role and status of the elderly so as to draw
analogies that will help us to understand New Testament texts by
illuminating the context which they take for granted.

The Legacy of Sohm

Rudolf Sohm was not by training a theologian or biblical scholar,
but an academic lawyer who published studies in jurisprudence. He

---

[13] Theissen, *Social Setting*, pp. 177–94.

is thus an unlikely source of views which have continued to be influential in both New Testament studies and sociology throughout the twentieth century. Yet the opening chapter of his book, *Kirchenrecht*,[14] in which he sets out to describe early Christianity, was not only to influence successive generations of scholars who agreed in detail neither with his methods nor his conclusions, but was also to provide Max Weber with the concept of *charisma* which in a secularized form has been an important subject of study by subsequent sociologists.[15]

Sohm was a devout Protestant, and his work was written to show how primitive Christianity degenerated into Catholicism.[16] That Catholicism was an aberration was a view Sohm shared with other Protestant scholars of the time, notably Lightfoot and Hatch in England and Harnack in Germany, but he differed from them in what he saw as the reason for its rise. Where Hatch attributed the decline of primitive Christianity to its achieving the status of a State religion, and Harnack to the corruption of simple faith by Hellenistic speculation, Sohm placed the blame on church law: the tendency of religious people to prefer to operate by law, rather than grace. This, Sohn insisted, is the original sin of the Christian movement. Where Hatch explained the forms of earliest Christianity in purely natural terms, its various offices modelled on Greek and Jewish counterparts, Sohm insisted that the church at its conception, as witnessed to by the New Testament, was a purely spiritual reality.[17]

---

[14] *Kirchenrecht* was published in 1892. It has never been translated into English, and copies are extremely scarce in England, even in University libraries.

[15] This debt is acknowledged by Weber himself. See Weber, *Theory*, p. 328. But Weber secularized the concept. 'Weber did not restrict his usage of "charisma" to refer only to manifestations of divinity... . All forms of genius, in the original sense of the word as permeation by the 'spirit', are as much instances of the category of charismatic things as is religious prophecy.' Shils, 'Charisma', p. 200, and *IESS*, Vol. 2, p. 387. See also Haley, 'Charisma', p. 196: 'By generalizing the concept "charisma", Weber emptied the idea, gift of grace, first of its Christian meaning, finally of all Christian content.'

[16] Sohm does not use the term *Frühkatholizismus*, which appears to have been coined at around the turn of the century, speaking simply of *Katholizismus*. Cf. Dunn, *Unity*, p. 341, who refers to Neufeld, '*Frühkatholizismus*', *ZKT*, 94 (1972), pp. 1–28. See also Lightfoot, *Philippians*, p. 207.

[17] Linton, *Problem*, pp. 49–67, Haley, 'Charisma', pp. 185–97.

The texts on which Sohm chiefly builds his theory of the church's original purity are the Pauline passages about the body of Christ and the gifts of the Spirit (1 Cor 12 and Rom 12), together with the Matthean ἐκκλεσία passages (Mt 16:16–19 and 18:15–20), supplemented by the evidence of the recently discovered *Didache*. These texts are treated as interpreting one another, and as direct evidence for the ways things were, and were understood by all. Just as there was only one political ἐκκλεσία in a Greek city-state, and just as in the Septuagint ἐκκλεσία refers to the whole people of God, so there is only one church, which is the body of Christ. It does not properly speaking exist on earth, but in heaven, being manifested on earth in its completeness wherever two or three Christians meet together (Mt 18:20). The phrase 'the church in your house' means just that: the one, spiritual, church is present, as Christ is present, whole and entire, in that person's house. Strictly speaking the local church, considered as a human society, does not exist. It has no place in the economy of God.

> The idea of the local church, especially a defined congregation in today's sense of the word, simply does not exist so far as the organization of the Church (i.e. Christianity) is concerned.[18]

Such a church knows nothing of legal organization. Christ is the Head of the church and his authority is recognized in the exercise of gifts of the Spirit. Everything rests on these *charismata*, which are the direct gift of Christ to his church, manifest from time to time in different people. 'There can be no legal constitution, and no official body with legislative power in the Ecclesia.'[19] This is not to say that the church is without order. Quite the opposite! But it is not a legal order, but a charismatic order. Christ rules his church through the gift of teaching brought by apostles, prophets and teachers.

> There is a gift, a *charisma*, which has responsibility for leading and ruling the congregation on Christ's name: it is the *gift of Teaching*.[20]

[18] Sohm, *Kirchenrecht*, p. 22.
[19] Sohm, *Kirchenrecht*, p. 25.
[20] Sohm, *Kirchenrecht*, p. 28.

Such people are not elected: their gifts are simply recognized and lovingly followed.

According to Sohm's contemporaries the emergence of the various offices in the early church could be explained in purely natural terms. Hatch for example saw the bishops as at first purely financial officers derived from the constitution of Greek clubs and societies and charged with administering the church's poor relief,[21] while the elders formed a court to deal with matters of discipline, exactly as in the synagogues.[22] Lightfoot, less extreme, nevertheless accounted for the development of the church's ministry in essentially natural and historical terms.[23] Of the elders he says:

> With the synagogue itself [the Christian congregations] would naturally, if not necessarily, adopt the government of a synagogue, and a body of elders or presbyters would be chosen to direct the religious worship and partly also to watch over the temporal well-being of society.[24]

For Sohm, by contrast, the ministry was to be seen as a divine creation, provided to meet the church's spiritual needs. The fundamental ministry, as we have seen, was the ministry of the Word as brought by the apostles, prophets and teachers in virtue of their *charisma*. The function of the bishop was to lead the eucharistic assembly and (as with Hatch) to administer the church's charity[25]. He was chosen from among the elders to offer the eucharistic prayer, for which purpose he too needed to have a teaching gift. He was not a teacher as such, but in the absence of an apostle, prophet or teacher he might stand in for them and teach the congregation[26]. At no time, before the end of the first century, did this confer on him any constitutional power or right to act in this capacity. His entitlement lay in being invited to act by the people of God who thus recognized his gift[27].

[21] Hatch, *Organization*, pp. 40f.
[22] Hatch, p. 64ff.
[23] Lightfoot, *Philippians*, pp. 181ff.
[24] Lightfoot, p. 192.
[25] Sohm, *Kirchenrecht*, p. 81.
[26] Sohm, *Kirchenrecht*, pp. 84f., 87.
[27] Sohm, *Kirchenrecht*, p. 151.

The elders on the other hand did not hold an office in the church at all, but rather enjoyed a position of honour in the congregation as senior members of proven Christian character. 'The elders of that earlier time are not an office, but a rank'.[28] The bishops as office-holders are drawn from among such elders, but the elders are not office-holders as such.[29] This is worked out by means of a detailed examination of the references to elders in 1 Clement, on the basis of which Sohm concludes that when bishops are spoken of as elders, it is because they are the *appointed* elders (οἱ καθεστάμενοι πρεσβύτεροι, 1 Clem 54:2), so that, 'the older man who is appointed, is appointed to the office of Bishop'.[30]

There is, of course, no *charisma* of age, but the elders are not just old. They are distinguished by their Christian character, and honoured for their length of faithful service, and as such are ranked as the church's most 'honourable' members.[31] Yet the elders are not without *charisma*, since everything in the church is governed by *charisma*. Theirs is the *charisma* of practical Christian service, 'the gift of love', 'the *charisma* of being a practical proof of Christianity itself'.[32] As such they were well-qualified to teach the young, and so from their ranks could be chosen someone to stand in for the apostle at the Eucharist and to offer the eucharistic prayer – the bishop or overseer of (that particular) eucharistic assembly. Those elders not so chosen occupied seats of honour in the assembly, sitting with the bishop at the eucharistic Table.[33]

Although not translated into English, Sohm was in fact taken up and interpreted for the English-speaking world by the American scholar, W. Lowrie.[34] Lowrie adopts the whole Sohmian schema, including

[28] Sohm, *Kirchenrecht*, p. 93.
[29] Sohm, *Kirchenrecht*, p. 95.
[30] Sohm, *Kirchenrecht*, p. 96.
[31] Sohm, *Kirchenrecht*, p. 103.
[32] Sohm, *Kirchenrecht*, pp. 109, 112.
[33] Sohm, *Kirchenrecht*, p. 137. A similar view was expressed by Harnack. While he disagreed with Sohm's central contention of a purely spiritual church (see *Constitution*, pp. 204–42), he nevertheless described the Pauline church as a 'spiritual democracy' where 'the charismata determine everything'. *Constitution*, p. 53. He took a mediating position on the elders, who were both 'honourables' and officers, pp. 58, 89f.
[34] Lowrie, *The Church and its Organization*, (*1904*).

9

the twofold pattern of early Christian meetings: the assembly in which the Word was ministered by those gifted to teach it, and the eucharistic assembly presided over by the bishop. The origin of the church's ministry lay in this gathering, not in the Jewish courts. When the church assembled, the older believers, as honoured people, sat in the chief seats, but had no office or function to perform. It was the overseer and deacons who presided and officiated. Only when the various house-meetings came together to form a large meeting was the profile of the elders enhanced, in that they now sat with the bishop at the Table and began to form his council. That is to say, those who had been overseers of smaller meetings now found themselves surrounding the one overseer of the now enlarged congregation and were known naturally as the elders. Lowrie says:

> The presbyters of the first century were not officers, but merely a class in the community, the class of elder disciples, the 'honourables' of the community, from whose number the bishop was chosen, and among whom he was ranked when it was rather dignity than office that was in question — just as were the apostles themselves. The presbyter as such was not elected or appointed, but enjoyed his informal position of leadership by common and informal consent: when an elder is 'appointed' there is nothing else he can be appointed to but the episcopate — the 'appointed elder' is *ipso facto* a bishop.[35]

What is lacking in both these scholars' accounts is any appreciation of the everyday social realities, especially the household, within which the earliest churches operated (and which the New Testament writers took for granted). It is made to look as if the early Christians set out to organize a religious institution guided by theological principles alone.

---

[35] Lowrie, *Church*, p. 347. Summarizing the implication of this view for the development of the threefold ministry M. H. Shepherd, 'Development', p. 149, says: 'The presbyterate as an order of ministry, and not simply as a position of honour, arose out of the episcopate by delegation, and not the episcopate out of the presbyterate by elevation.' Contrast Lightfoot, p. 196: 'The episcopate was formed not out of the apostolic order by localization but out of the presbyterial by elevation.'

The Heirs of Sohm

As already noted, hardly anyone was willing to go all the way with Sohm, but his central ideas influenced succeeding generations of scholars especially in Germany, but with significant modifications. Sohm's handling of the New Testament evidence had basically been uncritical, or pre-critical. For Sohm it was 'undenkbar' — unthinkable — that various different forms of church order should have existed side by side, or that different forms might have been fused together ('verschmolzen',[36]). The New Testament scholars who were influenced by his charismatic understanding of the church, however, found it perfectly 'denkbar'! As the heirs of F. C. Baur, they were accustomed to think in that way. Accordingly, what for Sohm was seen as the primitive constitution of the universal church, now became for them the distinguishing nature of the *Pauline* churches only. Elders on the other hand belonged to Jewish Christianity, 'unreformed' Christianity; they were guardians of the Law and of tradition, in which already lay the seeds of Catholicism. Sohm's understanding of the elders was quietly forgotten.[37]

Sohm's idea of the charismatic congregation found its classic and most influential statement in H. von Campenhausen's account of the Pauline churches.[38] Von Campenhausen does not, it is true, mention Sohm except briefly to disagree with him[39], but the influence of Sohm is clear. Von Campenhausen believes that Paul had an understanding of the church that was at variance with anything that preceded or followed him. The organizing principle is the idea of the Spirit who enables different members of the church to function in whatever way was needed from time to time. As a result,

> for an office of governor on the lines of the presbyterate or of the later monarchical episcopate there was no room at Corinth either in principle or in practice.[40]

---

[36] Sohm, *Kirchenrecht*, p. 105.
[37] So, for example, Bultmann, *Theology*, II, pp. 98–101.
[38] Von Campenhausen, *Authority*, esp. chapters 4 and 5.
[39] Von Campenhausen, *Authority*, p. 84.
[40] Von Campenhausen, *Authority*, p. 65.

The normal factors that propel people into positions of power and influence did not operate in the Pauline churches.

> The community is not viewed as a sociological entity ... For it is not the 'strong', the capable and the great who enjoy the 'honour' of precedence; instead, the weaker and more needy a member is, the more all the rest are to support him with their love and honour him. [41]

Paul's reference to local leadership in Thessalonica (1 Thess 5:12) is acknowledged, but then largely discounted.

> It can hardly be taken to imply a fixed office. Paul has in mind anyone who comes forward in one way or another within the congregation to take on its problems and provide material and spiritual help, since, when Paul uses the word [sc. προϊσταμένους] he is not thinking of any definite 'governing' office within the congregation, but quite generally of any work of advising and assisting that takes place there.[42]

Where von Campenhausen departs more seriously from Sohm is in his portrayal of the elders. Elders for von Campenhausen represent, in contrast to 'certain modest beginnings of an organization' such as we find in Paul's churches, the idea of:

> functionaries controlling all the members and responsible for them, called to this particular work and qualified by their appointment ... a fundamentally different way of thinking about the Church, which can only with difficulty be combined with the Pauline picture of the congregation, and certainly cannot be derived from it.[43]

The origins of this way of organizing the church lie in Judaism, since, 'There had for a long time been elders at the head of every Jewish congregation, especially in Palestine'.[44] The system of elders

---

[41] Von Campenhausen, *Authority,* p. 58.
[42] Von Campenhausen, *Authority,* p. 65.
[43] Von Campenhausen, *Authority,* p. 76.
[44] Von Campenhausen, *Authority,* p. 77.

had for this reason won acceptance with the Jewish-Christian congregations almost from the start, so that eldership is not to be
thought of as a later development *per se*. It existed before the rise of
Paul's churches, and contemporary with them, but when in due
course it spread to Paul's churches also, it represented,

> not merely a new phase but a new line of development, the first
> and decisive prerequisite for the elaboration of a narrowly 'offi-
> cial' and 'ecclesiastical' way of thinking.[45]

Not all German scholars have followed this line. In particular, of
course, Roman Catholic scholars have generally been resistant to
it.[46] Another notable exception is L. Goppelt, whose carefully expressed account of the church office explicitly criticizes Sohm and
Bultmann for failing to do justice to the historical-physical nature
of the church in the purposes of God, and charges von
Campenhausen with practically placing Paul in the very category of
pneumatic perfectionism that 1 Corinthians is written to combat.[47]
There is no purely charismatic church, and 1 Corinthians is not a
blueprint for church order. Goppelt notes but minimizes the differences between Pauline churches and Jewish-Christian churches and
sees the differences between the elders and the Pauline προϊστάμενοι
as 'simply relative'[48]. Nevertheless he follows the consensus in attributing elders to the constitution of the synagogue community.

---

[45] Von Campenhausen, *Authority*, p. 77. Other influential representatives of this point
of view have been E. Schweizer, *Church Order in the New Testament*, and E. Käsemann,
'Ministry and Community', *Essays on New Testament Themes*, pp. 63–94. Schweizer sees
the Sohmian view as true of the Pauline churches, so that, 'For Paul an ordination, any
explicit appointment on undertaking a form of service, is impossible' (p. 101). Käsemann
contrasts the Pauline churches where, 'All the baptized are office-holders' (p. 80), with
the Pastorals where we find, 'an office which stands over against the rest of the community', and which is 'now the real bearer of the Spirit', so that 'we can now speak ... of the
ministerial Spirit' (p. 87).

[46] See, for example, Schnackenburg, *Church*, pp. 22–34, p. 100ff., Gnilka, 'Amt', pp.
95–104, Hainz, 'Anfänge', pp. 102–7, and among scholars writing in English, Bourke,
'Church Order', p. 505. For a Catholic scholar who has embraced this consensus, see
Kertelge, *Gemeinde*, pp. 97–151.

[47] Goppelt, *Apostolic*, p. 187, n. 23.

[48] Goppelt, *Apostolic*, p. 187.

They represented the church to the outside world and cared for order and pastoral needs inside.

> Nevertheless, they did all this on the basis of the Gospel and not like their Jewish counterparts on the basis of the Law[49]

This distinction, as we have seen, is found in von Campenhausen too; one wonders how they know this! Furthermore we are told that, at least in Corinth, Paul had,

> wanted to give freedom to faith in accordance with its character and in opposition to Palestinian and Hellenistic influences. In doing so he opposed the historical and legal as well as the spiritual authorities, although the dislike which he displayed to the institution of elders should not be seen as an artificial opposition.[50]

It is not altogether clear what that last phrase means, but it is plain that the Sohmian legacy is still strong.

Until fairly recently this legacy has largely been handed down within German scholarship. In English writing on the origins of the ministry, from Lightfoot through Streeter to Farrer and Dix, interest has rather centred on the development of the episcopate, and on the relationship of elders to bishops than on the opposition of *charisma* to 'Amt'. The latter view is, however, now well represented in this country by J. D. G. Dunn in his *Unity and Diversity in the New Testament*.[51] Dunn begins by telling us that,

> Paul's concept of ministry is determined by his understanding of the church as the body of Christ.[52]

Romans 12 and 1 Corinthians 12 are to be taken as a *description* of

---

[49] Goppelt, *Apostolic*, p. 185.

[50] Goppelt, *Apostolic*, p. 186f.

[51] It is unfortunate that although we are told in the Foreword to the Revised Edition (1990) that, 'The topic of Chapter VI, "Concepts of Ministry", is one where sociological analysis has proved particularly fruitful', no changes to the main text have been possible. The work of Holmberg, and MacDonald is briefly referred to; that of Brockhaus and Chapple is not discussed.

[52] Dunn, *Unity*, p. 109.

14

the local church, which is for Dunn a wholly charismatic community, where each member has some function, and in which ministry belongs to all.[53] In the next section Dunn starts by telling us that *charismata* are particular manifestations of the Spirit's power, strictly speaking *events*, not aptitudes or talents possessed by individuals. Of course, some have more regular ministries than this, such as the apostle, and the prophets and teachers, and there is also a wide range of other ministries, including preaching and administration, but they are not established or official.

> Any form of service etc. which any individual member of the charismatic community found himself regularly prompted to by the Spirit, and which benefited the church was (or at least should have been) recognized as a regular ministry by the church (1 Thess 5:12f., 1 Cor 16:16, 18). Consequently these ministries should not be thought of as established or official ministries, and they were certainly not ecclesiastical appointments or church offices.[54]

The only apparent exception is the reference to 'bishops and deacons' (Phil 1:1), of which Dunn says,

> Some of the less well defined areas of administration and service ... had begun to cohere into more clearly defined forms of ministry.[55]

Dunn, following von Campenhausen, makes much of the fact that at Corinth Paul nowhere asks the local leaders to sort out the problems, even though the situation seems to be crying out for someone to take this responsibility. The fact that Paul does not do this leads Dunn to say,

> The implication is plain: if leadership was required in any situation Paul assumed that the charismatic Spirit would provide it

---

[53] Dunn, *Unity*, p. 111.
[54] Dunn, *Unity*, p. 112.
[55] Dunn, *Unity*, p. 113.

with a word of wisdom or guidance through an individual (cf. 1 Cor 6:5, 12:28).[56]

Paul assumed! Perhaps it is rather Dunn who assumes this. For all we know, Paul may have assumed that the lead would be taken by those who would naturally do so. In conclusion, Dunn endorses the view of von Campenhausen that Paul's concept of the church was one of,

> free fellowship developing through the living interplay of spiritual gifts and ministries without benefit of official authority or responsible elders.[57]

A variation of the consensus view is provided by the work of the feminist scholar E. S. Fiorenza.[58] At many points, of course, her reconstruction departs from consensus thinking. Thus, she rejects the opposition between Pauline and Jewish Christianity. Paul was a Jew, and in any case he did not initiate the early Christian movement, nor did he seek to radicalize a hitherto conservative community. Rather the reverse. Earliest Christianity was characterized by a radical egalitarianism derived from Jesus himself, and the seeds of the later patriachalization of the church are to be found in Paul's own letters, which show him struggling to relate his egalitarian inheritance to the pressures and demands of missionary work in the Graeco-Roman world. But although the roles in the story are assigned by Fiorenza to different characters, the story is still basically the same, granted the shift of interest from *charismata* to gender roles. It is still the story of the corruption of an unstructured church into one that is institutionalized and clericalized. Thus she can describe the original pattern as follows:

> Organizational equality is sustained by shifting and alternating authority and leadership among members of a group, all of whom — in principle — have equal access to authority, leadership and

---

[56] Dunn, *Unity,* p. 113.

[57] Dunn, *Unity,* quoting von Campenhausen, p. 70.

[58] Elisabeth Schüssler Fiorenza, *In Memory of Her,* subtitled, 'A Feminist Theological Reconstruction of Christian Origins'.

power. This was the case in the early Christian movement, inso-
far as all members of the movement were Spirit-gifted people of
God who had received the power and endowment of the Holy
Spirit for the building up of the community.[59]

This is pure Sohm! However, unlike Sohm, Fiorenza attributes this
not to the whole church but to part of it, and unlike Sohm's other
heirs, identifies that part not with Paul but with pre-Pauline Christianity. We shall return to her view when we look at the elders in
Acts.

For all the many differences of judgement between them on points
of detail, these writers, and many more, can all fairly be seen as the
heirs of Sohm in that they have insisted on the primacy of *charisma*
for a right understanding of the church. However, where Sohm saw
this as the teaching of the whole New Testament, his heirs have
generally confined it to Paul, and seen it as one pole of an opposition between Pauline Christianity (which was by implication right)
and Jewish Christianity (which was, of course, wrong!). In the process only part of the legacy has been accepted. The all-charismatic
picture of the church has been received, but what Sohm actually
said about the elders has been not so much refuted as largely ignored. This is particularly true of his insight that elders do not as
such hold an office in the church at all, being rather a class of
people from whom office-holders may very well be drawn. One of
the concerns of the present work will be to re-examine this idea in
the light of our present understanding of the New Testament house-
churches within the society of the Graeco-Roman world.

As we carry out this re-examination we shall do well to heed the
warning sounded over fifty years ago by O. Linton towards the end of
his review of the debate about early church government. So long as
we try to understand the government of the early church in western
democratic categories we shall miss the mark. By contrast, says Linton,
'In the Orient there is a phenomenon unknown to us of a legislative
assembly where all are not equal.'[60] He instances Luke's account of

[59] Fiorenza, *Memory*, p. 286.
[60] Linton, *Problem*, pp. 189f.

17

the Apostolic Council (Acts 15), which he thinks Harnack is wrong to have analysed in terms of a sovereign πλῆθος with the apostles and elders forming an executive that proposes legislation to it, and continues:

> In the first place there exists neither a separate Council, nor a separate Assembly. There are honoured older people, but their honour does not consist in the fact that they have been elected onto a board of elders, but in the fact that in the assembly they are honoured with the chief seats, and that people listen to them.

In such assemblies decisions are not made by majority vote but by the submission of the minority. This is made possible both by the patriarchal authority of the leaders and by the sense of collective solidarity enjoyed by the assembly as a whole. This suggests that in our search for the elders we shall need to be sensitive to the cultural assumptions of a world very different from our own.[61] Accordingly, before engaging directly with the arguments of the consensus or presenting our own reconstruction of the earliest churches, we shall turn our attention to the world in which those churches came to birth: first the world of Judaism and then the world of Greece and Rome to see who was honoured with the title of elder within it and how that title was understood. It is very easy to view both the early churches and the synagogues through the spectacles of our own experience of church or sect, and to forget that, in the words of L. P. Hartley, 'The past is a foreign country. They do things differently there.'[62]

To Sum Up

We have sketched out a line of thinking about the early church which has dominated Protestant scholarship for the last hundred

---

[61] Even professional studies of sect development do not seem to have asked what happens to the egalitarianism characteristic of modern western sects when a sect develops in a patriarchal and hierarchical society. See, for example, Wilson, *Religion*, pp. 89–120, and 'Analysis', pp. 22–45.

[62] L. P. Hartley, *The Go Between*, p. 1.

years. We have seen how it is imperfectly based on the ideas of Rudolf Sohm. What Sohm said about the elders has been largely ignored, while his insights about *charisma* have been used to set the Pauline churches apart from Jewish Christianity. This consensus has not been without its critics, as we shall see, and yet it survives. One reason for this we may find is that its assumptions about the elders have not been effectively challenged.

The elders have been the neglected people in our picture of the early church, neglected and misunderstood. Seen as bearers of an office taken over from the synagogue, their presence in Pauline churches has been denied and their appearance in the Pastorals seen as the surest evidence of spiritual decline. But this is a particularly Protestant view. During the last fifteen years we have learnt to stop looking at Paul's gospel through 'Reformation spectacles'. It is time to take a fresh look at his churches also. When we do so, we shall find neither precisely the 'threefold order' of the later Catholic church, nor the charismatic democracy of Protestant imagining, but a society in which *charmismata* operated within a framework of honour and respect, a society which belonged within its own social world even while it claimed to experience the in-breaking of another.

Chapter Two

The Elders in Ancient Israel and Early Judaism

The use of the word 'elders' to denote the leaders of a community of some kind has a long Jewish history behind it by the time we meet it in the emerging churches of the New Testament. At all periods of Israelite and Jewish history down to the fall of Jerusalem in 70 CE, and in all sizes of community, we find leadership being exercised by those to whom this title is applied, and it will be convenient to summarize the evidence under two headings: elders in Ancient Israel and elders in Early Judaism.

The Elders in Ancient Israel

The subject has been quite extensively covered in recent years, and the biblical evidence reviewed by a number of scholars,[1] from whom a reasonably agreed picture emerges, although the details remain somewhat elusive. This elusiveness is due to the fact that our sources say very little about the elders, so that in the words of one scholar,

---

[1] H. Frankfort, *The Intellectual Adventure of Ancient Man*, Chicago, 1946; Wolf, C. U., 'Traces of Primitive Democracy in Ancient Israel', *JNES*, 6 (1947), pp. 98–108; J. van der Ploeg, 'Les Chefs du Peuple d'Israel et leurs Titres', *RB* 57 (1950), pp. 40–61; M. Weber, *Ancient Judaism*, Glencoe, ILL.: Free, 1952; G. Bornkamm, 'πρέσβυς', *TWNT*, Vol. VI, pp. 655–58, Stuttgart, 1956; McKenzie, J. L., 'Elders in the OT', *Biblica* 40 (1959), pp. 522–40; R. de Vaux, *Ancient Israel*, ET, London: Darton, 1961; J. van der Ploeg, 'Les Anciens dans l'Ancien Testament', *Lex Tua Veritas: Festschrift, H. Hunker*, Trier: Paulinus, 1961, pp. 175–91; A. Malamat, 'Kingship and Council in Ancient Israel and Sumer', *JNES* 22 (1963), pp. 247–53; J. Conrad, 'זקן', *TWAT*, Vol. IV, Stuttgart, 1980, pp. 122–31; I. Eph'al, 'Political and Social Organization of the Jews in Babylonian Exile', *ZDMG*, Supp. 5, Wiesbaden, 1983, pp. 106–112; H. Reviv, *The Elders of Ancient Israel*, Jerusalem: Magnes, 1989.

'la personalité du zaqen-ancien est reśee un peu vague',[2] and of another, 'the total amount of information is minimal and the references to them [elders] do not reflect their true importance'.[3] Accordingly the fragmentary biblical evidence tends to be filled out and interpreted by reference to what is known of other contemporary societies in the Ancient Near East,[4] and from studies of Bedouin groups down to our own day.[5] We shall look first at the functions performed by the elders, then at the relationship of the elders to other office-bearers in Israel, and finally at the question of how a person came to be numbered among the elders of his community.

1. *The functions performed by the elders.* Israelite society was tribal and patriarchal. The nation consisted of tribes, which themselves consisted of clans which in turn consisted of extended families,[6] and each of these units and sub-units looked to the senior males among them for leadership.[7] The head of the house made decisions within his own home and also represented the family in the counsels of the village community. Such family heads collectively provided for the internal order of the community,[8] and also represented it to those outside.[9] These are the people described as the elders, and they are often, and by implication always, said to be the elders *of* something or somewhere, the elders of a city, of the land, of the people, of Moab and Midian and most commonly the elders of Israel. The functions performed by the elders are accordingly deliberative, representative and judicial.

A number of scholars have described the constitution of Israel before the monarchy in terms of primitive democracy. Frankfort wrote:

---

[2] van der Ploeg, 'Anciens', p. 190.

[3] Reviv, *Elders*, p. 9.

[4] Reviv, pp. 137–86.

[5] E.g., McKenzie, 'Elders', p. 533.

[6] The Hebrew expression is 'father's house', בית אב, rendered 'household' by RSV. See Josh 7:14ff.

[7] An excellent illustration of this is provided by the Gideon story, Judg 6:11–32, esp v. 15. Cf. Josh 7:14ff., and 1 Sam 10:20f.

[8] Conrad cites the story of Boaz and Ruth, Ruth 4:1–12.

[9] Like the elders of Moab and Midian in Num 22:7ff.

It was a primitive democracy, uncritical and unconscious, for there is no ground to suppose other than that every senior member of the group was admitted to the governing body purely on the basis of his age.[10]

On the basis of passages where 'elders' appears to be used interchangeably with 'all the men of Israel', or equivalent expressions, Wolf argued that the elders are to be equated with the 'entire free male population'.[11] This explains, he says, how a place like Succoth could be credited with seventy-seven elders, if all the men were eligible to assemble and speak, but this conclusion has been rejected by all subsequent writers.[12] It is anachronistic in that the popular assembly of biblical times was never an assembly of equal individuals as we understand it, but an assembly in which each person had and knew his 'place', and where the older took precedence over the younger. Moreover, it falls foul, for example, of a passage like Josh 9:18f., where leaders and congregation are explicitly differentiated. It is also against this interpretation that 'the elders' are linked in parallel with words that undoubtedly convey the sense of people in authority: heads, judges, officials and the like. It must surely be the case rather that these people can be described as all the men of Israel because they are seen as representative and inclusive of the members of their tribes and clans. It is therefore generally agreed that זקנים refers to the heads of the families or houses of which the clan or tribe consisted. But the fact that Wolf could make a plausible case for seeing elders as all free males indicates the difficulty of defining elders precisely, and strongly suggests that they were leaders whose authority came by recognition from below rather than by appointment from above.

The influence wielded and the role performed by the elders in Israel varied at different periods of her history. While the role of village elders probably remained largely unchanged, at the national

---

[10] Frankfort, *Intellectual Adventure*, p. 343. This was really based on his research into early Mesopotamia and only secondarily applied to Israel.

[11] Wolf, 'Traces', p. 99, cited particularly Josh 24:1f.; Jdg 8:14; 1 Kings 8:1f.

[12] Eg. by McKenzie, 'Elders', p. 353, Conrad, זקן p. 131, de Vaux, *Ancient Israel*, p. 69, Reviv, *Elders*, p. 7.

level so to speak it varied with the rise and fall of the monarchy. We first meet the elders of Israel in the Pentateuchal narratives where they form a largely silent group that accompanies Moses, witnessing the acts of the Lord through Moses and relaying to the people what the Lord has said to him (e.g. Ex 3:16, 24:1). In the view of Conrad[13] and Reviv,[14] this is anachronistic, serving to highlight the supreme role of Moses and the pristine unity of Israel, but actually reflecting the national role of elders under the monarchy. The historical reality prior to the monarchy is seen better from the role played by the elders of Moab and Midian in Numbers 22:7, where they function as diplomats, and by the elders of Gibeon who come to Joshua with authority to negotiate a covenant (Josh 9:11), and by the elders of Gilead who confer headship on Jephthah (Jdg 11:5–11). As heads of their tribes the elders will also have been military leaders, active in the conquest of the land, and only ceding power to a Jephthah, Saul or David in the face of a threat from outside that demanded greater unity.

Under the monarchy the elders tended to lose power relative to the royal officials and the king. It is true that they play a significant role in making David king in the first place (2 Sam. 2:17), and they then form a royal council of whose opinions the king must take account, but the king also violates the traditional channels of authority by appointing officers who take much of the day to day power out of the hands of the elders, and by appropriating power to himself.[15] Within the royal capitals, the elders become part of the upper stratum of an increasingly centralized government, becoming themselves in some cases royal officials.[16] The concentration of land in the hands of a few, against which the eighth-century prophets inveigh, meant, according to McKenzie, that 'a gap opened up

---

[13] Conrad, זקן, p. 130.

[14] Reviv, *Elders*, pp. 22–9. He shows that there is a persistent tendency in the OT narratives to write history in such a way as to overemphasize the role of the individual leader and the unity and harmony of the people of Israel.

[15] Reviv, *Elders*, p. 87ff.

[16] That is to say that שר (*sar*) comes to refer not only to tribal elders but also to royal officials. Since the officials were recruited from the elders, some elders at least became officials.

between the elders and the people as a whole which would have been inconceivable at a time when elders were representatives of the whole people.'[17]

With the disappearance of the monarchy, however, the elders regained something of their former role as representatives of the people. Elders head the list of those exiles to whom Jeremiah sends his letter (Jer 29:1); the elders of the exiled community come to consult Ezekiel (Ezek. 8:1); and elders take an active role in the restoration under Ezra (Ezra 5:5, 6:7) and Nehemiah.[18] In the view of van der Ploeg, however, as post-exilic Israel became a people of the Book, the elders tended to lose their popular judicial role, being overshadowed and to some extent replaced by scribes learned in the Law.[19] Nevertheless, as we shall see, the heads of prominent families continued to play an important role in both local and national government during the Second Temple period.

2. *The relationship of the elders to other office-bearers.* Biblical Hebrew has a rich and varied vocabulary of words that refer to leaders.[20] Over a dozen of these are listed by van der Ploeg, who notes that all of them can be used interchangeably for the same people, although the role played by the referents may change at different times of Israel's history. The commonest are שׂר (*sar*), נציא (*nasi*), נדיב (*nadib*) and ראשׁ (*rosh*), variously translated in the RSV as 'prince', 'noble', 'official', 'head' etc.

The word 'elders' is found linked in parallel with many of these, notably שׂרים (*sarim*, Num. 22:44f.; Jdg 8:6; Ezra 10:8), and ראשׁים (*rashim*, Josh. 24:1; 1 Kings 8:1). In Num 22:7ff., Balak sends the elders of Midian to Balaam and these are then called princes. Gideon vents his anger on the officials and elders of Succoth (Jdg 7:14). Solomon assembles 'the elders of Israel and all the heads of the tribes, the leaders of the fathers' houses' (1 Kings 8:1). It seems

---

[17]McKenzie, 'Elders', p. 539.

[18] The book of Nehemiah, however, does not use the term זקנים, preferring סגנים, probably due to Aramaic influence. See de Vaux, *Israel,* pp. 69–70.

[19]van der Ploeg, 'Anciens', pp. 188–9.

[20]van der Ploeg, 'Chefs', pp. 40–61.

unlikely that we can clearly distinguish between any of these terms either in terms of rank or function. On the basis of derivation van der Ploeg, followed by McKenzie, suggests that שׂרים refers to military commanders, but it seems better to say that the word שׂרים tends to be chosen when military action is in the writer's mind. Under the monarchy *sarim* comes to mean royal official, but this only shows that all of these words can be used to refer to whatever powers there be, without thereby changing their connotation. Reviv, after reviewing a number of passages in which 'heads' appear together with 'chiefs' and 'elders' concludes:

> These passages corroborate the fact that 'heads' were the leaders (the 'elders') at the sub-tribal and settlement levels, or parallel to the 'chiefs' at the tribal level. However, the 'elders' are invariably second in rank to the 'head' in the sense of 'chief', when these terms are both mentioned in a particular context. Consideration of the titles assigned to the 'chiefs', in the sense of tribal heads, such as 'heads of the fathers', 'heads of fathers' houses', 'heads of the people of Israel', implies that the individual tribal chiefs came from the ranks of the elders.[21]

In other words, each tribe consists of 'clans' (sub-tribal units); each 'clan' has a head, and the heads of the clans collectively are the elders; the head of the tribe comes from the ranks of these elders, but is never then called an elder (or *the* elder).[22]

Two things stand out in all this. The word 'elder' never occurs in the singular, referring to an office-holder.[23] Where a person is being

[21] Reviv, *Elders*, p. 21.

[22] An interesting parallel suggests itself in the leadership of the NT churches. The local church consists of households, and each household has its head; the heads of the households are collectively the Elders, and individually Overseers; the leader of the local church is drawn form the ranks of these Elders, but is never then called 'the Elder', but rather 'the Overseer'! (The writer of 2 and 3 John breaks this rule, and has baffled New Testament exegetes ever since. See p. 207–8.)

[23] Is 3:2 is not an exception to this, since the singular is a generic singular. It does not refer to an actual person. Lev 19:32 refers to an old man, not an office-holder, as the parallel expression 'hoary head' makes plain. The computer, using *Thesaurus Linguae Graecae* on CD-ROM, confirms that there are no genuine exceptions to this observation in the Septuagint.

considered in his capacity as the head of his house, clan or tribe, he is likely to be called 'head' or 'prince', but not 'elder'. This confirms that 'the elders' is a *collective* term for the leadership of the tribe, or of the ruling class under the monarchy and thereafter, but that it was never the title of an office to which an individual might be appointed. The other thing to note is the delight the biblical writers have in heaping up titles of honour to describe the leaders gathered together on any one occasion without there being any clear distinction to be drawn between them.[24] This partly reflects a desire on the part of the writer to emphasize the unity of the nation in the action being described, and the solemnity of the occasion, but it must also reflect a cultural trait, an oriental delight in paying courtesies, perhaps, or more generally a Semitic tendency to pile up near synonyms.[25] If so, we would expect it to be an enduring trait, extending into New Testament times, so that when we read the Old Testament narratives or those of the New Testament we should not conclude that just because the writer says that 'so and so summoned all the X and Y and Z' that there were necessarily three distinct groups or ranks of officer present.

3. *How a person came to be numbered among the elders.* To understand the nature of an office it is revealing to ask how one enters upon it. How did people become elders in Ancient Israel? It is nowhere recorded, but the silence itself may help to confirm the picture that has already emerged. For if the elder was 'le chef vénéré d'une grande famille, considerée comme partie de la nation',[26] then clearly there can be no candidacy nor procedure leading to such a

---

[24] So for example, Dt 19:10 (RSV), 'You stand this day all of you before the Lord your God; the heads of your tribes, your elders, and your officers, all the men of Israel… .'; and Dt 31:28 (RSV), 'Assemble to me all the elders of your tribes and your officers.'

The LXX for these verses is particularly striking in view of its likely impact on emergent Christian traditions. Dt 29:10 reads: οἱ ἀρχίφυλοι ὑμῶν, καὶ ἡ γερουσία ὑμῶν, καὶ οἱ κριταὶ ὑμῶν, καὶ οἱ γραμματοεισαγωγεῖς ὑμῶν. (Your tribal leaders, and your council, and your judges, and your scribes); Dt 31:28: τοὺς φυλάρχους ὑμῶν, καὶ τοὺς πρεσβυτέρους ὑμῶν, καὶ τοὺς κριτὰς καὶ τοὺς γραμματοεισαγωγεῖς ὑμῶν. (Your tribal leaders, and your elders, and your judges, and your scribes). Note how titles have multiplied in comparison to the Hebrew original.

[25] Cf. the many words for 'wisdom' in Prov 1:1–7, or for 'praise' in 1 Chron 16:4.

[26] van der Ploeg, 'Anciens', p. 189.

position of honour. Equally, during the time of the monarchy, the elders might serve as the king's council, but it was not a council that he appointed or whose membership he completely controlled. As we have said, elders represent leadership from below, not from above. Heredity had much to do with it. A person succeeded his father to the headship of his tribe or family, by which time he had probably also acquired the years normally associated with eldership. But it will also have much to do with the gradual acquiring of respect. Van der Ploeg expresses it this way:

> In 1947, I asked an Arab priest from Beisan in Palestine, who was well-acquainted with the Arab nomads or semi-nomads, how one became an 'elder' of the tribe. He replied that he was not able to say, for there are no rules or laws to determine it. It seems that when a man reaches the point where people often ask his counsel and he has the moral authority such as elders have, he is admitted by common, often tacit, consent into their 'college'. So there is tacit admission into the group of elders, no nomination, nor application of a rule according to which one becomes an 'elder'. The qualification is a man's moral authority. It is my clear impression that a person became an elder in Israel in the same way, and this explains why our texts say little of it.[27]

With regard to the elders of Ancient Israel also, we should conclude that they constituted a form of leadership at all levels of Israelite society that was collective, and representative, with an authority derived from their seniority relative to those they represented, and varying according to the size and wealth of the social group whose representatives they were, their own personal qualities, and the leadership being exercised by the king, priests or other bearers of authority. It is not so much an office of individual leadership as a body of people from whom leaders would be likely to spring or be chosen, and with whose opinions any such leader must undoubtedly reckon. Seen from below 'the elders' collectively represent the leadership which the people must follow; seen from above,

---

[27] van der Ploeg, 'Anciens', pp. 190–1.

from the king's throne for example, 'the elders' embody nothing less than 'all the men of Israel', whose heads they are and whose views they articulate.

In the succeeding centuries 'the elders' was a term applied to many different groups of leaders, but it never loses this character. It is collective, rather than individual, a matter of honor rather than of office, with power based in relationships that already exist rather than in appointment, election or ordination. As Reviv shows, there was a tendency from very early on to idealize the elders, providing them with an ideal number and a role of passive support for the ideal leader. This process of idealization probably involves reading back into the past aspects from the writer's own day, and the ideal picture thus created is then appealed to in still later times as the origin of patterns of government among the Rabbis and early Christians alike.

The Elders in Early Judaism: Jewish National Life

The period between the reforms of Nehemiah and the Maccabean uprising is a notoriously shadowy one so far as hard evidence goes, although it is unlikely that the role of the heads of important families changed much in this time. We shall pass over these centuries in silence and turn next to the evidence supplied by selected writings which date from the early years of the first century BCE to the end of the first century CE. This is a fruitful line of enquiry, first because we do in fact have a lot of evidence from this period, and second because this is the period surrounding the rise of the Christian church with which we are here concerned. Some of our witnesses lived in Palestine, others in the Diaspora, but their evidence is remarkably uniform. Its value is all the greater in that it emerges quite incidentally. None of these writers was concerned to read back into the narrative the structures of a later period, or the structures they thought ought to have been obtained, so we can hope to learn from them how a word like 'elders' was used in this period and to whom it referred.

1. *1 Maccabees.* The first book of the Maccabees tells how the

Jews gained their independence from Syrian rule through the exploits of the Maccabees between 175 and 134 BCE. It starts with Mattathias' defiance of the decree of Antiochus Epiphanes and reaches its climax in the establishing of his son Simon as high priest and ruler of an independent Judaea. Written most probably between 103 and 90 BCE,[28] it is a primary source for Jewish history and institutions of the period. The action takes place for the most part on the national stage.

There are several important references to elders and other leaders in 1 Maccabees, and what is striking is the apparent lack of precision in the use of terms referring to persons in authority, and the habit of grouping various different titles together. Thus we find expressions like: ἄρχοντες καὶ πρεσβύτεροι ('rulers and elders', 1:26), τῶν πρεσβυτέρων Ἰσραὴλ καὶ τῶν ἱερέων ('some of the elders of Israel and the priests', 11:23), ἐπὶ συναγωγῆς μεγάλης ἱερέων, καὶ λαοῦ, καὶ ἀρχόντων ἔθνους καὶ τῶν πρεσβυτέρων τῆς χώρας ('before a big meeting of priests and people, rulers of the nation and elders of the land', 14:28). This is not peculiar to 1 Maccabees, but can be found in other ancient Jewish writers.[29]

We have already noted in the Old Testament a tendency to heap up titles in the interests (we suggested) of inclusiveness and solemnity, and this occurs here too. Thus we read: Καὶ ἐστενάξαν ἄρχοντες καὶ πρεσβύτεροι, παρθένοι καὶ νεανίσκοι ἠσθένησαν (the rulers and elders groaned, young men and maidens lost their strength, 1 Macc 1:26). The passage means no more than that *everyone* was affected. We cannot safely differentiate ἄρχοντες and πρεσβύτεροι, since either they are two largely overlapping circles or the writer is referring to the same people in two different ways.

[28] Goldstein, *1 Maccabees*, p. 93.

[29] In his account of the unhappy relations between the last Roman procurator, Florus, and the people of Jerusalem (*BJ* 2.293–405), Josephus speaks of the Jewish leaders as, οἵ τε ἀρχιερεῖς καὶ δυνατοὶ τὸ τε γνωρομώτατων τῆς πόλεως (301), οἱ δυνατοὶ σὺν τοῖς ἀρχιερεῦσιν (316), τοὺς τε ἀρχιερεῖς σὺν τοῖς γνωρίμοις (318). There is a reference to οἱ τῶν Ἱεροσολύμων ἄρχοντες (333), and to action taken by οἵ τε ἀρχιερεῖς ἅμα τοῖς δυνατοῖς καὶ ἡ βουλὴ (336). We note the way in which titles are piled up, and the imprecision of those titles. The passage is discussed by Sanders, *Judaism*, p. 485f.

Again when we read of 'a big meeting of priests and people, rulers of the nation and elders of the land (1 Macc 14:28, quoted in the previous paragraph), we are surely not dealing with *four* distinct groupings — priests, people, rulers of the nation and elders of the country. It is much more likely that terms are being heaped up to signify comprehensiveness, for, while the people can presumably be distinguished from the other three, it must be very doubtful whether ἀρχόντων ἔθνους, καὶ τῶν πρεσβυτέρων τῆς χώρας (rulers of the nation and elders of the land) are distinct groups at all.[30] Slightly more plausible is the suggestion that πρεσβύτεροι are laymen in contexts where they are paired with ἱερεῖς,[31] but can this be considered a safe conclusion? When we read in 1 Maccabees 11:23 that Jonathan gambled his life in preparing an embassy to Ptolemy for which he chose 'some of the elders of Israel and the priests' (τῶν πρεσβυτέρων Ἰσραὴλ καὶ τῶν ἱερέων), is it not just as likely that πρεσβύτεροι and ἱερεῖς are linked expexegetically to show that Jonathan chose for his delegation people who were in every way worthy of respect? We need not doubt that there were prominent non-priestly people to whom the term πρεσβύτεροι certainly applied, simply that the term *excluded* priests. 'Priests and *other* elders' probably conveys the sense better.

Underlying much conventional thinking about the elders in Jewish national life has been the enduring notion of the Sanhedrin, the Great Council that is supposed to have ruled Jerusalem and all Judaea during the whole of our period. πρεσβύτεροι are then seen as members of this body, or more specifically *lay* members of it. From this idea it has been an easy step to suppose that πρεσβύτεροι are members of a council wherever they are found.[32]

---

[30] Contra Bornkamm, πρέσβυς, p. 660, who sees them as specifically rural leaders. He wants to press this meaning of χώρα also in discussing Jer 26:17, so as to set up an opposition between capital and country. Reviv p. 112f. gives good reasons for rejecting this for the period of the monarchy, and his arguments would hold for the Maccabees reference too.

[31] So Bornkamm, πρέσβυς, p. 659.

[32] This is the view of Bornkamm who speaks of the Sanhedrin as 'a clearly delineated supreme ruling body of the Jews with its seat in Jerusalem' (p. 658). It is the view put forward also by Schürer, *History*[2], Vol. II, pp. 199–226, and by Jeremias, *Jerusalem* p.222.

Belief in the existence of this Sanhedrin rests largely on accepting at face value the picture given by the Mishnah in the tractate of that name, interpreting all references to council meetings in the literature of the period as references to that body (however much individual writers may seem to have got the details wrong!), and allowing modern ideas of elected legislatures to colour the resulting picture. On this basis we have all been brought up to believe that Jewish life was controlled by a sovereign parliament, existing independently of the wishes of kings and governors, with a fairly fixed membership of priests and elders divided into parties. In the light of recent scholarly work this whole idea is open to serious question. The case for an alternative picture may be summarized as follows.[33]

In the first place the picture given by the Mishnah is contradicted at crucial points by the accounts of actual trial proceedings given by Josephus and the New Testament writers.[34] While the possibility of inaccuracy or distortion in these writers is not ruled out, it is perhaps even more likely that the rabbinic evidence is designed to legitimate the constitutional arrangements of their own day by attributing to them a spurious antiquity. Secondly, although our sources refer frequently to a council in Jerusalem, they use a variety of different names for it, which is very odd if in fact there was a Sanhedrin with the prestige and permanency traditionally ascribed to it.[35] Thirdly, the picture presented by m. Sanhedrin is not borne out by the rest of the Mishnah itself, which is silent about the involvement of the Sanhedrin when recounting disputes from the Second Temple period.[36]

A more likely picture seems rather to be as follows. First, there was certainly some sort of council in Jerusalem throughout our

---

[33] M. Goodman, *Ruling*, pp. 112–16, J. S. McLaren, *Power*, pp. 211–7, E. P. Sanders, *Judaism*, pp. 458–90. Methodologically all three proceed by examining actual cases as recorded in the first century sources, rather than starting with the Mishnaic evidence.

[34] Goodman, *Ruling*, p. 113.

[35] Goodman, p. 114. γερουσία, βουλή, πρεσβυτέριον and τὸ κοινόν are all found. All of them may be translated 'council', the context deciding who or what is meant.

[36] McLaren, *Power*, pp. 50–1, concludes: 'The evidence from the tannaitic literature tends to suggest that the Sanhedrin/ *bet din* of the Mishnah has no practical application, or even existence, in the Second Temple period.'

period, as in other cities. Josephus refers to a γερουσία under the Seleucids, and to a βουλή in the Roman period, but this body should probably be seen as administrative rather than as having legislative or executive powers. Its principal functions were to collect taxes and to ensure law and order. Second, when our sources speak of τὸ συνέδριον we should not think of a permanent institution with constitutional powers. Effective power lay at all times with the ruler, whether the Hasmonean high priest, or Herod, or the Roman governor. But rulers were in the habit of convening συνέδρια when it suited them, either to seek advice or to conduct a trial.[37] Most references to the συνέδριον in our literature are to this latter function, but we should not think of the συνέδριον as an independent court, since the ruler in convening the court was also likely to determine its membership, and the court in turn was expected to deliver the verdict for which it had been convened.[38] Third, people of rank and influence often acted without recourse to any formal council at all.

> People who, because of birth, wealth, abilities, or position, were 'leaders' often acted on their own or collaboratively to get things done, with no reference to a formal body.... These people did not become officials; they had no titles (except the High Priest); they were simply responsible to maintain order and see that tribute was paid.[39]

Such were in fact the elders of a community.

In the light of this, when we encounter references in 1 Maccabees or elsewhere to kings or high priests addressing or deliberating with the elders we should not think of men who have been elected or appointed to an office of elder, in virtue of which they sit on a

---

[37] 'The Sanhedrin was not a regular political council at all, but only met at the request of the high priest as his advisory body.' Goodman, p. 114.

[38] 'The evidence does not permit a firm decision about the formal existence of a supreme court with a fixed and known membership. We can be certain, however, that even if there was supposed to be a supreme court, rulers could nevertheless empanel a group of their supporters for a trial.' Sanders, p. 488.

[39] Sanders, *Judaism*, p. 485.

council with a right to be consulted, but rather of people dignified by wealth, birth, and seniority, whose opinion or support the ruler is likely to seek when he needs to legitimate his actions. There were of course councils of various kinds with various administrative and legal functions, and the people who served on them could properly be described as the elders, but we should probably not say that they were elders because they served on the council, but rather that they served on the council because they were the elders of the community. References to πρεσβύτεροι in 1 Maccabees are therefore to be seen not as references to lay members of a permanent governing council, but rather to distinguished members of the community acting on their own or at the behest of a ruler.

2. *3 Maccabees.* Written at about the same time as 1 Maccabees,[40] the book that bears the name 3 Maccabees has in fact nothing to do with the Maccabees at all, being an account of the miraculous deliverance of the Jews from persecution at the hands of Ptolemy IV (221–203 BCE). While no one would give much credence to the story 3 Maccabees tells, it is nevertheless good evidence for the way in which titles of leadership functioned at the time of its composition.

There are three significant references to elders in 3 Maccabees. In the first, the Jews send a delegation to Ptolemy, described as follows: τῶν δὲ Ἰουδαίων διαπεμψαμένων πρὸς αὐτὸν ἀπὸ τῆς γερουσίας καὶ τῶν πρεσβυτέρων τοὺς ἀσπασομένους αὐτὸν (the Jews also having sent some of their council and elders to greet him, 1:8). The use of γερουσία and πρεσβύτεροι together like this is simply two ways of saying the same thing and well illustrates the way that titles of honour are reduplicated.

In the second, the younger men are with difficulty restrained by the older people from offering armed resistance, the event being described as follows:

μόλις τε ὑπό τε τῶν γεραιῶν καὶ τῶν πρεσβυτέρων ἀποτραπέντες ἐπὶ τὴν αὐτὴν τῆς δεήσεως ἔστησαν στάσιν (they were with difficulty brought back by the aged and

---

[40] Anderson, *OT Pseudepigrapha*, Vol. 2, p. 512.

the elders to the station of prayer which they had occupied before, 1:23)

Again we note the pleonastic use of γεραίοι καὶ πρεσβύτεροι, a phrase that perhaps underlines their age and dignity. Their function and authority are brought out two verses later when they are called: οἱ δὲ περὶ τὸν βασιλέα πρεσβύτεροι ('the elders who surrounded the king', 1:25).

The final passage makes plain the fluidity with which these terms can be used.

'Ελεαζάρος δὲ τις ἀνὴρ ἐπίσημος τῶν ἀπο τῆς χώρας ἱερέων, ἐν πρεσβείῳ τὴν ἡλικίαν ἤδη λελογχὼς, καὶ πάσῃ τῇ κατὰ τὸν βίον ἀρετῃ κεκοσμημένος, τοὺς περὶ αὐτὸν καταστείλας πρεσβυτέρους ἐπικαλεῖσθαι τὸν ἅγιον Θεὸν προσηύξατο τάδε. (Eleazer, a distinguished member of the priests of the land, having already attained the dignity of old age, and a life adorned with every virtue, restrained the elders who were about him from calling on the holy God, and prayed as follows, 6:1)

These verses tell us of one Eleazer, who is described as an illustrious priest, explicitly commended on account of his age and virtue. This man restrains 'the elders who were about him'. Here then is a man who is both a priest and an elder, a priest so far as his office is concerned, but an elder among priests, able to call on the elders about him. It seems plain that we should be cautious about neat divisions of priests and elders into clergy and laity. They are not terms of equal precision. A man was either as priest or he was not, and that was a matter of birth. But anyone who by virtue of age, rank or wisdom counted for something in the counsels of his community might be described as belonging to the elders. In particular while older people could not be called priests in virtue of their age or honour, priests who enjoyed respect and participated in the councils of the community could readily be included among the elders.

3. *Judith*. The Book of Judith tells the story of the deliverance of the Jews from the power of a foreign invader by the bravery and resourcefulness of a Jewish woman. Although the story is set in the

time of Nebuchadnezzar, it provides evidence for Jewish institutions at the time of its composition, most probably early in the first century BCE.

The relationship between the terms 'priests' and 'elders' in 3 Maccabees is similar to that between ἄρχοντες and πρεσβύτεροι in the book of Judith. First we hear of a letter sent from the national government described as:

ὁ ἱερεὺς ὁ μέγας, καὶ ἡ γερουσία παντὸς δήμου Ἰσραὴλ, οἳ ἐκάθηντο ἐν Ἰερουσαλήμ (the high priest and the council of the whole people of Israel who dwelt in Jerusalem, 4:8).

This language presumably echoes the terms in which the high priest's letter was couched and is typical of the way that a ruler would invoke the authority of a council and magnify its status to give weight to his own decision. This body sends instructions to the city of Bethylia. In Bethylia we meet three people described as ἄρχοντες, named Ozias, Chabris and Charmis (6:14–16). On receipt of instructions from Jerusalem they then call together all the πρεσβύτεροι of the city, and a general assembly takes place including women and children. Later (7:23) the people come together to confront Ozias 'and the rulers of the town' (καὶ τοὺς ἄρχοντας τῆς πόλεως), and make a protest 'in front of all the elders' (ἐναντίον πάντων τῶν πρεσβυτέρων). Judith hears what is said about Ozias (8:9–11), who is described as ὁ ἄρχων. She sends a message to him and to Chabris and Charmis, who are described there as οἱ πρεσβύτεροι, but whom she addresses as ἄρχοντες. Finally Ozias, Chabris and Charmis, who were earlier called οἱ ἄρχοντες are now called οἱ πρεσβύτεροι τῆς πόλεως (10:6). The conclusion to be drawn from this evidence is that for this writer — Ozias and his colleagues are both ἄρχοντες and πρεσβύτεροι. Yet the terms are not fully identical, since, while Ozias can be described as ὁ ἄρχων, he could not be described as ὁ πρεσβύτερος. Furthermore the elders are clearly a wider body than these three men, since it is they who call the elders together (6:16), and the elders hardly form a closed circle, since what results from the call is a general assembly of the citizens. The evidence permits the conclusion that the day-to-day running of

35

the town was in the hands of the ἄρχοντες, who function as an executive, presumably appointed to the task, and that these men were drawn from a circle of senior family heads whose approval and advice could be sought at a meeting of the whole population in times of need. If this is so, then we may say that ἄρχοντες are πρεσβύτεροι, for that is the group from which they are drawn, but πρεσβύτεροι are not necessarily ἄρχοντες unless they have been appointed to that office.

4. *The Story of Susannah.* The Story of Susannah, which forms one of the additions to the canonical book of Daniel,[41] tells the story of a beautiful, young Jewish woman, who is maliciously accused of adultery by two wicked elders and saved from death by the wise intervention of the young Daniel. According to the story the elders first conceive a secret passion for Susannah, who is the wife of a leader of the Jewish community in exile, and then proposition her. When she refuses, they accuse her of adultery with an unnamed young man, and demand her execution. Because of their eminence they are believed, and Susannah is only rescued from death by the intervention of Daniel, who proves the elders to be lying by the device of questioning them separately. Susannah is saved and the elders are stoned to death.

Various theories have been propounded about the origin and purpose of this story, but attached albeit tenuously to the book of Daniel it surely intends to convey the message that God never abandons those who are faithful to his Law.[42] However, it can hardly be without significance that the villains of the piece are two elders. The story begins by claiming to demonstrate the truth of a word of

---

[41] It has been preserved for us in two versions in the LXX and the text of Theodotion respectively. These are most conveniently set out in Engel's commentary (see bibliography). The history and relationship of these two texts need not concern us, but, according to C. A. Moore, *Additions*, p. 33, 'There is a growing consensus among Septuagint scholars that the Θ of Daniel was not done by the second-century translator Theodotion but by an earlier Palestinian translator, and that the Additions (sc. to Daniel) seem to have been part of that translation.' In the case of Susannah the Θ version is much the more coherent of the two and is the form in which it has been read in the Christian Church since the Fathers.

[42] So Delcor, *Daniel*, p. 278.

the Lord to the effect that, 'Wickedness came forth from Babylon through elders who as judges only seemed to guide the people'.[43] The point is then made that it was because they were elders and judges that the people believed them.[44] Finally at the turning point of the story the elders who are judging the case invite Daniel to join them, even though he is a youth, because, as they say, 'God has given you τὸ πρεσβεῖον' (v. 50).[45] The story thus has a subversive and anti-establishment feel to it. Wisdom, it says, is the gift of God and not the preserve of those authorities with whom (perhaps) the writer and his group were in dispute.[46]

The story in its Theodotion-form makes two interesting contributions to our understanding of the elders in Early Judaism. In the first place it makes plain that while elders were appointed to office, it was not to the office of elder that they were appointed. In this case we have two elders appointed as judges for the year.[47] More important, when the young Daniel appeals against the two elder-judges to the wider body of elders (who here make a somewhat belated appearance in the story as told by the Θ text),[48] they welcome him into their number on the ground that his wise intervention shows that God has given him τὸ πρεσβεῖον, that is, the same authority as themselves.[49] Despite the subversive purpose of the

[43] Θ-Susannah v. 5. The translation used is that of C. A. Moore, *Additions*. The prophetic word is generally thought to be a garbled version of Jer 29:20–3.

[44] Θ-Susannah v. 41. Cf. LXX *Susannah* v. 51: 'Daniel said to the congregation, Have no regard for the fact that these men are elders, or say to yourselves, They will never lie.'

[45] Cf. m.Sanh V. 4c 'If one of the rabbis' pupils says: I have something to bring forward about the accused for his acquittal, they let him come up and sit with them, and he does not get down from there for the whole day. If there is something to what he says, they listen to him.' But which has influenced the other?

[46] According to Wright, *NTPG*, p. 220, the story is aimed at the Hasmonean authorities.

[47] Θ-Susannah v. 5 reads: v. 5 Καὶ ἀπεδείχθησαν δύο πρεσβύτεροι ἐκ τοῦ λαοῦ κριταὶ ἐν τῷ ἐνιαυτῷ ἐκείνῳ. Lxx lacks this verse but conveys the same point by repeatedly calling them οἱ δύο πρεσβύτεποι καὶ κριταὶ, v. 29, 41.

[48] Engel believes that the Theodotion writer has introduced the idea of a council of elders into the LXX text at v. 50 in order to make the story more plausible, since the idea that just two elders could be both witnesses and judges in their own capital case is not likely. Engel, *Susannah*, p. 167.

[49] ὅτι σοὶ δέδωκεν ὁ θεὸς τὸ πρεσβεῖον, Θ-*Susannah* v. 50. The word πρεσβεῖον is not common in Greek, but it is helpfully defined for us by Plutarch

story, this is incidentally good evidence for the assumptions that it is challenging. Dignity and authority normally belong to age and experience. If Daniel possesses them, that is because God has miraculously given them to a mere youth in order to shame those who are elders by nature. This serves to show that eldership was not thought to be a constitutional office but something that is recognized, normally in wisdom born of experience. In this case it is recognized in the young Daniel through the wisdom of his intervention, and is evaluated as a gift of God.

5. *Aristeas.* The letter of Aristeas, written probably in Alexandria and usually dated to the second half of the second century BCE,[50] tells the story of how the Jewish scriptures came to be translated into Greek by seventy two Jews sent to Alexandria for this purpose. The King sends to Jerusalem to ask the High Priest to send: τοὺς μάλιστα καλῶς βεβιωκότας καὶ πρεσβυτέρους ὄντας ἄνδρας, ἐμπείρους τῶν κατὰ τὸν νόμον τὸν ἑαυτῶν (32). This phrase is difficult to translate without prejudging the issue. Hadas renders it: 'elders who have led exemplary lives and are expert in their own law'.[51] Shutt offers 'men of the most exemplary lives and mature experience, skilled in matters pertaining to their law'.[52] This nicely points up the difficulty in identifying the elders in Jewish society. Since the accent is on character and skill, 'mature experience' is much to be preferred to 'elders', and yet they are likely to have been people of social position as well. This serves to confirm the understanding of eldership that we have already formed from other literature. Eldership is primarily a matter of honour based on age and nobility. The translation was not entrusted to obscure and penniless scholars but to persons of influence and affluence and of ripe experience.

There is, however, a more difficult mention of elders in Aristeas. When the work is completed it is read aloud to a gathering of the

---

(Moralia, 787D), who speaks of τὸ δ᾽ ἀπὸ τοῦ χρόνου πρωτεῖον, ὃ καλεῖται κυρίως πρεσβεῖον, or 'the primacy that comes from time, for which there is a special word *presbeion* or 'the prerogative due to seniority in age'''. (Loeb translation)

[50] So Shutt, *OT Pseudepigrapha*, Vol. 2, pp. 8–9.
[51] Hadas, *Aristeas*, p. 111. In his note he calls them 'authoritative representatives'.
[52] Shutt, *OT Pseudepigrapha*, Vol. 2, p. 15.

Jewish community in Alexandria who receive it with acclaim, and the leaders declare that the translation must remain inviolate. This provides us with a second even more difficult reference to the elders: στάντες οἱ ἱερεῖς καὶ τῶν ἑρμηνέων οἱ πρεσβύτεροι καὶ τῶν ἀπο τοῦ πολιτεύματος οἵ τε ἡγούμενοι τοῦ πλήθους εἶπον ... (310) (the priests and the elders of the translators and some of the corporate body and the leaders of the people rose up and said ...) (Hadas).

There are several difficulties with this. If οἱ πρεσβύτεροι is taken with the preceding τῶν ἑρμηνέων, what sense does this make? Hadas simply says, 'In point of age'. But it is certainly strange to learn that only some of the translators made this statement. Since the whole group have previously been called 'elders', it is also odd to find a group within their number being called in effect 'the elders of the elders'. Moreover, why would it be appropriate for the translators to acclaim their own work?

At least three possible ways of understanding the text have been suggested. In the first place, many scholars have taken οἱ πρεσβύτεροι both with τῶν ἑρμηνέων which proceeds and with the phrase following, καὶ τῶν ἀπὸ τοῦ Πολιτεύματος, so as to make them 'elders of the people from the community'. Thus Meecham begins his note on the passage with the words, 'The "elders of the city", a term frequently found in the early period of the history of Israel... '.[53] However, Tcherikover is surely right to object that, if this interpretation is followed, Aristeas would be using πρεσβύτεροι in two different senses in the same passage without explanation.[54]

Accordingly Tcherikover prefers a second solution, taking πρεσβύτεροι only with τῶν ἑρμηνέων, and understanding the following phrase as, 'and the men (i.e. representatives) of the community, those who were the leaders of the people', the second phrase defining the first. In this way πρεσβύτεροι refers throughout to the

---

[53] Meecham, *Oldest*, pp. 186–7. Similarly Burtchaell, *Synagogue*, p. 219, cites *Aristeas* 310 to show that 'even before they had an Ethnarch the Alexandrian Jews composed a single community, with elders and an assembly.'

[54] Tcherikover, *CPJ*, Vol. 1, p. 9., n. 24.

reverend translators and not to 'elders' of either community, but it involves disregarding the particle τε, and it does not address the problem of the translators acclaiming their own work.[55]

A more radical proposal has recently been revived, namely that τῶν ἑρμηνέων should simply be omitted, so that the translation is then acclaimed by the leading Alexandrians, priests, elders, and leaders of the people.[56] This produces a smooth story but does not explain how τῶν ἑρμηνέων got into the text in the first place. I would tentatively make the proposal that the genitive is appositional, and that the phrase intends to say 'the elders who were the translators'.[57] A very early copyist, knowing that οἱ πρεσβύτεροι has hitherto always referred to the translators, added τῶν ἑρμηνέων here to make plain that he thought they were still being referred to.

If this proposal is accepted, it means that in this second passage 'the elders' originally referred to the leading men of Alexandria. There is nothing odd about that, for 'the elders' is an imprecise and flexible term of honour, equally at home in describing the scholars who came from Jerusalem and the leading men of the community that received them. In style, the passage agrees closely with the pattern we observed in 1 Maccabees, titles of honour being heaped up to show that all the people of importance were identified with this solemn moment.

6. *Josephus*. References to elders in the writings of Josephus agree well enough with the picture so far built up, but add very little to it. When he is writing the earlier history of his people, he refers to leading and influential people as elders. Thus in retelling the story of Israel's defeat of Amalek he speaks of the leaders as φύλαρχοι (tribal leaders) and as οἱ ἐν τελεῖ (those in authority) and goes on to call them οἱ πρεσβύτεροι (*AJ* 3.47.2). In most places he is

---

[55] Tcherikover was following a suggestion of Wilamowitz. This is apparently how Josephus understood the text, paraphrasing as follows: ὅ θ' ἱερεὺς καὶ τῶν ἑρμηνέων οἱ πρεσβύτεροι καὶ τοῦ πολιτεύματος οἱ προεστηκότες (*AJ* 12.108).

[56] D. Schwartz, 'Priests', p. 569, reviving a suggestion of Reinach.

[57] This suggestion will be helpful also if the present text is judged authentic. It may be compared with the notorious 'scribes of the pharisees' in Mark 2.16. This harder reading is perhaps equivalent in meaning to the more familiar 'the scribes and the pharisees', itself an epexegetic phrase. Alternatively see Cook, *Leaders*, pp. 66, 88–91.

simply following the biblical record, so that, for example, Abner consults the elders of Judah in seeking to make David king; Rehoboam rejects the advice of the elders in favour of that of the younger men; Josiah coming to the throne while still young is guided by the advice of the elders; Jeremiah is defended by the elders against the opposition of the priests; and the returning elders disparage the rebuilt temple in comparison to the earlier one (*AJ* 7.27.6, 8.216.5, 10.51.1, 10.91.1, 11.81.1). In this last passage he calls them τῶν πατρίων οἱ πρεσβύτεροι (the elders of the families), confirming that these people owe their position to birth and age rather than to appointment. The vagueness of the description can be seen from another place where the Persian governor receives instructions to assist τοῖς πρεσβυτέροις τῶν Ἰουδαίων καὶ τῶν γερόντων ἀρχοῦσιν (the elders of the Jews and the rulers of the elders, *AJ* 11.105.4), a phrase that exactly captures the assumption that age and authority will go together without being clear about any particular rank or office.

The story of Josephus' assumption of command in Galilee is particularly instructive, however (*BJ* 2.570–1). Josephus tells us that on arrival he judged it politic to involve local people of influence (τοὺς δυνατοὺς) in his administration, both to conciliate the powerful and to gain the consent of the people as a whole.

> He therefore selected from the nation seventy persons of mature years and the greatest discretion and appointed them magistrates of the whole of Gailiee ... τῶν μὲν γηραιῶν ἑβδομήκοντα τοὺς σωφρονεστάτους ἐπιλέξας κατέστησας ἄρχοντας. (*BJ* 2.570)

Josephus' purpose is to appoint ἄρχοντες. His assumption is that these will need to be drawn from among οἱ δυνατοί, and moreover that they will be γηραιοί, and σωφρονέστατοι. That is the way people thought, and Josephus is anxious to present his action as a reasonable one. He needs wise councillors and powerful allies, and it is among the senior citizens that he expects to find them. Josephus does not use the word πρεσβύτεροι to describe them, but it is clear that he could rightly do so. He does not, of course, *appoint* them to be elders, or δυνατοί, or γηραιοί. They are that already, and as

41

such they antedate his arrival. He appoints them to be ἄρχοντες, making clear the distinction between rank and appointed office. It is the same distinction that we were able to make when reading Judith.

Reading through Josephus' Jewish War one is impressed by two things. On the one hand the wide variety of terms used to describe the people in charge, and on the other the comparative rarity of the actual term πρεσβύτεροι. Two conclusions follow: Jewish society at the time was aristocratic rather than democratic in character; and πρεσβύτεροι, being merely one synonym among many others, denoted no fixed office whose title Josephus was obliged to use.

7. *New Testament.* The final witness to the role of the elders in the national life of the Jews in the period leading up to the destruction of the temple is provided by the New Testament in those places where it refers to the Jewish leadership. The evidence clusters in two places: the Synoptic passion narrative and predictions, and in the accounts of the arrest of the apostles and of Paul in the book of Acts. In only one place (Lk 7:3, to be discussed in a later section) is there a reference to elders outside Jerusalem.

Mark has five references to the elders.[58] In all of them πρεσβύτεροι are mentioned with ἀρχιερεῖς and γραμματεῖς, in one case first, but otherwise as the second or third member of the trio. Matthew has all five of Mark's references, and adds another six of his own, in which πρεσβύτεροι are associated with ἀρχιερεῖς.[59] Luke has three references, only one of which is peculiar to himself.[60] He also has an interesting variant on Mark 15:1, in which he speaks of τὸ πρεσβυτέριον τοῦ λαοῦ, ἀρχιερεῖς τε καὶ γραμματεῖς (the elders of the people, both high priests and scribes, 22:66), in which it is plain that τὸ πρεσβυτέριον *consists* of priests and scribes, confirming the impression that 'elders' should not necessarily be

---

[58] Mk 8:31 // Mt 16:21, Lk 9:22.
  Mk 11:27 // Mt 21:23, Lk 20:1.
  Mk 14:43 // Mt 26:47.
  Mk 15:1 // Mt 27:1. Cf. Lk 22:66.
[59] Mt 26:3; 27:3; 27:12; 27:20; 27:41.
[60] Lk 22:52.

taken to refer to a body distinct from other leaders mentioned in the same sentence.

We may note that 'the elders' never appear alone, but always in the company of other groups. Yet this does not so much tell us they were in fact a subordinate group, as that the evangelist uses the word to reinforce his picture of the whole leadership working together. It seems very doubtful whether we can learn much from these references about the historical composition of the leadership of Judaea in the first century. Van Tilborg doubts whether Matthew, in particular, has any interest in distinguishing between these leadership groups, Pharisees, Sadducees, scribes, high priests and elders, while Cook similarly doubts whether Mark has any first hand knowledge of the distinctions between them, or intends to distinguish them.[61] This means that we should not say, with Bornkamm, that when mentioned with priests the elders are laymen.[62] The way in which Matthew speaks of οἱ πρεσβύτεροι τοῦ λάου might seem to suggest this, but his phrase is probably rather to be seen as reflecting a desire to show that responsibility for the rejection of Jesus lies with the whole nation. The elders are not laymen so much as representatives, and their presence with the high priests, as well as being a convenient way of referring to 'the authorities', agrees with the stylistic pattern we have already observed where titles of dignity and authority are heaped together so as to indicate comprehensiveness and authority.

The case is no different when we turn to the Acts of the Apostles. Jewish elders appear in the story seven times (with one further reference to the whole πρεσβυτέριον).[63] All the references are to the Jerusalem authorities. In harmony with what we have seen elsewhere, we find that οἱ πρεσβύτεροι never appear *alone*, never appear *first*, and never appear in the *singular*. Their presence in the narrative adds weight to the statements made, but not precision. They are evidence of the patriarchal character of first-century Jewish society, and of the

---

[61] Van Tilborg, *Leaders*, pp. 1–4, Cook, *Leaders*, p. 17.
[62] Bornkamm, πρεσβύς, p. 659.
[63] Acts 4:5, 8, 23; 6:12; 22:5; 23:14; 24:1; 25:15.

collective nature of decision making, but do not appear before us as those appointed to an office of 'eldership'. Luke's usage conforms to that of other writers of the period, as we have seen.

The evidence thus presented shows that eldership was not an office among the Jews of this period, but was rather a collective term for leaders of whatever kind, and is usually found accompanying other more precise terms. It can be applied both to national leaders and to local leaders. It often adds a note of unity, solemnity and importance to the actions taken by leaders on behalf of their communities. It is evidence of a way of thinking about society, but is not the title of an office within it.[64]

The Elders in Early Judaism: The Synagogues

As we noted in the last chapter, proponents of the consensus have generally attributed the appearance of elders in the earliest churches to the influence of Jewish institutions. Elders were taken over from the synagogues. This is a very old view, going back at least to Vitringa in the seventeenth century, and is fundamental to the recent work of J. T. Burtchaell.[65] Yet it has not been without its critics. As long ago as 1904 Lowrie could say, following Sohm:

> Schürer's admirable study of Jewish organisation has disposed of the idea that the Synagogue could have furnished the pattern of Church government.[66]

[64] I have not extended this discussion to include the Mishnah, because of the well-known difficulty of determining how far it can be taken as evidence for the period before 70 CE. 'The elders' is used to refer to the men of old time (m.Aboth 5.1). In the singular it appears following the names of Shammai and Hillel (m.Or. 2.5, m.Arak. 9.4), and it sometimes refers to community leaders and teachers (m.Sanh. 11.2, cf. Mk 7:3). This is consistent with its having been a term of honour, applicable to scribes among others, rather than a distinct office, especially before 70 CE.

[65] Burtchaell, *Synagogue*, pp. 228–33, 292–99. We shall discuss his work in Chapter 4. Vitringa published a number of works in Holland between 1685 and 1696. His view is repeated by Lightfoot, *Philippians*, p. 193, Streeter, *Primitive*, p. 73; Farrer, 'Ministry', p. 142; von Campenhausen, *Authority*, p. 77; Bornkamm, πρέσβυς, p. 662; Roloff, 'Amt', p. 514.

[66] Lowrie, *Church*, p. 96. Cf. Schürer, *History*, II.2, pp. 54–68, 243ff. The view has not changed in the second edition. The same point was made by a number of scholars in

The problem has rarely been acknowledged. It continues to be assumed as something beyond question, not merely that there were people in the Jewish communities honoured with the title of 'the elders' (nobody disputes that), but that these formed a ruling council in the synagogue of a sort that the earliest churches would be likely to imitate. In seeking to resolve this question within the scope of the present study we shall not ask whether the ancient synagogue 'had' elders. Instead we shall borrow Sanders' blunt terminology and ask, Who ran the ancient synagogues?[67]

That this is a hard question to answer is partly due to the fragmentary nature of our evidence, much of it is significantly later than the period with which we are concerned, so that evidence from the third or fourth centuries should not simply be read back into the first century. It is also partly due to the diversity of situations in which the Jewish communities found themselves, so that evidence drawn from the Diaspora cannot automatically be transferred to Palestine and vice versa. Even within the Diaspora, the situation in Alexandria seems to have been quite different from that in Rome, while in Palestine conditions were not the same between largely Gentile cities and areas of Jewish control.[68]

> The word 'synagogue' covers a wide variety of phenomena, and a definition that fits one place and time may not be appropriate for another.[69]

A degree of caution is therefore appropriate here and a willingness to admit the provisional nature of all conclusions.

The word συναγωγή itself appears in our sources with different meanings. It is used in the Septuagint to translate both עדה ('edah) and קהל (qahal) with reference to the whole congregation of Israel.[70]

---

the 1970s, notably Sobosan, 'Role', p. 133; Harvey, 'Elders', p. 325; Powell, 'Ordo', p. 303; and is acknowledged by Karrer, 'Ältestament', p. 159 and MacDonald, *Pauline Churches*, p. 215.
[67] Cf. Sanders, *Judaism*, pp. 458ff. 'Who Ran What?'
[68] Schürer, *History*[2], Vol. II, p. 183, 427.
[69] Cohen, *Maccabees*, p. 114.
[70] Schrage, 'συναγωγή', p. 802.

Used with reference to the institution we are studying it may mean a meeting in the sense of a particular event (Acts 13:43), a congregation that regularly meets, the Jewish community in a place, or the building in which meetings take place. In Jewish inscriptions from the Diaspora it refers most commonly to a local congregation, rather than to the building, which was usually known by the term προσευχή.[71] This is Philo's normal usage,[72] and we meet it also in Acts 16:16. In Palestine, however, as we know from the Gospels, συναγωγή was used metonymously of the building, and this use is found also in Josephus,[73] and in the 'Theodotus' inscription discussed below.[74] So although 'the senses "congregation" and "building" cannot be sharply differentiated',[75] and to the congregation that assembled there,[76] it would not be wide of the mark to say that in general προσευχή is a Diaspora συναγωγή, and that συναγωγή is a Palestinian προσευχή.[77]

The origins of the synagogue are disputed. A minority of scholars seek to trace its origins to pre-exilic times, but most would see its emergence as a response to the strains of the Exile and the resulting Dispersion,[78] although there is no definite evidence of it before the mid-third century. At any rate it is a widely held view that the synagogue originated in the Diaspora, and only became widespread in Palestine after the Maccabean period.[79]

---

[71] See for example *CIJ*, I, 683, an inscription from the Crimea. For συναγωγή as the congregation rather than the building, see LXX *Susannah* 28, 41.

[72] Philo, *Leg* 132, 156, *Flacc*, 47, 74. An exception is *Quod Omn. Prob.* 81.

[73] Josephus *BJ* 2:285, 289, 7:44; *AJ* 19:300.

[74] *CIJ*, II, 1404, Frey gives the date as first cent. BCE/CE.

[75] Schrage, p. 807.

[76] Safrai, *Synagogue*, p. 908. Sometimes indeed this occurs in the same inscription. See Reynolds, 'Inscriptions', n. 16 (= *SEG* 17 n. 823), for an inscription from Cyrenaica dated 56 *CE* which reads: 'It was resolved by the congregation (τῆ συναγωγῆ) of the Jews in Berenice that the names of those who donated to the repairs of the synagogue (εἰς ἐπισκευὴν τῆς συναγωγῆς) be inscribed on a stele of Parian marble.' See Oster, 'Anachronism', p. 187.

[77] Levine, *Synagogue*, p. 22, Cohen, *Maccabees*, p. 112, Hengel, 'Proseuche', pp. 157–84. However, Oster shows that these are only two of a wide range of terms found in the ancient sources. See Oster, 'Anachronism', p. 186.

[78] *Encyclopedia Judaica*, Vol. 15, pp. 579–83.

[79] Schürer, *History²*, Vol. II, p. 200.

From the ancient sources it appears that the main purpose of the synagogue was the reading and study of the Law,[80] but it dealt with much else besides. At least in the Diaspora, but probably everywhere, synagogues provided a place for prayer (as evidenced by the name προσευχή), and a forum for discussion of community affairs.[81] Tcherikover writes:

> It may be assumed that any reference to a synagogue indicates the existence of an organized Jewish community.... A synagogue was a place of meetings and deliberations as well as of prayer and the study of the Torah; it was in some sense even a hostelry, since special rooms for strangers were attached to it. In small towns and villages the synagogue probably also accommodated all the public institutions of the community (such as the court or the notary's office).[82]

This can be seen from the earliest Palestinian synagogue inscription known to us, the 'Theodotus' inscription already referred to, which reads as follows:

> Theodotus the son of Vettenus, priest and ruler of the synagogue, son of a ruler of the synagogue, son's son of a ruler of the synagogue, built the synagogue for reading of the law and for teaching of the commandments, and also the strangers' lodging and the chambers and the conveniences of waters for an inn for them that need it from abroad, of which (synagogue) his fathers and the elders and Simonides did lay the foundation.[83]

Situated in Jerusalem in the first century CE,[84] this synagogue provided not only a place for study but also hospitality, catering for the needs of pilgrims to Jerusalem.

---

[80] Sanders, *Jewish Law*, cites Philo, *Hyp* 7:13, *Spec Leg* 2.62; Jos. *Apion*, 2.175. But his citing of Philo, *Quod Omn. Prob.* 81 is dubious: it refers to the Essenes. Also relevant are NT references to the synagogue: Lk 4:16ff., Acts 15:21.

[81] Jos. *Vita* 276–303.

[82] Tcherikover, *CPJ*, Vol. I, p. 8.

[83] Deissmann's translation, *Light*, p. 440.

[84] According to Deissmann and most scholars, although the first century date has recently been challenged by Kee. See next note.

Much of the published work on the ancient synagogue is concerned with the building, and there has been a lively debate in
recent years over whether there were in fact special synagogue buildings in Palestine before 70 CE. Hoenig argues that before this date
כנסת (*kenesset*) in Judea was a meeting of the community to transact
public business, and that it met in the town square, as it had done
from early times, or else in a private house or public building.[85]
Only after the destruction of the temple did the practice of desig-
nating buildings specifically for religious purposes בית הכנסת spread
from the Diaspora and Galilee to Judea. A similar view is argued by
Kee, who in a recent article questions the assumption that prior to
70 CE 'synagogue' refers to a religious building. Rather the archaeological record shows that it refers to a meeting, and the meeting
took place in private homes and public buildings and not in buildings set aside for worship.[86] Such synagogues were plentiful in
number. According to a late source there were over four hundred in
Jerusalem at the time of its destruction.[87] According to Philo, there
were 'many' synagogues in Alexandria, while inscriptions so far attest
eleven separate synagogues in Rome.[88] They should be seen not as

[85] Hoenig, 'City Square', pp. 448–76.

[86] Kee, 'Transformation', pp. 1–24. This view has been vigorously opposed by Sanders (*Law*, pp. 341–3, n. 28, 29), who instances the remains of the synagogue at Gamla in
the Golan Heights and references in Josephus to synagogue buildings at Caesarea and
Tiberias (*BJ* 2:285–90, *Vita* 276–303) as evidence of designated synagogue buildings in
Palestine as early as the first century (Cf. Lk 7:3). At the heart of the discussion is the
date of the Theodotus inscription, which clearly attests the existence in Jerusalem of a
designated synagogue building for 'reading the law and teaching the commandments'
among other things. Kee seeks to dispose of this evidence by redating the inscription to
the second century, but Sanders is surely right to argue that only before 70 *CE* would
there be wealthy priests in Jerusalem providing facilities for Jewish pilgrims. This lends
solid support to his conjecture that the reason for the absence of much architectural
evidence for synagogues in Judea in the first century is mainly due to chance and to the
fact that later synagogues were built on the sites of earlier ones so obliterating them.
   Oster, 'Anachronism', pp. 188–194, makes similar points from Josephus (*BJ* 7.43–4,
AJ 19.299–305), and Philo (*Quod Omn. Prob* 81). He argues that the archaeological
evidence does not so much show that the synagogues met in private houses, but that in
some cases they met in what *had been* private houses — a very different matter.

[87] TJ, Meg. 3:1, and Ket. 105a.

[88] Leon, *Jews*, pp. 159f. Contra Frey, *CIJ*, p. lxviii, who had argued for thirteen. Leon
also notes that, 'It is very likely that not all eleven of these congregations existed at the
same time' (p. 166). Both Leon and Frey are at this point talking about congregations
rather than buildings.

mere buildings or as groups of worshippers, but as the vital focus and embodiment of a community of Jewish people.

Who then ran the synagogues as we have described them? We may distinguish between the day to day running of the synagogue and its activities, especially its religious meetings, from the leadership of the community of which it was the centre.[89] From inscriptions,[90] and also from the accounts of synagogue life in the New Testament,[91] we know that the meetings of the synagogue were supervised by the ἀρχισυνάγωγος. This was clearly an important office, as we can see from its prominence in inscriptions. Its holder is likely to have been a well-to-do person of some education, chosen by the leading members of the Jewish community from among their own number. In the case of the famous Theodotus he was in fact a priest, although it was not a priestly office that he held in the synagogue.[92] It is possible that there was more than one in a synagogue at one time (Acts 13:15), and three inscriptions all later than our period name women as holders of the office.[93] While ἀρχισυνάγωγοι did not themselves read the Scriptures, teach or lead prayer, they were responsible for inviting people to do so (Acts 13:15), and for the good order of the service (Lk 13:14). Other functions of the synagogue were carried out by the חזן / ὑπηρέτης, who looked after the building, administered discipline and taught the children.

Yet the separate synagogues were not in our sense of the term independent congregations. Meetings for worship and the other activities of the synagogue took place under the authority of the Jewish community, so that the people who ran the community ran the synagogues. The constitutional nature of this community varied

---

[89] For this distinction, see Frey, *CIJ*, p. lxxxii.

[90] Over thirty of these are known and from a wide geographical spread, Brooten, *Women Leaders*, p. 23, Frey, *CIJ*, p. xcvii.

[91] Mark 5:22, Acts 13:15, 18:8, 17.

[92] For the prominence of priests in the synagogue services see Sanders, *Judaism*, pp. 170–82, who argues that they provided the synagogue with a pool of educated and respected men, free from farming responsibilities and able to meet the needs of village communities for teachers, judges and scribes (Philo, *Hyp* 7.13).

[93] See Brooten, *Women Leaders*, pp. 5–33 for these inscriptions and the various interpretations they have received.

widely. In the Jewish homeland, where Jews had freedom to run their own affairs under Roman suzerainty, Jewish towns had their officers and councils, and the local aristocracy (who, as we have seen, might be called οἱ πρεσβύτεροι among other things) controlled the affairs of the community, providing the ἄρχοντες from among themselves and meeting in council when necessary. The authorities in larger towns exercised jurisdiction over the surrounding villages, and the authority of the high priest and his council extended at least over Judaea.[94] In such areas, according to Schürer, 'the elders of the community will also have been the elders of the synagogue'.[95] We catch a glimpse of them when the elders of Capernaum petition Jesus on behalf of the centurion (Lk 7:3), and when 'the elders' lay the foundation of Theodotus' synagogue. Although in both cases elders are mentioned in connection with a synagogue, we should not think of them as religious officials or as elders of the synagogue as such. They are more likely to be members of the local council delighted to be associated with the opening of a synagogue in their area.[96]

Things were different in the Diaspora, and in Palestinian cities where the Jews had no political control. It should be said once again that our knowledge here is extremely patchy. Almost nothing is known, for example about conditions in the eastern Diaspora until much later than the first century. Elsewhere the Jews formed a distinct community within the Gentile cities where they lived. This community was in some places called τὸ πολίτευμα, as in Alexandria and Berenice, but might also be known as ἡ κατοικία, ὁ Λαός, το Ἔθνος, and later as ἡ συναγωγή.[97] The form of this community also varied widely, although only those of Alexandria and Rome are known to us in any detail, and these present a contrast. In Alexandria the πολίτευμα appears to have exercised authority over Jewish life throughout the city and to have been led

[94] Schürer, *History²*, Vol. II, p. 197.
[95] Schürer, *History²*, Vol. II, p. 429.
[96] Schürer, *History²*, Vol. II, p. 185.
[97] Schürer, *History²*, Vol. III, pp. 90–1.

by an Ethnarch together with a council.[98] In Rome we have no evidence of this, but only of various individual συναγωγαί functioning as 'private associations',[99] each with their own officers, whose tombs and memorial inscriptions provide us, as we have seen, with evidence of some eleven synagogal communities. It is likely that most places in the Diaspora more closely resembled Rome than Alexandria, but, as for the most part we have only one or two fragmentary inscriptions to go on, it is impossible to be sure.

The inscriptions mention various community offices, including the γερουσιάρχης,[100] and even in one case of an ἀρχιγερουσιάρχος.[101] Following Schürer,[102] and Frey,[103] scholars have generally considered that this person will have held the position of President of the Council, or γερουσία, that is presumed to have existed in each community, a sort of Diaspora counterpart to the high priest in Jerusalem.[104] There are also frequent references to men having been ἄρχοντες, the most general term for administrative officials in the Jewish communities as in the rest of the Graeco-Roman world,[105] to people with the title of φροντιστής, γραμματεύς, προστάτης, and πατήρ/μητήρ συναγωγῆς. We can only guess for the most part at the responsibilities involved. What is important to note is that all these titles refer to officials

---

[98] Josephus AJ, 14.7, 2. Phil. Leg 132.

[99] Schürer, History², p. 91.

[100] For example, CIJ, Nos 9, 95, 106, 119.

[101] Horsley, Documents, I, No. 73.

[102] Schürer, History², Vol. II, p. 435; Vol. III, pp. 98–100.

[103] Frey, CIJ, I, p. lxxxv.

[104] Burtchaell (Synagogue, pp. 237–40) challenges this consensus, arguing that it may be no more than an honorary position of senior elder, either the senior elder, something like the 'Father of the House' in the British parliament, or else a senior elder, equivalent to being an alderman in a British town council. Executive power over the community lay, Burtchaell argues, with the ἀρχισυνάγωγος, whom Schürer was wrong to characterize as merely responsible for arranging the worship in the local synagogues (see Schürer, History², Vol. II, pp. 433–6). One has to say that the Theodotus inscription tells against this, since clearly in Jerusalem Theodotus cannot have been more than leader of his own congregation.

[105] Like their counterparts in Greek cities, archons were elected annually. Leon, Jews, p. 175f., argues that only one held office at a time within each congregation and acted as an executive officer, but this is conjectural.

with responsibility for the secular concerns of the community as a whole, unlike the official in charge of the meeting for study and prayer, the ἀρχισυνάγωγος, whose role we have already discussed in relation to the synagogues of the homeland.

Among all these titles, that of 'elder' is comparatively rare. There are less than a dozen inscriptions listed by Frey which mention πρεσβύτερος/οι at all.[106] Horsley gives one other.[107] They are either epitaphs or dedicatory inscriptions and the earliest is dated 244/5 CE. The majority have πρεσβύτερος in the singular following a man's name, identifying him as an elder of the community. Little can be gleaned from these. A rather smaller number refer to 'the elders', apparently as a body or group of some kind. For example from Syria we have the following:

ἐπι, τῶν τιμιωτάτων ἀρχισυναγώγων Εὐσεβίου καὶ Νεμίου καὶ Φινέου, καὶ Θεοδώρου γερουσιάρχου καὶ τῶν τιμιωτάτων πρεσβυτέρων Εἰσακίου καὶ Σαούλου καὶ λόιπων... .[108] (in the days of the most illustrious archisynagogoi Eusebius and Nemias and Phineas, and Theodoros the gerousiarch, and the most illustrious elders Eisakios and Saoulos and the others... .)

We may wonder why it is so rare. The probable answer to this question will itself help us to understand the meaning of the title. We may take it for granted that there was in all of these Jewish communities a γερουσία, but if so, then it is not likely to have been a body with defined membership or fixed constitutional rights and duties.[109] In the light of what we have seen of the Sanhedrin in Jerusalem, it is more likely to have met as required to rule on matters of dispute in the community, and to have consisted of the senior representatives of the leading families. Its members could be

[106] Frey, *CIJ*, Nos. 378, 663, 739, 790, 800, 803, 829, 931 and 1404.
[107] Horsley, *Documents* IV, p. 215.
[108] Frey, *CIJ*, No. 803, Syria, 391 CE.
[109] This would explain why, according to Leon, *Jews*, p. 181, there is no direct mention of it in the Roman inscriptions.

referred to as 'the elders', but this was everywhere an imprecise term of honour of fairly widespread application. When it came to remembering a man's achievements, people preferred to mention the offices in the community which the deceased had held, ἄρχων, γερουσιάρχης, above all ἀρχισυνάγωγος.[110] It goes without saying that people who had held these offices were also to be numbered among the elders of the community, but 'elder' was probably not an office as such and that is why it is so little mentioned.[111] This, of course, is consistent with what we have observed about this title in other places.

A glimpse of the way things probably worked in the local congregational meeting is provided by a passage of Philo preserved for us by Eusebius which, if it does not use the word πρεσβύτεροι (it uses a synonym, γέροντες), nevertheless bears on our subject.[112]

> And indeed they do always assemble and sit together, most of them in silence except when it is the practice to add something to signify approval of what is read. But some priest who is present or one of the elders — τῶν ἱερέων δέ τις ὁ παρὼν ἢ τῶν γερόντων εἷς – reads the holy laws to them and expounds them point by point till about the late afternoon, when they depart having gained both expert knowledge of the holy laws and considerable advance in piety. (Philo, Hyp 7:13)

Sanders argues that this shows that the ancient synagogues were 'run' by priests and elders, the heads of prominent lay families living in the area, but we should notice that the elders no more occupy an office in the synagogue than do the priests, but, like the priests, they are among the leaders of the local community, men of education and influence and as such likely to be called on by the

[110] 'The rank of simple member of the Council doubtless appeared too unimportant to be commemorated in an epitaph.' Reinach, 'Inscription', *REJ*, 26 (1893), p. 170–1.
[111] 'Not so much office-holders as counsellors and leaders spontaneously recognized by the people, probably the heads of the foremost and noblest families.' Krauss, *Synagogale*, p. 143. 'Such "elders", being relatively numerous, were probably not regarded as congregational officers,' Leon, *Jews*, p. 181.
[112] This is discussed by Sanders, *Law*, pp. 77–81.

ἀρχισυνάγωγος to teach and lead when the community meets for prayer and study of the Torah.

To summarize, the ancient synagogues were 'run' on a day to day basis by their officers, the ἀρχισυνάγωγος and the ὑπηρετης. Men who were recognized as the elders of the community exercised great influence in its life, but they did not as such hold office. The synagogues existed not as independent congregations but as expressions of the life of the community to which they belonged. The elders ran the synagogue as much and as little as they ran the community, that is, they did not themselves hold an office, but their corporate judgment probably decided who did, namely, the ἄρχοντες. This would be true both of the scattered communities of Rome and the more structured πολίτευμα of Alexandria. The elders ran the synagogues, but it was not as the elders of the synagogue that they did so. They ran the synagogues because they ran the community, and they did so not in virtue of an office they held but because of the honour they enjoyed as senior men from traditionally powerful families.

The Elders in Early Judaism: Qumran

We might have hoped that the Qumran community, as a Jewish sect whose last years were contemporary with the rise of another Jewish sect, the Christian church, would provide helpful information on the role of elders and the meaning of the word, but in fact the elders prove to be as elusive in the Qumran writings and those ancient writers who refer to the Essenes[113] as everywhere else — indeed more so because of the special difficulties of interpretation presented by the Dead Sea Scrolls themselves.

In the first place the text itself is sometimes poorly preserved and the correct translation a matter of dispute.[114] Secondly, although we

---

[113] I accept the judgement of the editors of the new 'Schürer' that 'the hypothesis equating Qumran sectaries with Essenes appears to be endowed with the highest degree of probability.' History², Vol. II, p. 584.

[114] This is specially so for the document variously called The Messianic Rule, or The Rule of the Congregation (1QSa). All quotations from the Scrolls in this chapter are taken from Vermes, DSSE³.

have a number of documents providing rules for the ordered life of the community, they are not all talking about the same thing. The Community Rule (1QS) legislates for the community that lived in conditions of monastic separation by the Dead Sea, whereas The Damascus Rule (CD) provides for the life of those who were living away from Qumran in the towns and villages of Judaea, which the Rule calls 'camps', where they engaged in many of the same everyday activities as their non-sectarian neighbours, rearing children and engaging in trade and agriculture. On the other hand The Messianic Rule (1QSa) presented an ideal constitution for the life of the community in the new age, so that, as with The War Rule (1QM), it is a matter of dispute how far the actual state of affairs in the Essene communities can be read off from them.[115] Thirdly, the documents as we have them appear to have come to their present form over a period of time, with new legislation being added alongside the old as the community developed.[116] The Scrolls may therefore present something of a moving target.

Finally, precisely because the sect sought to legitimate itself from the Scriptures at all points, it is not always clear whether the various terms used actually refer to separate realities, or what in fact these realities were. For example, The Damascus Rule quotes Ezekiel 44:15 and then interprets it as follows:

> As God ordained for them by the hand of the prophet Ezekiel, saying, *The Priests, the Levites, and the sons of Zadok who kept the charge of my sanctuary when the children of Israel strayed from me, they shall offer me fat and blood.*
>
> The *Priests* are the converts of Israel who departed from the land of Judah, and the *Levites* are those who joined them. The *sons of Zadok*, are the elect of Israel, the men called by name who shall stand at the end of days. (CD 3:21 — 4:4)

---

[115] Schiffman, *Community*, can speak of 1QSa providing 'a mirror image of the society described in the Manual of Discipline' (p. 9). Others, for example Knibb, *Qumran*, (p. 145), are more cautious.

[116] Schiffman, for example, thinks that the role of the priests at Qumran is in the process of becoming ceremonial as the sect is becoming 'more democratized', *Law*, p. 4, *Community*, p. 35.

Does this mean the founding members were in fact priests, or does it mean that the true interpretation of this verse is that the founders (and their successors in leadership?) are the true fulfilment of this prophecy and the real priests before God (rather than the corrupt priesthood in Jerusalem)? What cannot be disputed is that 'sons of Zadok', which is here used for ordinary Israelites, or members of the community, is elsewhere used as a synonym for the priests in distinction from the ordinary members (1QS 5:2–3). This flexibility in the use of terms will need to be borne in mind when interpreting other passages that refer to elders or Levites, for example.

All of this means that any attempt to reconstruct the institutions of the Qumran community or its satellite groups is an extremely complex and uncertain undertaking, and one which falls outside the scope of the present work. Nevertheless some attempt must be made to sketch the character and constitution of the sect so as to be able to explain the few references to 'elders' that occur in the Scrolls. The very difficulty of doing this is not without significance for our topic, since if we can see *why* it is so hard to define the place of the elders at Qumran, we may understand why that is so in the church as well.

The Dead Sea Scrolls bear witness to a community dedicated to living in the highest degree of ritual purity, and to that end engaged in the study of the Old Testament Scriptures. Those who lived at Qumran and those who lived outside in the 'camps' shared the same outlook and values, but only by living at Qumran itself could members actually achieve that ideal of purity to which all were committed. The Community Rule (1QS) refers to those able to separate themselves physically from the contamination of normal Jewish society. The Damacus Rule (CD) provides for those who must seek to follow the rules of the sect while still living 'in the world', while The Messianic Rule (1QSa) appears to envisage a time when the Messiah has come and the whole people, men, women and children, will live together in holiness.

Life at Qumran was regulated according to a strict hierarchy. References to rank are frequent. For example:

And they shall all sit before [the priest] according to their rank and shall be asked their counsel in all things in that order. (1QS 6:4)

This rank appears to be a matter of merit, not of birth. Members are ranked 'one after another according to the perfection of their spirit' (1QS 2:20). This is explained a little later as follows:

> But when a man enters the Covenant to walk according to all these precepts that he may join the holy Congregation, they shall examine his spirit in community with respect to his understanding and practice of the Law... . They shall inscribe them in order, one after another according to their understanding and their deeds, that every one may obey his companion, the man of lesser rank obeying his superior. (1QS 5:20–3)

This rank is not fixed or constant. There is an annual examination, and men can be moved up or down. Rank is thus according to understanding of and obedience to the Scriptures as interpreted by the sect.

By contrast, rank does not appear to have been by age. From The Messianic Rule we learn that a person could become a full member of the community at twenty, and could hold a position of leadership at thirty. However, when he becomes 'advanced in years' he must relinquish his office, and when he manifests symptoms of senility he is excluded from the meetings of the community in the same way as are other crippled or handicapped people. While, as we have seen, The Messianic Rule envisages the conditions of the 'last days', the stipulations concerning age were presumably applied by the community in the present time, as is confirmed by the fact that The Damascus Rule directs that Judges are not to serve beyond sixty years of age, and that the Guardian of all the camps shall be from thirty to fifty years old. These age limits, like so much else in the constitution of the sect, appear to have been taken directly from Scripture, being inspired by the age stipulations regarding the Levites in the Pentateuch,[117] and perhaps also the age for military service,

---

[117] For example, Num. 4:3, 23, 30, 35, 47. See Schiffman, *Community*, p. 25f. for the suggestion that it is the requirements of the holy war that have influenced the retirement age.

the sect being seen as the army of the Lord mobilized for war. It is not possible to know how strictly these limits were enforced, but at least they place no particular value on old age per se. Age, we may say, is thus a necessary but not a sufficient condition of rank at Qumran. A man was not admitted to a position of responsibility without a minimum age, but age by itself neither secured him honour nor kept him in it.

One of the signs that The Messianic Rule paints an ideal picture of the congregation is that there is no individual at the head of the congregation, apart, of course, from the Messiah himself. Instead, as befits the true Israel, the congregation marches under a collective leadership whose titles are derived from the description of Israel in the Wilderness.

> At the age of thirty years he may ... take his place among the chiefs of the Thousands of Israel, the chiefs of the Hundreds, Fifties and Tens, the Judges and the officers of their tribes, in all their families, under the authority of the sons of Aaron the Priests. (1QSa 1:13–15)

This is clearly an idealized description and tells us nothing about the actual organization of the Essene communities.[118]

By contrast, in The Community Rule and also in The Damascus Rule, which must provide for the administration of the community in this present age, there is an overall leader of the community, who is referred to by various titles. Sometimes he is called מַשְׂכִּיל (maskil, 1QS 3:13; 9:14), translated by Vermes as 'Master', and by Knibb 'the wise leader'. Sometimes he is called פָּקִיד (paqid, 1QS 6:14), which Vermes renders 'Guardian' (Knibb calls him 'the officer in charge'). Most commonly he is called מְבַקֵּר (mebaqqer, 1QS 6:11–12; CD 13:7ff.), which Vermes also renders 'Guardian', Knibb 'overseer'. He is responsible for teaching the community (1QS 3:13; CD

---

[118] Vermes (DSSE³, p. 2) points out, for example, that the Qumran community cannot have numbered more than about 200 people at a time, and that according to Josephus (AJ 18:21) the total number of Essenes was only slightly above 4000. The reference to leaders of Thousands is therefore impossible, and the whole list is probably quite idealized.

13:7ff.). Within the 'camps', or communities of Essenes external to Qumran, his duties closely resemble those of a pastor ('He shall love them ... carry them in all their distress ... he shall loosen all the fetters that bind them' CD 13:9–10). He presides at meetings (1QS 6:11–12), where his authority interpenetrates that of the congregation, as they in turn follow the lead he gives.[119] He also apparently acts as Bursar, since he is called 'the overseer over the property of the Many' (1QS 6:19–20), and receives the offerings of the congregation (CD 14:13). In CD, in addition to the Guardian of the camp, we also meet someone called 'the Guardian of all the camps' (CD 14:8–9), whom Vermes suggests is in fact identical with the Guardian at Qumran, each of the camps having its own Guardian, but recognizing the primacy of the head of the community at Qumran.[120] Some scholars assert that this figure was a layman,[121] but in view of the prestige of priests at Qumran it is surely more likely, as Vermes says,[122] that he was a priest, and we may suppose that the reference to 'the priest who enrols (יפקד) the Congregation' (CD 14:6–7) is another reference to the Guardian of the camp. We shall consider the role of the מבקר again when we come to look at the leadership of the earliest Christian house-churches.[123]

The most characteristic institution at Qumran was the congregational assembly, which appears to have met under the presidency of the Guardian to eat and drink the Covenant meal and to deliberate together.

> Every decision concerning doctrine, property and justice shall be determined by them (i.e. by the men of the Community meeting under the authority of the Priests). (1 QS 5:3)

Aspiring members were questioned by the Guardian at a meeting of

---

[119] Reicke helpfully compares the interlocking roles of leader and congregation in Luke's account of the Jerusalem Council in Acts 15. See 'Constitution', p. 147.

[120] Vermes, DSSE³, p. 17.

[121] Knibb, Qumran, p. 96, 118, and Sanders, Judaism, p. 365.

[122] Vermes, DSSE³, p. 3.

[123] See Chapter 5, pp. 155–8.

the assembly, with whom lay the decision whether to admit them to their number or not. All full members of the sect belonged to this assembly, and took part in the trial of those accused of transgressions.

The passage that gives the Rule for an assembly of the Congregation begins as follows:

> Each man shall sit in his place: the Priests shall sit first, and the elders second, and all the rest of the people according to their rank. (1QS 6:8)

Although this might seem to be clear evidence for the existence of a council of elders, or at least the position of elder, in the Qumran community, this is actually unlikely. In the first place, this is in fact the only passage we have that appears to give a role to elders in the government of the community, compared with many references to the role of the Guardian, the Priests and the Congregation (or 'Council of the Community'). Secondly, two other passages, which are in other respects similar, do not use the word 'elders', substituting 'Levites' instead:

> The priests shall enter first, ranked one after another according to the perfection of their spirit; then the Levites; and thirdly, all the people one after another in their Thousands, Hundreds, Fifties and Tens. (1QS 2:19)

and:

> The Rule for assembly of all the camps. They shall all be enroled by name: first the Priests, the Levites second, the Israelites third, and the proselytes fourth. And thus shall they sit and be questioned on all matters. (CD 14:6)

The Levites can only be understood by reference to the Priests. In the scriptural model on which The Community Rule is based, the Levites are assistant priests. In the life of the Community, 'Priests' on occasion denotes those who are the founder members of the community (CD 4:2), and more generally those who direct its counsels by virtue of their continual study of the Law (1QS 6:3–6). Accordingly, 'Levites' refers to those who were subsequently added to the community (as CD 4:3 says) and presumably assisted the Priests in the practical administration of the community.[124]

It is impossible to be sure why the word 'elders' has been substituted for Levites in this one passage, but it must surely be another term for the same people,[125] and can hardly be taken as evidence for a separate rank or body of leaders in the community. The likelihood is that it is a term which commended itself because of its biblical resonance as a way of honouring those whose status as Levites elevated them above the rank and file.

Elders appear in only one other place in the Scrolls, and here too there is a closely parallel passage in which another term is substituted for them. In The War Rule we read:

> (The High Priest) shall come, and his brethren the Priests and the Levites, and all the elders of the army shall be with him. (1QM 13:1)

But earlier we are told of:

> The priests, the Levites and the heads of the tribes ... the priests as well as the Levites and the divisions of the fifty two heads of the family of the congregation. (1QM 2:1)

Here the elders of the army is another way of describing the heads of the family of the congregation, the elders being the heads of the fathers' houses, exactly as we have seen them to be in the Pentateuchal narrative.

A similar passage of The Messianic Rule speaks of 'the heads of the families of the congregation, the leaders, the judges, and officers' (1QSa 1:24). These people could of course quite properly be referred to as the elders. However, the passage is hardly describing any constitutional reality at Qumran, but rather painting a picture of the mustering of Israel before the Messiah, so that if the passage is not evidence for the presence at Qumran of anybody called 'the heads of the families of the congregation etc.', neither is it evidence for the presence of a body of elders.

---

[124] Nothing explicit is said about this, but see 1QSa 1:23–5.
[125] So Reicke, 'Constitution', p. 150.

It might be thought, however, that there is evidence of a council of senior men at Qumran, in addition to the assembly, to whom the title of elders might apply, in other words that although the word is not used, the concept of a council of elders is present. This is doubtful. The only evidence for it is provided by a passage which reads:

> In the Council of the Community there shall be twelve men and three Priests. (1QS 8:1)

But a little earlier we have been told that,

> Every man, born of Israel, who freely pledges himself to join the Council of the Community shall be examined by the Guardian at the head of the Congregation concerning his understanding and his deeds.

This implies that 'the Council of the Community' is none other than the congregational assembly itself, in which case the word 'Council' is not so much a body of people as an event, the holding of a meeting of members.[126] The reference to 'twelve men and three Priests' most probably refers to a quorum for an assembly of the congregation, or else possibly to the initial core group at the time when the sect was coming into being.[127]

We should conclude from these references that 'elder' was never the title of an office at Qumran. In The Damascus Rule provision is made for people to do the things elders do. The panel of ten judges (CD 10:4–10) could very well have been called 'elders', but they are not, and the emphasis of the passage is on their retiring before they get too old! To repeat, the word 'elder' is extremely rare in the Scrolls, and where it occurs it is simply a biblical honorific for the Levites or other leading figures in an idealized Israel.

There is nothing in Josephus' or Philo's accounts of the Essenes to disturb this conclusion. Josephus says:

---

[126] Knibb, *Community*, p. 129.

[127] Schiffman, *Law*, p. 25. 'There can be no question that the text deals only with a minimum number of members for the sect or of a particular settlement of its members.' Otherwise, Reicke, 'Constitution', p. 151 and Draper, 'Apostles', p. 47ff.

They also regard it as a good thing to obey the elders (τοῖς πρεσβυτέροις) and the majority (Jos *BJ* 2:146).

We may compare 1QS 5:2:

> They shall be answerable to the sons of Zadok, the priests who keep the covenant, and to the multitude of the men of the community.

Josephus is saying no more than the Scrolls themselves say, but the fact that he uses the word πρεσβυτέροις is hardly evidence for the existence of a rank or office of elder at Qumran. Josephus is merely referring to those who are in charge, whom we know from the Scrolls to be the Guardian and the Priests.[128] In any case, the passage in which this comes is concerned with describing the piety and high ethical standards of the Essenes rather than constitutional niceties. In the world of Josephus' day respect for elders was generally prized as a mark of godliness, and it takes its place here between reverence for God and for Moses on the one hand, and not spitting in the midst of the group and burying their excrement on the other!

Similarly Philo's reference to 'elders' among the Essenes makes him a witness to the hierarchical nature of life in the community, not to its constitution. The passage reads:

> They proceed to sacred spots, which they call synagogues. There arranged in rows according to their ages, the younger below the elder, they sit decorously as befits the occasion with attentive ears. (Quod Omn. Prob. 81)

From our knowledge of The Community Rule we can see that he is reliably informed, but his purpose is to praise what his readers would have seen as their old-fashioned virtue.

From the fact that the word 'elders' is extremely rare in the Scrolls, and that there does not seem to have been a body or rank at

---

[128] See Sanders, *Judaism*, p. 366. Otherwise Beall, *Essenes*, p. 94, who speaks of the elders and the majority as 'authoritative bodies who are obeyed by the Essene members'. But the passage speaks of the submissiveness of the individual, not the structures of the community.

Qumran to which the title of 'elder' belonged, it might be thought that Qumran contributes little to our subject or that the contribution is at best entirely negative. This is not so. In fact when we enquire as to the likely reasons for this absence, we shall find that it serves to confirm what we know of the elders from our study so far and also to illuminate the emergence of the term in the Christian churches.

The reason that the term 'the elders' appears so rarely in Qumran is that the community saw itself as a community of priests. The purity in which all seek to live, and by which they are ranked, is priestly purity. As we have seen, even the ordinary members of the sect can on occasion be described as 'the sons of Zadok' (CD 4:3). It is priests who dominate the life of the community (1QS 5:2), and who act as its authoritative teachers (1QS 6:3). Priests, we may say, *fulfil the role of the elders* at Qumran, but 'the elders' is not a usual way to describe priests. A people whose every waking moment was governed by the Pentateuch and by a desire to be conformed to the model of priestly holiness it contains would know perfectly well that the elders in the Pentateuch are the heads of the fathers' houses — and in the celibate community of Qumran there were no fathers' houses! It is then not the absence of the term from The Community Rule that is surprising, but its one rogue appearance.

A second reason suggests itself. 'The elders' wherever it appears in our literature is a collective term, referring quite generally to the people of weight and honour in the community. Individual rulers or chiefs are not known as 'the elder'. Among the Essenes, both at Qumran and in the 'camps' of The Damascus Rule, we find a single overseer or Guardian at the head of each community. He presides over the congregational assembly at Qumran, and exercises pastoral oversight in the 'camps'. It would not be natural to refer to the Guardian as 'the Elder'. We do not know how many Essene communities there were, whether monastic communities in the desert or 'lay' communities in the towns, but it would only be natural to refer to their overseers as 'the Elders' of the community if in fact the overseers met together in some representative capacity to deliberate on behalf of the community, or if someone wished to refer collectively to the overseers as a body or rank. There is no opportunity in the Scrolls for anyone to do this.

'Elder' is thus not a natural word to find either in a monastic setting where the community is not based on family units, or to describe a single overseer acting within his own community. By contrast, we shall not be surprised to see the term emerging within the household-based Christian churches, nor that as a collective term it appears when the households begin to multiply. But this is to anticipate!

Conclusions

This chapter has sought to follow through the use of the term 'the elders' in Jewish sources that between them span a period of over a thousand years. Since this enquiry is but a preliminary to our main task of studying the use of the term in earliest Christianity, the treatment has necessarily been selective rather than exhaustive. Yet what strikes one is how uniform in meaning the term proves to be. We may sum up our findings by addressing two questions.

Were the elders holders of an office? The answer must surely be No. Whether we look at the history of ancient Israel or the political life of early Judaism, at the nation as a whole or the life of a town or village within it, the answer is the same. The elders are the senior men of the community, heads of the leading families within it, who as such exercise an authority that is informal, representative and collective. It is a term both flexible and vague. It neither denotes particular office-holders, nor excludes them, but can easily associate with more precise official titles. An author who does not wish to do so is not obliged to use it at all, and can describe the local aristocracy by a range of other titles. The term cannot be shown to have denoted the officers of a religious organization, whether in the synagogue congregation or in the Qumran sect, and for most Jewish people in our period it was a term more commonly associated with what we would call the 'civic' community. To speak of the elders as officers is thus something of a category mistake, since 'the elders' does not so much denote an office as connote prestige. The holders of office may be included, but the word is a sign that prestige in the community is not confined to such people.

Secondly we may ask, *Were the elders then necessarily old men?* Again the answer is No. Their authority did not rest on age alone, but on the prestige of the families whose heads they were. The society we have been studying can properly be described as an aristocracy.[129] Age, of course, was an important factor in a man attaining headship, but hardly a sufficient or necessary cause. In a society prone to disease and death in war, many men must have succeeded their fathers at a comparatively young age. At the same time, we should not neglect the probability that there was an ideal of eldership at work. Eldership connotes age, wisdom and honour, even when not all of those denoted by 'the elders' in a particular context possess these qualities.

---

[129] Josephus in fact uses this term both of pre-monarchic Israel and of Roman Judaea, *AJ* 4:223, *BJ* 1:169.

Chapter Three

The Elders in Graeco-Roman Society

Earliest Christianity was a movement within Judaism that experienced its first great period of growth within the Graeco-Roman world. To the Jewish inheritance with which it was born was added the influence of the social environment in which it grew up. It is for this reason that we have examined the Jewish background first before moving to the Graeco-Roman. Dictionaries, tracing the history of a Greek word, operate the other way round. They start with the earliest Greek literature, move through the classical period to the Hellenistic age and come in due course to the Septuagint and so to the Jewish background to the New Testament. Our concern is not with the history of a word, but with the formation of an institution, the Christian ministry in its earliest forms. If we think of this as a river rising within Judaism, Graeco-Roman influences may be seen as tributary to it, entering the main stream at a point lower than the source. Accordingly, having surveyed the Jewish background, we shall now consider the Graeco-Roman.

This chapter will first sketch very briefly some aspects of the constitutional history of the Graeco-Roman world, from its beginnings in Homeric Greece, through the democratic experiment of classical Athens, to the rise of the Hellenistic kingdoms and their eventual absorption within the Roman Empire. This will show that, while the term οἱ πρεσβύτεροι is rarely used to describe those in authority, the underlying social patterns are very similar to those of the Jewish world. Although Athenian notions of democracy posed a challenge to their rule, the senior members of well-to-do families continued to wield power and influence at most times and in most places. The usual term for them is οἱ γέροντες, and they are conceptually equivalent of οἱ πρεσβύτεροι in Jewish society and exercise a similar function.

We shall then consider the status of older people within Graeco-Roman society, taking issue with the view that older people were not in fact accorded much respect there. The evidence here is mainly literary, and it will be shown from a variety of ancient authors that respect for the senior man was as deeply rooted in the Graeco-Roman world as in the Jewish. The relevance of this evidence has been questioned, in that many of the authors are upper-class literary men who lived a long time before the period with which we are concerned, but it must be remembered that the classical authors, from Homer to Aristotle, were used as textbooks in Graeco-Roman schools, so that generations of children imbibed the attitudes they inculcated. Respect for one's elders was a deeply ingrained attitude and an almost universally accepted mark of virtue, which was institutionalized within the ancient household, where the role of ὁ κύριος, or *paterfamilias*, was performed by the senior male. Evidence from comparative anthropology will underline the importance of the extended family in preserving the status and influence of the elders in society.

A Brief Survey of Graeco-Roman Constitutional History

We have seen that in constitutional terms the form of government enjoyed by the Jewish people, whether in Ancient Israel or Second Temple Judaism, was that of an aristocracy or oligarchy. In Ancient Israel we saw that the elders were the heads of leading families, and that this continued to be the case in the Second Temple period. The high priests and the heads of wealthy non-priestly families formed an aristocratic oligarchy whose members were loosely referred to as 'the elders'. At the village level a similar pattern prevailed. Those possessing property or other means of influence, whose families traditionally took a lead, and who were moreover at the head of such families by reason of seniority — these were the elders of the community whose opinion tended to carry the day in a gathering of the people. Politically speaking, then, a society where the rulers are called 'elders' may be termed an aristocracy.[1]

The earliest form of government enjoyed by the Greeks, as we see from the Homeric poems, is also a form of aristocracy. There is a king, or tribal leader, who is responsible for the well-being of his people, from whom he in turn receives honour and tribute in the form of the first share of the spoil. The qualities required of such a king closely resemble those required of the king in the Old Testament.[2] The king is surrounded by a council of elders, who are themselves sometimes called kings, and are the heads of powerful clans and families. The king calls them together at his discretion and summons a general assembly of the people when necessary. The leading speakers are the elders, and people indicate their assent by acclamation.

Two examples will suffice. In the first, Agamemnon calls a council of the elders: βουλὴν δὲ πρῶτον μεγαθύμων ἷζε γερόντων (Iliad 2.53) (But the king first made the council of the great-souled elders to sit down). Nestor, as the oldest of them, replies favourably and counsels action, whereupon the council breaks up, and the other 'sceptred kings' rise from their seats and follow the 'shepherd of the people':

οἱ δ'ἐπανέστησαν πείθοντό τε ποιμένι λαῶν σκηπτοῦχοι βασιλῆες· ἐπεσσεύοντο δὲ λαοί (2.85f.) (and the other sceptred kings rose up and obeyed the shepherd of the people, and the people hastened after)

The second example is provided by the story of Odysseus in the court of the Phaecian king Alcinous. Odysseus finds the king sitting

---

[1] Arnheim, *Aristocracy*, defines aristocracy as 'a state dominated by a section of the population whose position was hereditary' (p. 10). The term 'gerontocracy', so far as I know, refers to a purely theoretical concept. There never has been a people ruled simply by the old, as opposed to the oldest members of specific families, and the term 'gerontocracy', being of modern origin, is basically a term of abuse.

[2] Mentor reproaches the people of Ithaca as follows: 'Never henceforth let sceptred king with a ready heart be kind and gentle, nor let him heed righteousness in his heart, but let him ever be harsh and work unrighteousness, seeing that no one remembers divine Odysseus of the people whose lord he was; yet gentle was he as a father' (*Od* 2.230ff. (*LCL* translation.) Cf. Ps 72, Ezek 34.

in the midst of his elders; he appeals to the king, and the first to speak is

> the old Lord Echeneus, who was an elder among the Phaecians, well skilled in speech and understanding all the wisdom of the old (Odyssey 7.136ff.)

At a more humble level, the Shield of Achilles portrays a typical village scene where the elders take their seats to settle a village dispute, in a manner not dissimilar to their role at the end of the book of Ruth.

> And the elders (οἱ δὲ γέροντες) sat on the polished stone seats in the sacred circle, taking the rod in their hands as they received it from the loud-voiced heralds: they should each stand forward with the rod and give his judgment in turn. (Iliad 18:503ff.)[3]

The early history of Athens, about which we are much better informed than about other Greek city-states, is the history of the replacement of aristocracy by democracy. The reforms of Solon (594 BCE) ended the power of the hereditary aristocracy. He redistributed the land, made the archonship open to people of wealth irrespective of family, and made the archons answerable to the assembly, by whom they were to be elected. The ancient council of the Areopagus, which had originally been the king's council, Solon made the guardian of the constitution and supreme court for trying cases of homicide, and its ranks were swelled by ex-archons at the end of their year of office. This body has the best title to be called 'the elders' in the Athenian state, but it had little real power, especially after 487 BCE when the archons themselves were appointed by lot and ceased to be politically important.

Subsequent reforms further strengthened the position of the citizen assembly, known as ὁ δῆμος, or ἡ ἐκκλησία, so that by the fifth century power lay with a mass meeting of the male citizens

---

[3] Translated by M. Hammond, Penguin Classics, 1987. Homeric society is discussed by G. M. Calhoun in Wace and Stubbings, *Companion to Homer*, pp. 432ff. According to T. L. B. Webster, the poems in their present form combine memories of the Myceanaean Age with descriptions of life in eighth century Greece, ibid. pp. 452ff.

over thirty years of age. From among them was chosen (by lot) a council, the βουλή, which prepared business for the assembly, and the nine archons, or magistrates, who were also chosen by lot each year, and were responsible for carrying out the wishes of the ἐκκλησία.[4] The great age of Athenian democracy was the fifty century. Athens suffered a humiliating defeat in the Peloponnesian War (431–404 BCE), and although democracy was quickly restored in 403 BCE, it never fully recovered its confidence, and in 322 BCE Athens was forced finally to submit to Macedon. Thereafter, her democratic institutions continued to function with much reduced authority under the suzerainty of first the Macedonians and then the Romans.[5]

Because the fifth and fourth centuries were the most creative period of Greek art and literature, and because most of this was produced in Athens, it is easy for us to suppose that Athens was typical of Greek civilization at all times and in all places. This would be a serious mistake. In reality Athenian democracy was a comparatively short lived episode in the long story of Greek history, albeit one with momentous consequences. It is also all too easy to exaggerate the egalitarianism of the Greeks. Arnheim shows the idea that 'excellence', ἀρετή, is hereditary runs through Greek society from Homer to Aristotle and beyond.[6] Even under democracy, a disproportionate number of people of noble birth can be shown to have exercised political power, and many Greek states were not democracies at all, but aristocratic oligarchies, of which the best known is Sparta.

Sparta gained its classical constitution at an earlier date than other Greek cities, and then retained unchanged what seemed to others a rather primitive form of government. Power was distrib-

---

[4] OCD², 'Athens', 'Boule', 'Ekklesia'. Also, Aristotle, Ath Const; Jones, Athenian Democracy, pp. 99–133, Ehrenberg, Greek State, pp. 52–74.

[5] According to Arnheim, Aristocracy, p. 156: 'From 323 Athens was ruled by an aristocracy of wealth, but, since wealth tended to be hereditary, oligarchy soon gave way in practice to aristocracy.'

[6] Arnheim, Aristocracy, p. 181: 'The idea that the Greeks were believers in equality must be buried for ever.' See, Aristotle, Pol IV. vi. 2, 3.

71

uted between the two kings, the annually elected Ephors, the popu-lar assembly and a council of elders, known as the Gerousia, in a way that favoured the last named institution. There were in the classical period twenty eight γέροντες, men over sixty years of age elected by the assembly from a restricted circle of aristocratic fami-lies, who then held office for life.[7] The senior Ephor was apparently known as πρέσβυς τῶν ἐφόρων.[8]

In the Hellenistic and Roman periods the power of the γερουσία was greatly curtailed, its members made subject to annual election. The γέροντες still feature in inscriptions of the Roman period, and lip service was paid to the assembly, but this seems to have been part of an 'archaizing facade' maintained by both the Spartans them-selves, who prided themselves on preserving their ancestral constitu-tion unchanged, and by the Roman rulers. The Romans in particu-lar greatly admired the traditional Spartan constitution attributed to Lycurgus, seeing in it a reflection of their own senatorial govern-ment. So none of this should be seen as a symptom of increased democracy. In Roman Sparta power lay not with the assembly but with the magistrates and council working together, so that Spawforth's judgement is that, 'The Roman city was scarcely less an oligarchy than Classical Sparta had been.'[9]

Democracy, then, had never been universal, and in the Hellenis-tic period it withered away as the autonomy of the Greek city-states came to an end. Following Alexander's death his empire split into separate states ruled by kings. It was, of course, in this form that the Jews first experienced Greek civilization, under the Ptolemies and Seleucids. The kings were Macedonian Greeks who ruled in virtue of their military achievements. Like the kings of old, and kings everywhere, these kings had their councils, but they did not consist of the local nobility, but of other Greeks, chosen by the king and styled as Friends.[10] Accordingly we do not find the title 'elders'

---

[7]   *OCD*, p. 465. Aristotle, *Politics*, II.vi.iff.

[8]   *IG*, 5, 1, 51, 27, and see Bornkamm, *TDNT*, VI, p. 653.

[9]   Cartledge & Spawforth, *Sparta*, p. 143–59, 190–211.

[10] Since the new monarchies were the personal creation of their founders and had no roots in the native population, there was no indigenous nobility on whose help the king could draw. Walbank, 'Monarchies', *CAH²*, VII.1, p. 69.

being used with respect to those kingdoms, since the kings felt no need to reckon with the representatives of leading families as the early Greek and Israelite kings, or the Jewish high priest, had to do. While democracy withered, aristocracy was not restored, although local aristocracies flourished among the subject peoples of the various kingdoms, as we see in the case of the Jews.

The Hellenistic kingdoms were overthrown in their turn by Rome, but not in the name of democracy. Rome had a long tradition of hostility to kings, but was herself a great aristocracy. Under the Republic power lay, in practice if not in theory, with the Senate, a body of some three hundred men, drawn mainly from the landed aristocracy, who remained senators for life and held the chief magistracies. Within that body effective control rested in the hands of some twenty to thirty families who kept appointment to the higher magistracies, and so to the ranks of the Senate, largely in their own hands.[11]

When after a century of civil war and revolutionary challenges to the Senate's authority, Augustus became Princeps, he treated the Senate with great respect, while largely robbing it of real power. The Senate became a hereditary order, since, except for new men introduced by the emperor, only the sons of senators could become senators. Most high offices of state were reserved for senators.[12] This was the body with whom the Roman emperor associated himself in the government of the Graeco-Roman world. Within that world, over a period of 800 years, the pattern of government had moved full circle, from the leadership of kings and their elders to that of the Emperor and the ultimate eldership.

In the eastern provinces Rome encouraged the formation and recognition of γερουσίαι. The evidence for this is provided by inscriptions from a number of places, principally in Asia Minor, though also in some of the islands, from the third century BCE onwards, but mainly in the Roman period.[13] According to Ramsay

[11] Scullard, *Gracchi*, pp. 5ff.

[12] *OCD*, 'Senatus', p. 825.

[13] These were fully discussed by W. M. Ramsay, *Cities*, pp. 110–14, 438–40; I. Lévy, 'Études', pp. 203–50; F. Poland, *Vereinswesens*, p. 98ff. No new views are expressed by A. D. Macro, 'Cities', pp. 658–97.

these were 'bodies of great importance, but their character is rather obscure'.[14] However, there now seems general agreement that they are to be distinguished from the βουλή, having no administrative functions or executive power.[15] In some places they appear very much as social clubs for the older citizens, parallel to the νέοι, with their own gymnasium,[16] showing that πρεσβύτεροι in this context are not dotards, but probably men over forty. They were however, more than this. As well as having a restricted number and conditions for enrolment, the γερουσία had honorary duties and a ceremonial role alongside the ἐκκλησία and βουλή, and dispensed considerable funds for civic purposes. Originally it had been more than this, and in the view of Lévy its decline mirrors that of the democratic life of the Greek city generally.[17] It suited the Romans very well to promote bodies with prestige but without power, which would, like the House of Lords in Gilbert's phrase, do 'nothing in particular and do it very well!'

Two things are of particular interest for our present purpose. In the first place, the γερουσία could also be known as 'the corporate body (σύστημα), or council (συνέδριον), of elders', and in the second place the institution was particularly prevalent in just that part of the world in which the Pauline churches developed, Asia Minor, including Ephesus, Smyrna and Philadelphia. By the first century CE, according to Lévy, it had spread throughout Asia Minor,[18] and this means that during the period of the rise of the

[14] Ramsay, *Cities*, p. 110.

[15] Jones, *City*, pp. 225f.

[16] E.g. Pliny, *ad Traj* 33, referring to Nikomedia. 'The imperial gerousia, then, was a high-class club'; Ramsay, *Cities*, p. 440. 'Une maniére de cercle de vieillards', Lévy, 'Etudes', p. 239.

[17] Lévy, 'Etudes', p. 249.

[18] Lévy, 'Etudes', p. 239. More recently discovered and discussed inscriptions show that it was not confined to that region. Entries in *SEG* for the period 1976 to 1988 refer to πρεσβύτεροι in Illyria, Ionia, Thrace, Chios, Amphipolis in Macedonia and Ephesus. See *Supplementum Epigraphicum Graecum*, Vols. XXVI–XXVII, ed. H. W. Pleket & R. S. Stroud, Amsterdam: Gieben, 1979. See especially Vol. XXVI, 1976, No 785, (Thrace, Roman period); No. 1021, (Chios, first century BCE; Vol. XXX, 1980, No. 546, (Amphipolis, Macedonia, first century BCE; Vol. XXXIII, 1983, No. 946 (Ephesus, first century CE). Cf. Jones, *JRS*, 73 (1983), pp. 116–23; Vol. XXXVIII, 1988, No. 521, (Illyria, second century BCE); No. 1218, (Ionia, Roman Imperial period).

Christian churches and in the first area of its expansion the term
'the elders' was in regular use to denote well-to-do citizens of a
certain age and seniority. We need not suppose that the early Christians copied the civic institution (why should they want to?), but it
is reasonable to think that the kind of people connoted by οἱ
πρεσβύτεροι in the Greek cities were found in the house-churches
too, especially as time went by, and that the use of the term would
have seemed quite normal both to those inside the churches and
those outside, and that it would have suggested not office but dignity based on age and social status.[19]

There is only one place where οἱ πρεσβύτεροι appears as a title
of office, and that is in papyri dating from the Ptolemaic and Roman periods, where it refers to local authorities and village officials
in Egypt.[20] The fullest and most recent discussion of these is that of
A. Tomsin,[21] who traces a development of the role of these village
committees during three hundred years.

At the beginning of the Ptolemaic period they fulfill the role of
village elders the world over.[22] Tomsin describes them as a spontaneous organization created by the indigenous population. As such
they arbitrated in conflicts and were recognized by government
officials as having an authority that all would respect. Their title
rested both on age and also on wealth, since, as Tomsin says, "in a
patriarchal society, like the Egyptian, the two generally go together".[23]

By the end of the second century the elders have acquired a more
official role, charged by higher authority with collecting dues and

---

[19] Deissmann says: 'Just as the Jewish usage is traceable to Egypt, so it is possible that
also the Christian communities of Asia Minor may have borrowed the word from their
surroundings and may not have received it through the medium of Judaism at all.' *Bible
Studies*, p. 156.

[20] Deissmann (*Bible Studies*, p. 154) even suggested that it was the use of this word in
Egypt that influenced the LXX translators so to translate זקנים in the OT (in preference
to using γέροντες presumably).

[21] Tomsin, 'Étude', pp. 95-130, 467-532. See also R. Taubenschlag, *Law*, but he has
little to say about the πρεσβύτεροι.).

[22] "The πρεσβύτεροι are the 'notables' who enjoy among their own people an
authority based on age and social position, and who possess an extensive experience of
the business and people of the village." Tomsin, 'Etude', p. 98.

[23] Tomsin, 'Etude', p. 102.

imposing order.[24] They have begun to assume the functions of a local police force, and are now styled in papyri as πρεσβύτεροι γεωργῶν.[25] However, by the close of the Ptolemaic period and under Roman rule the worsening economic situation and government pressure forced the πρεσβύτεροι to become tax-collectors, no longer representatives of the people so much as of the government, not so much a defence against tyranny as themselves agents of it.[26]

The role and history of these elders is probably typical of that played by village head-men and notables throughout the Ancient Near East under successive oppressive empires, and I would certainly suggest that their presence in Egypt is a legacy of Asia and not Europe.

With this exception, the word πρεσβύτερος rarely appears in the history of Greek and Roman institutions. It was not usually the title of an office, nor in the plural does it refer to any group possessing legislative or executive power or administrative duties, for whom the normal term seems to have been οἱ γέροντες.[27] πρεσβύτερος, by contrast, denotes age and dignity, as will now be demonstrated by reference to the writings of Plutarch.

The Connotation of 'The Elders' in the Graeco-Roman World

The evidence of Plutarch is of particular relevance to this discussion. In the first place he is contemporary with the rise of the Christian churches, being born before 50 CE and dying after 120

[24] "At one and the same time representatives of the peasants and agents responsible to the government". Tomsin, 'Etude', p. 114.

[25] BGU, I, 85, 9ff.

[26] These are the people referred to in papyri as πρεσβύτεροι τῆς κώμης (P. Oxy., XVII, 2121, 4.).

[27] I have tested this statement with the help of a computer search of a number of relevant Greek authors: Plato, Republic and Laws, Aristotle, Politics, and the whole of Xenophon, Epictetus, Aristides, Dio Chrysostom and Plutarch. The search was conducted using Thesaurus Linguae Graecae on CD-ROM courtesy of Tyndale House, Cambridge.

CE;[28] and secondly his voluminous works are concerned with a wide range of behavioural issues. Even when he writes history he is really concerned with behaviour, with the study of history as a means to moral improvement, while the volumes of his *Moralia* deal with a variety of social behaviour and show us how a well-educated person of the first century thought, and the associations which the word πρεσβύτερος might be expected to have for him.

Occasionally οἱ πρεσβύτεροι appears to mean 'the men of old time', 'the ancients' or 'our fathers'. For example:

Among the ancients this same thing is said of Thrasymedes the son of Heraieus

(τῶν δὲ πρεσβυτέρων ταὐτὸ τοῦτο λέγεται περὶ Θρασυμήδους τοῦ Ἡραιέως)[29]

Or again:

μαρτυρεῖ δ' αὐτοὺς τῶν μὲν πρεσβυτέρων Ἑλλάνικος, τῶν δὲ νεωτέρων Ἔφορος,[30]

(Evidence in their favour comes from Hellanicus and Ephorus, to mention one older and one later writer.)

Or again:

To us also the ancients handed down as a tradition nine Muses

οἱ δὲ πρεσβύτεροι Μούσας παρέδωκαν καὶ ἡμῖν ἐννέα[31]

The same usage is found in Philo,[32] and also in the New Testament: 'By faith the men of old (πρεσβύτεροι) received divine approval' (Heb 11:2).

However, usually in Plutarch οἱ πρεσβύτεροι refers to people living at the time of the story and denotes senior citizens. Occasion-

---

[28] *OCD*, p. 848. All the dates of authors given in this chapter are taken from the relevant entries of *OCD*.
[29] Plutarch, *Moralia*, 437F.
[30] *Moralia*, 869A.
[31] *Moralia*, 1029C.
[32] Philo, *De Post Caini*, 181.4.

ally it is as non-combatants that they are referred to,[33] but usually the point implicitly or explicitly is that they are old and wise and worthy of respect. This can be seen from the company kept by the word, for example:

τῶν δὲ πρεσβυτέρων καὶ νοῦν ἐχόντων πολιτῶν οἱ μὲν ...[34]

(Of the elderly and sensible citizens, some ...)

τοὺς μὲν οὖν εὐπόρους καὶ πρεσβυτέρους τῶν γεωργῶν τὸ πλῆθος ...[35]

(The men who were well-to-do, and the elderly men, and most of the farmers ...)

πρεσβυτέρων καὶ φρονιμωτέρων παρόντων ...[36]

(there were older and more competent men present)

As such, of course, in some of Plutarch's narratives the elders appear as members of the Council (βουλή, or Senate in his Roman stories),[37] and undoubtedly that could be the public sphere in which the elders of a Greek city exercised their influence, as also the Assembly, but they were not officers or magistrates as such. Magistrates are consistently known, and not only by Plutarch,[38] as ἄρχοντες and these can generally be distinguished from πρεσβύτεροι. Indeed we gain the impression that by the time a person deserves to be called an elder he has probably finished holding office and that his having been ἄρχων contributes to the honour in which he is held. I shall return to the relation of elders to officials shortly. Meanwhile some further passages in Plutarch's *Moralia* will serve to give the flavour of the respect conveyed by the word πρεσβύτεροι.

---

[33] *Pyrrh* 27.71.
[34] *Pyrrh* 13.2.7.
[35] *Nic* 9.4.2
[36] *Ages* 10.6.3.
[37] E.g. *Cor* 6.2.2.
[38] See e.g. Xen *Cyr* I v. 10, but the distinction is quite general and extends to Jewish sources too.

In his essay, *On the Education of Children*,[39] Plutarch says that through philosophy one learns how to behave towards gods, parents, elders, the laws, strangers, those in authority (τοῖς ἄρχουσιν), and with friends, women, children, and servants, and how one should revere the gods, honour parents, respect elders, be obedient to the laws, yield to those in authority, and so on. Nothing could make plainer the honour implied by the term elder, and yet its distinction from actual office. In another passage, Plutarch writes to console Apollonius on the death of his son, among whose many virtues is listed that he 'respected the elderly among his friends as fathers'.[40] In *Table Talk*, Plutarch links older men with foreigners and magistrates as those to whom a certain formality must be observed in conversation, in contrast to young men, fellow citizens and intimates.[41] Occasionally the claims to respect of age and office might conflict and in that case, according to Plutarch and the authorities he quotes, office takes precedence. He tells the story of how Fabius Maximus was an old man when his son was consul. When the two men met in the street the son ordered his father to dismount as a sign of respect for his office. The bystanders were horrified, thus showing the respect in which an elder was usually held, but Fabius Maximus was apparently delighted![42]

The Status of Older People in the Graeco-Roman World

The evidence we have surveyed might be thought sufficient to show that Graeco-Roman society from the archaic period down to the time of Plutarch respected the old and deferred to their authority, an authority that was unwritten, yet pervasive. Yet it has been argued that the opposite is the case. G. Minois, in his review of old age in many historical societies from the Ancient Near East to six-

---

[39] *Moralia*, 67.7.D.
[40] *Moralia*, 120A. αἰδουμένος τοὺς πρεσβυτέρους τῶν φίλων ὥσπερ πατέρας.
[41] *Moralia*, 617A.
[42] *Moralia*, 196A.

teenth century Europe characterizes the lot of the old in the Greek world as 'Sad Old Age;.[43] He points to the way in which Greek literature from Homer onwards glories in the beauty and grace of young men, and laments the decay of body and mind that characterizes old age. Among the playwrights, the tragedians portray old age as a curse,[44] while the comedians show old men as ridiculous.[45] Aristotle's unflattering description of the failings of the old, in contrast to the young and those in the prime of life (οἱ ἀκμάζοντες), is taken by Minois to reflect the prejudices of his time and place.[46] This picture, it is held, is borne out by the facts of political and social history, such as that in the Greek cities, with the exception of Sparta, the γερουσίαι lost their power, that the Athenians needed to pass laws requiring people to support their aged parents, and that in Athens men came of age at eighteen and could hold office at thirty.[47]

In reply we may say, in the first place, that the fact that the Greeks hated old age as an experience does not mean that they hated old people, or that the old did not wield power. There is a genuine ambiguity here, arising from the facts of the situation: on the one hand the old are worthy of respect, on the other hand old age is a time of weakness. When Aristophanes reports the young taking advantage of the old, he does so to deplore it, not to encourage it. When the old are attacked and lampooned in comedy it is precisely because they did represent an authority against which the young chafed. Minois admits this in the case of the Latin dramatist Plautus, whose plays make fun of the Roman *paterfamilias* (of whose continuing power there is no doubt). Moreover, the comedians attack not so much the old as the old behaving inappropriately, in

---

[43] Minois, *Old Age*, pp. 43–76.

[44] See especially Sophocles, *Oedipus at Colonus*, 1166–83, and Euripides, *Herakles*, 1540–4. However, the characters are railing at life and fate, rather than at the old as such.

[45] See especially Aristophanes, *Clouds*, 1321ff., *Birds*, 755–9, but the 'new comedy writer, Menander, reflects strong respect of sons for fathers', *Greek Literary Papyri*, 56.4.

[46] Aristotle, *Rhetoric* II.13, Minois, pp. 60–2.

[47] He refers to Haynes, 'The supposedly golden age for the aged in Ancient Greece (a study of literary concepts of old age)', *Gerontologist*, III, 1963.

ways unworthy of their age and status (such as running after young girls).[48]

Secondly, while ancient Greek writers often lament the drawbacks of aging, they also allow us to see that respect for age was a deeply entrenched assumption. Of course, there are limits to the usefulness of this evidence. Some of the writers I shall be quoting lived some centuries before the rise of the Christian churches, but in this case this is not a very serious problem, since the same sentiments are expressed by Plutarch who is contemporary with it. More serious is the fact that these writers are upper-class literary men whose ideas may not reflect the realities of everyday life. Plato and Xenophon in particular write as people of strongly conservative views who lament the decline in respect paid by the young to the old and long for a return to old-fashioned virtues. Does this not show the opposite of what I am arguing: that by the time of these authors the old had largely lost their traditional respect and authority, as Minois argues?

Athenian democracy in the fifth century certainly led to a massive challenge to the old on the part of the young. The democratic ἐκκλησία placed fathers and sons on a level of political equality. The older generation of leaders was held to have been discredited by Athens' defeat in the Peloponnesian War, and a play like Sophocles' *Antigone* is thought to reflect this.[49] But the old hit back. Socrates was impeached for corrupting the young, certainly not a charge brought by the young themselves. Plato and Xenophon are best seen as part of the backlash, while other fourth century writers, such as Aristotle and Aeschines, were still able to appeal to the validity of traditional norms. It seems best to conclude, with Reinhold, that the challenge of fifth century Athens to the hegemony of the old was exceptional and short-lived.[50] As democracy withered away in the Hellenistic age, generational conflict died down too, in much the same way as in Roman history the Augustan peace brought an

[48] Minois, *Old Age*, pp. 92–4.
[49] See, *Antigone*, 718–23, 728–9. Contrast, 639–48.
[50] Reinhold, 'Generation Gap', pp. 25–47.

end to the generational conflicts that plagued Rome exceptionally in the first century BCE.

To turn then to the evidence of Greek literature, the traditional understanding of the relationship of the older to the younger can be seen from the following passage from Plato (429–347 BCE):

> Very well, said I; what then have we next to determine? Is it not which among them shall be the rulers and the ruled?
>
> Certainly.
>
> That the rulers must be the elder and the ruled the younger is obvious.
>
> It is.[51]

Describing polite conventions which the young no longer observe as they should, Socrates speaks of:

> Such things as the becoming silence of the young in the presence of their elders; the giving place to them, and the rising up before them.[52]

And:

> As for the older man, he will always have the charge of ruling and chastising the younger.
>
> Obviously.[53]

By contrast one of the signs of a society breaking down in disorder is that,

> And in general the young ape their elders and vie with them in speech and action.[54]

---

[51] Plato, *Republic*, 412C. The relevant line reads:"Ὅτι μὲν πρεσβυτέρους τοὺς ἄρχοντας δεῖ εἶναι, νεωτέρους δὲ τοὺς ἀρχομένους, δῆλον;

[52] σιγάς τε τῶν νεωτέρων παρὰ πρεσβυτέροις, ἅς πρέπει, καὶ κατακλίσεις καὶ ὑπαναστάσεις καὶ γονέων θεραπείας. *Republic* 425A.

[53] Πρεσβυτέρῳ μὴν νεωτέρων πάντων ἄρχειν τε καὶ κολάζειν προστετάξεται. *Republic* 465A.

[54] οἱ μὲν νέοι πρεσβυτέροις ἀπεικάζονται (ape) καὶ διαμιλλῶνται (vie with) καὶ ἐν λόγοις καὶ ἐν ἔργοις. *Republic* 563A.

The same picture emerges from *The Laws.* πρεσβύτεροι refers to older people, apparently those over thirty (845C), to whom great respect is owed. *The Laws* is a strongly conservative work, and it articulates the view of an older person who sees standards slipping in the modern world. It is a great sin, but presumably not unknown, for a young man to strike an old man (879B). The old are the natural rulers of the young (690B), to whom they are to set a good example (729B). The old are, or ought to be, to the state what reason and memory are to the individual 'because of their eminent wisdom' (964E).

It is no different with Aristotle (384–322 BCE), as can be seen from the following two quotations:

> For the male is by nature better fitted to command than the female ... and the older and more developed person than the younger and immature.[55]

That the old should lead and the young obey is seen as part of the natural order of things, as unquestioned as the rule of male over female! It is interesting to note in passing that while Paul was to question one of these hegemonies, that of male and female, he nowhere questions the other, that of the old and the young (Gal 3:28). The other reference from Aristotle is:

> And no one chafes or thinks himself better than his rulers when he is governed on the ground of age, especially when he is going to get back what he has thus contributed to the common stock when he reaches the proper age.[56]

The philosopher takes it for granted that the young man can afford to put up with subordination in his youth, since, when he reaches the proper age, he will have the chance to rule others in his turn.[57]

---

[55] τό τε γὰρ ἄρρεν φύσει τοῦ θήλεος ἡγεμονικώτερον ... καὶ τὸ πρεσβύτερον καὶ τέλειον τοῦ νεωτέρου καὶ ἀτελοῦς. *Politics* I. v. 2.

[56] ἀγανακτεῖ δὲ οὐδεὶς καθ' ἡλικίαν ἀρχόμενος, οὐδὲ νομίζει εἶναι κρείττων, ἄλλως τε καὶ μέλλων ἀντιλαμβάνειν τοῦτον τὸν ἔρανον ὅταν τύχῃ τῆς ἱκνουμένης ἡλικίας *Politics* VII. xiii. 3.

[57] Reference has already been made to Aristotle's acceptance of the idea that noble birth and virtue tend to go together. He says that the rich are called καλοὶ κἀγαθοί and γνώριμοι by the people, and that 'noble birth is inherited wealth and excellence'. *Pol* IV. vi. 2. 3.

Our third classical witness is Xenophon (c 428/7–c 354 BCE). From the *Memorabilia* comes the following dialogue:

> Strange sentiments, these, Socrates! It's quite unlike you to urge me, the junior (νεώτερον ὄντα), to lead the way. And surely all hold the contrary opinion, that the senior, I mean, should always act and speak first? (τὸν πρεσβύτερον ἡγεῖσθαι παντὸς καὶ ἔργου καὶ λόγου)
>
> How so? said Socrates. Is it not the general opinion that a young man should make way for an older when they meet, offer his seat to him, give him a comfortable bed, let him have the first word?[58]

Regardless of Xenophon's personal conservative bias, the force of this argument depends on the premise being true — that such respect being due from young to old would have been generally agreed, even by those who did not themselves choose to pay it. Some did not, and we find Xenophon lamenting:

> When will Athenians show the Lacedaimonian reverence for age (πρεσβυτέρους αἰδέσονται), seeing that they despise all their elders, (καταφαρονεῖν. τῶν γεραιτέρων) beginning with their own fathers (ἀπο τῶν πατέρων ἄρχονται)?[59]

Then, in the *Cyropaedia*, we find the dying Cyrus speak as follows, a word which may be fittingly taken to sum up not only Xenophon's view of the matter, but that of Greek society as a whole:

> I too was thus trained by my country and yours to give precedence to my elders — not merely to brothers but to all fellow citizens — on the street in the matter of seats and in speaking (τοῖς πρεσβυτέροις οὐ μόνον ἀδελφοῖς ἀλλὰ καὶ πολίταις καὶ ὁδῶν καὶ θακῶν καὶ λογῶν ὑπείκειν) and so from the beginning, my children, I have been training you also to honour your elders above yourselves and to be honoured above those who are younger. Take what I say therefore as that which is

---

[58] Xenophon, *Memorabilia*, II, iii.
[59] *Memorabilia* II.v.15.

approved by time, by custom, and by the law (ὡς, οὖν παλαιὰ καὶ εἰθισμένα καὶ ἔννομα λέγοντος ἐμοῦ οὕτως ἀποδέχεσθε)[60]

From the speeches of Aeschines (c 397–c 322 BCE), a younger contemporary of Xenophon, we gain the following picture of the respect traditionally accorded to the older citizens in the Athenian assembly:

The herald then asks, 'Who of those above fifty years of age wishes to address the assembly?' When all these have spoken he then invites any other Athenian to speak who wishes ... Consider, fellow citizens, the wisdom of this regulation. The lawgiver does not forget, I think, that the older men (οἱ πρεσβύτεροι) are at their best in the matter of judgment, but that courage is now beginning to fail them as a result of their experience of the vicissitudes of life. So, wishing to accustom those who are wisest to speak on public affairs ... he invites them to the platform and urges them to address the people. At the same time he teaches the younger men to respect their elders, to yield precedence to them in every act, and to honour that old age to which we shall all come if our lives are spared.[61]

In another passage Aeschines expresses similar sentiments (*Ctes* 2–4), though he admits that the rules of the assembly that give precedence to the old are honoured more in the breach than in the observance.

Even though these writers lived hundreds of years before the first-century period with which I am chiefly concerned, it should not be forgotten that they continued to exercise influence by becoming 'classics', used in education of the Hellenistic period.

The primary function of the *grammatikos* or professor of letters was to present and explicate the great classic authors: Homer first of all, of whom every cultured man was expected to have a deep

---

[60] Xenophon, *Cyropaedia*, VIII, vii, 10.
[61] Aeschines, *Tim* 23–24.

knowledge, and Euripides and Menander — the other poets being scarcely known except through anthologies. Although poetry remained the basis of literary culture, room was made for prose, from the great historians, from the orators, Demosthenes in particular, even from the philosophers.[62]

Plutarch, writing five hundred years later, stands in the same tradition. The clearest and most extended passage to throw light on the subject is the essay in the *Moralia* entitled 'Whether Old Men should Engage in Public Affairs'.[63] By 'public affairs' it becomes clear Plutarch means attendance at and participation in the debates in the ἐκκλησία. Plutarch writes to encourage his friend to continue his active participation and not retire to the country and sit in the sun. It is clear that he is not urging him to stand for office, but to exercise his privilege as a citizen and to fulfil his responsibility as someone who has a worthwhile contribution to make. Plutarch suggests (787C) that in the assembly the opinion of older people would be sought first as an honour. He goes on to speak of the primacy (πρωτεῖον) that comes with age as something 'for which there is a special word *presbeion*, or "the prerogative due to seniority in old age"'.[64] This is clearly not an office, but the weight attached to the opinions of a senior person, which is why, as he says, states in difficulties yearn for the leadership of older men.[65] This phrase makes it plain that even if in a crisis older men may hold office, it is not any office of eldership that they hold. What it is that elders have is spelt out a few lines further on: good sense, prudent thought and conservatism,[66] since, as he says, echoing Aristotle, πειθαρχικὸν γὰρ ἡ νεότης, ἡγεμονικὸν δὲ το γῆρας (It is for youth to obey, and age to lead)

S. Byl is therefore surely correct to dispute the verdict of Simone de Beauvoir that Plutarch displays a morose attitude to old age.[67]

---

[62] *Enc. Brit.* [15], Vol. 18, p. 9, Chicago, 1990.

[63] *Moralia*, 783–797 (ΕΙ ΠΡΕΣΒΥΤΕΡΩΙ ΠΟΛΙΤΕΥΤΕΟΝ).

[64] τὸ δ' ἀπὸ τοῦ χρόνου πρωτειὸν, ὃ καλεῖται κυρίως πρεσβεῖον (787D, *LCL* translation).

[65] πρεσβυτέρων ποθοῦσιν ἀρχὴν ἀνθρώπων, 788C.

[66] νοῦν ἔχοντος καὶ φροντίδα πεπνυμένην καὶ ἀσφάλειαν 789D.

[67] Byl, 'Plutarche', pp. 107–23. Cf. de Beauvoir, *Old Age*, p. 126.

Like other Greek writers, he knows the pains and limitations of old age, and he disapproves of old people marrying or concerning themselves with sexual relations, but that is because old age is for other, better things! According to Byl:

> Of all the Greek authors, Plutarch is the one who has left us the finest lesson in optimism in the face of old age. His whole life long he did not cease to extol activity on the part of the older man, and to affirm that in many spheres the old man was much more competent than the young.[68]

Turning to some of Minois' other arguments, while it is true that in comparison to the *patria potestas* of the Roman *paterfamilias*, the Athenian father's hold over his children was quite relaxed, this does not mean that parents were not to be respected. It is significant that a young man, though coming of age at eighteen, was not able to hold office or be fully a citizen until he was thirty, a serious and irksome disability. For some senior judges, the minimum age was sixty. In this connection we need to note that what Minois sees as Aristotle's diatribe against the old is part of an artificial comparison of the failings of young and old designed to present maturity as a golden mean. It transpires that, in Aristotle's view, maturity of mind is not attained until the age of forty-nine, while even marriage was not recommended until a man was thirty-seven. In the context of the life expectancy of the times this is hardly a charter of youth! If Athenian society was not ruled by the aged, it was at least ruled by the mature.

Above all, even if the old men of the γερουσία suffered loss of power in the state, (and we have seen that this was by no means always so), this does not mean that they lost power in their own homes and families. It is the *mores* and assumptions of family life that are of most relevance to us because it was in the matrix of the family that the earliest churches grew up. Just as the Jewish elders are not a likely model for the churches when they are the elders of

[68] Byl, 'Plutarche', p. 113.

the city, so the lack of elders among the officers of a Greek city tells us little about what to expect in the emergent churches.

The ancient Greek family as classically defined by Aristotle, consisted of husband, wife, slave(s), and children (who were necessary to make it a 'full' οἶκος (house/household).[69] The οἶκος is seen as the smallest unit of the state, yet still itself a community over which the man, its κύριος, ruled as king and leader. He was not, of course, necessarily an *old* man, since a father often handed over his management of the οἶκος to his eldest son upon the occasion of the latter's marriage, while himself continuing to live in the house. In addition, we should think of adult sons, prior to marriage, as well as small children. Then, since there was a legal obligation on children to provide for their parents in old age,[70] the household will typically have contained old people; and since in Athens women were unable to own property in their own right, there will also have been widows who had placed themselves under the protection of a male relative.[71] Finally, included in the idea of the οἶκος were outsiders, ξένοι, both those who came into the household to work and those whom ties of hospitality bound to the family.[72] Such a household is what would today be called an 'extended family'.

The fact that the Athenians had to enforce the care of aged parents tells us that people are selfish. It does not tell us that parents were widely neglected, any more than the repeated calls in Proverbs for sons to obey and listen to parents tells us that parents were widely despised and disobeyed. Respect for the old always exists in tension with human selfishness and pride, but a society that passes

[69] Aristotle, *Pol* I. ii. 1–2. 'The household in its perfect form consists of slaves and freemen. The investigation of everything should begin with its smallest parts, and the primary and smallest parts of the household are master and slave, husband and wife, father and children.'

[70] Lacey, *Family,* pp. 106–7.

[71] Lacey, *Family,* p. 25. The legal status of women improved considerably in Hellenistic Egypt, and under the Roman empire, Verner, *Household,* pp. 35–44. The NT bears witness both to wealthy and independent women (Acts 16:11ff., Col 4:15), and to the continuing need of widows and the expectation that they would be looked after by their own kin (1 Tim 5:8).

[72] Lacey, *Family,* pp. 30–2.

laws requiring the support of aged parents is a society that believes in the duties of children.

Reference has already been made to the power wielded by the Roman *paterfamilias*. The Roman household was not typically very large, consisting simply of the conjugal family together with their dependents, but not usually more remote relatives.[73] Yet within it the authority of the Roman father was absolute and lifelong. 'The family was organized as a miniature monarchy, that is, under the rule of one person with one purse and one worship.'[74] The Roman jurist Ulpian (d. 228 CE) put it as follows:

> In the strict legal sense we call a *familia* a number of people who are by birth or law subjected to the *potestas* of one man.[75]

Notoriously, this power included the right of a father to put his own children to death in the event of their being guilty of serious crime or of disrespect towards their father. This power was by no means merely notional even as late as the first century BCE.[76] It is true that the *paterfamilias* was expected to summon a family *consilium* to consider matters of life and death, and there is some evidence that, 'in the classical period the sovereign power of the *paterfamilias* over the household underwent a gradual but substantial curtailment.'[77] Yet, according to Reinhold:

> Despite the mitigation by custom of the absolute power of the *paterfamilias* over his household beginning with the second century BC, the Roman government was disinclined to interfere with *patria potestas*, and the total power it embodied remained as a legal right until the end of Roman civilization, and indeed into the Christian period.[78]

Although the turmoil of the first century BCE produced a rare outbreak of intergenerational conflict in Roman society, the Augustan

[73] Rawson, *Family*, pp. 7, 14.
[74] Plescia, 'Potestas', p. 144.
[75] Ulpian, *Digest*, 50.16.195. See Gardner and Wiedemann, *Household*, pp. 3–4.
[76] Sallust, *Cat* 39.5.
[77] Plescia, 'Potestas', p. 146.
[78] Reinhold, 'Conflict', p. 49.

settlement restored harmony and massively reinforced the authority of fathers. Augustus called himself *pater patriae*, and in calling for loyalty to himself in terms of that owed by children to their father, implicitly endorsed the authority of the latter. Both in the republic and under the early empire, Lacey writes,

> *Patria potestas* was the fundamental institution of the Romans, which shaped and directed their world view or *Weltanschauung*.[79]

The significance of this for the present study is that, according to MacMullen, 'when the Romans extended their law and citizenship throughout the empire they likewise extended the ancient rights of the *paterfamilias*.'[80] This means that in the societies of the eastern Mediterranean, already to some extent influenced by oriental notions of patriarchy, the traditional Greek respect for elders and fathers received a massive institutional reinforcement. The dominant position of the head of the household, affirmed and attested from time immemorial, was now additionally endorsed as a matter of government policy.

Suggestive Evidence from Comparative Anthropology

To the evidence provided directly by the ancient Greek and Roman writers and from historical study of the period, we may add an insight drawn from comparative anthropology.

Until recently the place and role of the elders, in societies ancient and modern, has been neglected, as is admitted by Amoss and Harrell, who speak of a 'massive neglect of old age by the discipline of social anthropology'.[81] However, the subject is now receiving a good deal of attention, as the aging populations of the western world force the subject of the aged onto the sociological agenda.

Much of this study has focused on primitive societies extremely remote not only from ourselves, but also from the biblical and

---

[79] Lacey, 'Potestas', p. 140.

[80] MacMullen, *Social relations*, p. 80. Cf. *Cod Just* 8.46.3 (227) and 4 (259).

[81] Amoss & Harrell, *Other Ways*, p. 1. This neglect has not yet been made good by, for example, Rogerson, *Anthropology and the OT*.

classical worlds. Close comparison is obviously impossible across vast distances of place and time, not least because field work and case studies are impossible to carry out on societies now extinct. Hence we must be very circumspect in trying to fill the gaps in our knowledge of the ancient world by reference to modern parallels. After all, there is clearly a danger of circular argument, the modern parallel being selected because of its similarity to the ancient world and then being used to show that the ancient world was similar. However, what Duverger calls 'distant comparisons' may be fruitful in the area of 'general ideas, theories, elements of typologies and systems', as some recent New Testament studies have shown.[82]

The modern study of primitive society all over the world appears to present a fairly uniform picture with regard to the status of older people. Amoss and Harrell, in their study already referred to bring together case studies by twelve different researchers on societies as diverse as Afghanistan, Micronesia and the Kalahari. These studies confirm that,

> In most societies older people gain access to positions in which the laws and customs of society give them considerable political power.[83]

In some societies this is automatic for all older people, and the elders as a corporate group wield power. In other places political power is exercised by certain older people to the exclusion of others. Universally, leadership within family groups goes with age, especially in wealthier families, and there is a natural tendency for senior people in the wealthier families to be the leaders of the community.[84]

---

[82] Duverger, *Introduction to the Social Sciences*, p. 266f. Cf. Maier, *Social Setting*, p. 7, Stanton, *Gospel*, p. 84.

[83] Amoss and Harrell, p. 12.

[84] See for example the study by M. N. Shahrani of the Kirghiz, a people living in the mountains of Afghanistan (Amoss & Harrell, pp. 175–91), where we learn that among the Kirghiz the process of growing old is seen as one of achieving greater wisdom, respect and privilege. Senior members of the community are never completely retired; they retain their managerial and decision-making privilege over the family (p. 183). Their arrival is received with many acts of courtesy and respect, and in public gatherings they can expect to occupy the places of honour and to be served first and with the best portions available.

But, of course, however true this may be in primitive societies, and however much light this may throw on Ancient Israel, the social world of the Graeco-Roman empire was very different. It was urbanized, sophisticated, literate and in process of change. It was precisely not the primitive society its peoples had once enjoyed. How then can comparative anthropological studies bear on it?

In their study, *Aging and Modernization*, Cowgill and Holmes bring together studies made of fifteen separate societies and cultures, including not only preliterate societies in Africa, but modern societies, such as Japan, Russia and Israel, and intermediate societies, like Thailand and Mexico, and seek to correlate the role and status of old people with the degree of modernization experienced by the community as a whole. This study is thus more relevant to our purposes than one which concentrates only on primitive societies.

Modernization is, they admit, hard to define, but easy enough to recognize, and is expressed in such things as higher per capita national income, and the level of literacy. It is usually accompanied by increased rates of mobility, urbanization and social change. Some of their findings confirm those of Amoss and Harrell: in all societies, some people are classified as old and are treated differently accordingly. There is a widespread tendency for older people to shift to more sedentary, advisory, or supervisory roles, and in all societies, some older persons continue to act as political, judicial, and civic leaders.[85]

From their number are chosen, on the basis of wealth, seen as a sign of effectiveness, those who exercise power as Camp heads, Lineage heads and as the Khan, or leader of the whole society. Individual leaders interviewed by Shahrani were aged between fifty and seventy. All were active in settling disputes. Access to all these positions comes through a combination of wealth, ability and seniority within the kinship group. Holders of these various offices are usually among the oldest, as well as the wealthiest, of the household heads within the units they lead, and Kirghiz respect for the aged generally is magnified in the case of the political leaders, who are by definition elders.

The same picture emerges from P. N. Wachege's study of eldership among the Agikuyu in Kenya, *Jesus Christ Our Ideal Elder* (Nairobi, 1992). Not every elderly person is an elder, but the qualifications for eldership are those likely to be possessed by those who are older, since they have to be the leaders of their families (p. 36), within a society structured according to age. Indeed, 'one cannot be an elder without having a family' (p. 71). They settle disputes, and are the guardians of the social and religious life of the community.

[85] Cowgill and Holmes, *Aging*, pp. 305–21.

The variations are more interesting than the universals, however. The studies show that people are classified as old at an earlier age in primitive societies, while they live longer in modernized societies. Longevity is directly related to the degree of modernization, more people live longer in modern societies, hence modern societies have proportionately more older people.

Of most relevance to our purpose is the finding that the status of old people varies inversely with the degree of modernization, old people being universally honoured in primitive societies, and enjoying a more ambiguous status in countries like Austria and Norway. It is particularly interesting that the status of older people is changing in Japan in step with rapid modernization, while in Israel the status of the elderly is much higher among immigrants from the East than from the West. The authors comment:

> It is particularly significant that the higher status of the aged among the Oriental migrants is associated with the persistence of the extended family.[86]

They see Russia as the exception to the rule that increased modernization correlates with decline in respect for the elderly, the study tending to show that older people enjoy a markedly more honoured place in Russia than their counterparts in the USA. This too is seen to be related to the preservation of the extended family in Russia.

Other factors which correlate with the status of the elderly are the rate of social change generally, and the mobility of the population. Where these are high, the status of the elderly tends to decline. Not surprisingly, therefore, the status of the elderly tends to be high in agricultural societies and lower in urban ones.[87] MacMullen makes this point with respect to the difference between rural and urban life in the Roman empire.[88] City life, then, as now, tended to be

---

[86] Cowgill and Holmes, *Aging,* p. 311.

[87] Wachege's study agrees with this too. Traditional respect for the elderly is undermined in Kenya by such factors as modernization and urbanization (p. 79ff.), which have tended to deprive the elders of a role and break up the family on which their status depends.

[88] MacMullen, *Social Relations,* p. 27.

characterized by mobility, and change, whereas agricultural societies were more conservative.

This suggests that in the Graeco-Roman world also we could expect less reverence for the elderly in the cities than in the country, and less in areas characterized by mobility, literacy and rapid social change. The Roman Empire is known to have afforded its citizens increased opportunities for travel, and the New Testament abundantly illustrates this. The surviving literature of Greece and Rome is a testimony to a society where literacy was widespread, but presumably mainly in the cities. That the first century was a time of social change is attested by the moralists of the time who hanker after the stricter standards of an earlier age, and there is some evidence of social tensions centred on the changing role of women.[89]

All of this might suggest that respect for the elders would have been a thing of the past in the cities of the Graeco-Roman world with which we are chiefly concerned, and we should certainly not ignore the likelihood that their status was less compared to earlier times. On the other hand, we should not exaggerate the degree of modernization anachronistically. In the first place, society was changing much more slowly compared to our experience today. The differential between city and country would have been much less marked than that between advanced and primitive societies in the modern world. Second, two further findings of Cowgill and Holmes are of particular significance here. In their survey of aging and modernization in the modern world they found that the status of older people remained high in places where they had a continuing role, and in societies where they could be part of extended families.[90]

Both these factors apply to the Graeco-Roman world. In the first place, there was no retirement age in the ancient world, and no institutionalized sidelining of all those past a certain age. Secondly, as we have seen, the term 'extended family' may fairly, if loosely, be used to describe the traditional Graeco-Roman household. This, as Lacey remarks,

---

[89] Verner, *Household*, pp. 64–79.
[90] Cowgill and Holmes, *Aging*, p. 317.

'continued uninterruptedly as the fundamental social unit of the Greeks, and at the centre of civil law, through centuries of foreign occupation, till it emerged as firmly entrenched as ever in the Greek Civil Code of 1946, which is still in force today'.[91]

Conclusions

This necessarily brief survey of a vast subject has tried to show that in constitutional terms there are similarities as well as differences between the Graeco-Roman and Jewish worlds. Both emerge from an archaic period whose government may be called aristocratic, in which the elders as local chieftains play a prominent part. In both worlds their peoples experienced, for much of the time, the autocratic rule of local kings and distant empires. Democracy, whether of the Athenian or modern variety, was not often, or for long, the experience of the peoples of the Graeco-Roman world. In most places at most times power lay with those born to wealthy families, whose senior members were leaders in the state, city, or rural community. The leaders owed their position in society to the power of their family, and their position in the family to their relative seniority.

They were not often called οἱ πρεσβύτεροι. This is partly because the preferred term for the ruling oligarchy is οἱ γέροντες, or ἡ γερουσία. In this respect Greek usage differed from Jewish, though we have seen that the terms came together in the γερουσίαι that flourished in the cities of the eastern Roman empire at the turn of the eras. οἱ πρεσβύτεροι connoted rather a class of person to whom respect was instinctively felt to be due, not so much the leaders of the state or town, but *one's own elders* within family, clan or acquaintance. Although the Greeks held this respect in tension with a fear of the aging process, and a willingness on occasion to lampoon the failings of the old and to strain against the leash of

---

[91] Lacey, *Family*, p. 233. The date is 1968, but the sentence stands unchanged in the 1980 edition.

their authority, there is no reason to think that it ceased to be a cohesive force in the home and in the community.

The work of comparative anthropologists tends to show that respect for older people has been typical of most human societies, but that there is a tendency for this respect to be eroded in the face of rising living standards, increased literacy, social mobility, urbanization and the whole process that can be called 'modernization'. We would therefore expect to find within the ancient world a high respect for the old, but also a tendency for this to be challenged by increased urbanization.

Comparative studies of societies in the modern world also show, however, that the erosion of respect is arrested wherever people live in extended families that preserve a strong sense of belonging. The typical Graeco-Roman household, especially in the case of the well-to-do, can fairly be described as an extended family, and we should expect that the senior people within such families would continue to enjoy considerable respect. The writings of Plutarch show that this expectation is justified for the world of the first century.

This was the world in which earliest Christianity spread. Starting within the patriarchal world of Judaism, in which 'the elders' was an imprecise, inclusive, term of respect for the leaders of the community at many levels, it grew particularly within the matrix of the Graeco-Roman household whose head exercised authority over wife, children and slaves alike. Not all such heads of families were old men, but all owed their position to seniority relative to others within the household. This fact exercised, I shall argue, a profound formative influence on the way in which the earliest churches developed.

Chapter Four
Paul and the Elders

The starting point of this chapter is the surprising fact that Paul,[1] so far as we know, called no one 'elder', and yet within a generation of Paul's death the term 'elders' was freely used in his churches. On the one hand, there is no mention of elders in the letters confidently ascribed to Paul by modern scholars.[2] On the other, we find references to them in the Pastorals (1 Tim 5:17–22; Tit 1:5), 1 Peter (5:1–5), 1 Clement (1:3, 21:6, 44:5, 47:6) and the letters of Ignatius (e.g. Eph 2:2; Mag 6:1; Trall 3:1; Smyrn 8). Luke takes it for granted that Paul appointed and dealt with elders in the churches he founded (Acts 14:23, 20:17). All these writings can be attributed

---

[1] We begin with the letters of Paul as the earliest Christian documents, written between 50 CE (1 Thess) and about 60 CE (depending on the date and provenance of Philippians). The character of pre-Pauline Christianity will be considered in the next chapter when the evidence of Acts is discussed.

[2] It is also missing from Colossians and Ephesians among the letters whose Pauline authorship is doubted. Only in the Pastorals do we find Paul giving instruction about elders, and this is itself one of the many reasons scholars doubt if these can be dated to Paul's life time. Accordingly, I shall deal with the Pastorals in another chapter. On any showing, they reflect a more developed state of congregational development than any of the other letters, and it is reasonable on this ground alone to see them as later, though not, I would argue, much later. The marked differences of style and vocabulary suggest that we should credit them to a Pauline circle concerned to preserve the apostle's legacy in the churches he founded.

The same may well be true of Ephesians. On the grounds of style and theology many scholars think that it comes from a 'Paulinist' rather than from Paul himself, but so far as its contribution to our understanding of leadership in the Pauline churches is concerned, I believe that Ephesians is best considered together with the earlier Paulines, and I shall discuss it briefly in this chapter. Colossians, which in any case I believe to be genuinely Pauline, does not contribute much to this discussion beyond the tantalizing reference to Nypha and the church in her house (4:15).

without undue controversy to the years between 70 and 110 CE, and most of them are addressed to churches in the broad area of Paul's evangelistic work: 1 Clement to Corinth, 1 Timothy to Ephesus, 1 Peter to churches in Galatia and Asia among others, while Ignatius writes to churches in Asia, including Ephesus again.

In none of these letters do we detect any sign that elders were an innovation or that their introduction had been in any way controversial. As Holmberg says:

> The amalgamation of 'presbyterial' [sic] and 'episcopal' order seems to have been a painless process, as Luke (in Acts 20), the Pastoral letters and 1 Clement all see it as a matter of course and as having its origin in the days of the apostle(s).[3]

How then are we to explain Paul's silence on elders together with the presence of elders in all his churches by the end of the century? Was this a natural development of the leadership structures Paul himself had sanctioned, or was it the result of harmonizing two quite different approaches to church government?[4] Or was it an accommodation of his thought to prevailing social norms that Paul himself had rejected, in von Campenhausen's words, 'a different way of thinking about the church'?[5]

This latter view has been popular with Protestant scholars for the last hundred years, and we need do no more than restate it briefly here, having already summarized it in some detail in the first chapter. There we saw that it is reached by combining the legacy of Sohm with the legacy of Baur to construct a model of the first century church divided into Pauline congregations led by the Spirit, and Palestinian congregations subject to the Law.

According to this view, 'Paul develops the idea of the Spirit as the organizing principle of the congregation.'[6] Hence, even though there

---

[3] Holmberg, 'Order', p. 194.

[4] Roloff, 'Amt, Ämter', p. 523 says: 'Auf breiter Front vollzog sich in nachpaulinischen Zeit die Verschmelzung der paulinischen Episkopen-verfassung mit der palästinischen Ältestenverfassung.'

[5] Von Campenhausen, *Authority*, p. 76.

[6] Von Campenhausen, *Authority*, p. 58.

may be people who give leadership in the congregation, the question of how such people are appointed is 'futile and ought not even to be asked'.[7] Recognizing leaders, still more appointing people to office, on the basis of seniority or natural endowments is to be seen as incompatible with this, 'a different way of thinking about the church', leading inevitably to 'a narrowly official and ecclesiastical way of thinking'.[8] Paul's teaching about *charismata*, taken together with the fact that, 'Paul consistently avoids using words which in Judaism denoted leadership of worship or of synagogue or priestly office', and that 'nowhere in his letters, with the probable exception of Phil 1:1, does Paul address one single class or group of people as though they were responsible for the organization, worship or spiritual well-being of others',[9] leads Dunn to the conclusion that, 'the word "office" is best avoided completely in any description of the Pauline concept of ministry', since, 'only he who ministered could have authority and that only in the exercise of his ministry.'[10]

As a result, where this line of interpretation holds sway, the Pastorals are assessed in terms of 'fading vision',[11] or 'drift', [12] and nothing provides a clearer sign of this than the appearance of elders. Elders, being Jewish in origin, and deriving their office from nature rather than grace, represent tradition as opposed to *charisma*, and the triumph of Law over the freedom of the Spirit.

This view has not been without its critics, who have in recent years attacked it on sociological, exegetical and historical grounds. These criticisms will be rehearsed here and further developed. First it will be shown that concentrating too narrowly on theology to the neglect of sociological factors has led scholars to produce a utopian picture of the Pauline churches. There follows an alternative exegesis of key texts in the debate concentrating on the character and purpose of 1 Corinthians in particular, after

---

[7] Von Campenhausen, *Authority*, p. 67.
[8] Von Campenhausen, *Authority*, pp. 76f.
[9] Dunn, *Spirit*, p. 285.
[10] Dunn, *Spirit*, p. 290.
[11] Dunn, *Spirit*, p. 345.
[12] Banks, *Community*, p. 192.

which we shall consider how a distorted view of the ancient synagogue may have contributed to an unhistorical view of the church. This will be the right point at which to interact with a fresh assault on the consensus view which differs significantly from my own, and to show why the household rather than the synagogue, or the association, best explains the development of the earliest churches.

We shall then be in a position to attempt an alternative explanation which proceeds along three lines. In the first place, we shall rehearse the evidence for regular leadership in the Pauline churches, so as to suggest that the seeds of the later development can be found even in Paul's earliest letters. It will be argued, secondly, that the rapid growth of the churches provided the right conditions for the seeds to germinate, so that talk about elders appears naturally at a certain point in the churches' development, in accordance with the dynamic of the word 'elders' itself. Finally, the suggestion will be made that Paul wrote and thought in terms more applicable to his own work as an apostle than to the work of those who took over from him in the development of the churches, and this produces a different terminology in his letters from that which became familiar in the churches.

The Fallacy of Idealism[13]

From the standpoint of the sociology of knowledge, there is a certain tendency to naivety shown by the theologians of the Sohmian tradition in attributing social realities to the application of ideas, or of theology, alone. To the man in the street (or indeed the man in the pulpit!) it might seem as if Paul, armed with certain convictions about the church in the purposes of God, set out from Antioch and founded his churches accordingly, and that the principles we see him enunciating in his letters are those which directed the construction of the churches, in such a way that they can do duty as descrip-

---

[13] The phrase was coined by Holmberg, *Power*, p. 205.

tions of those churches *simpliciter*. In fact, however, the principles Paul formulates in his letters are themselves partly shaped by the form his churches actually took, including not only patterns of behaviour and social organization of which he approved, but also those of which he did not approve and others which he simply took for granted.

Berger and Luckmann show that the relationship between social realities and ideas is dialectical in the sense that, while social institutions are created by people, once created they return to confront their creators as objective realities ('the way things are'), forcing their creators to formulate new ideas to explain and control them. This means that there is a continual dialectic between theological ideas and social realities. The structure of the church, for instance, is not only created by people in response to their theological ideas; the structures of the church may also act upon its creators to produce new theological ideas.[14]

Applied to the Pauline churches, this means that we cannot simply attempt an historical reconstruction of them, based on the ideas Paul puts forward in his letters.[15] For example, when Paul says that God has appointed in the church first apostles, second prophets, third teachers, we cannot simply read off from this statement a description of the Pauline church created according to this idea. The sentence itself is formulated in the heat of debate. The chaotic reality of the Corinthian church is reacting upon its creator to produce a new and powerful idea. In the same way, Paul's idea of the church as the body of Christ is more a response to the reality of the Corinthian church than the idea that brought it into being. To forget this not only ignores the possibility that Paul was not wholly successful in imposing his ideas on the church to which he was writing; it also assumes that a man like Paul could formulate his ideas in total freedom of the events and conditions confronting him, and forget that people act as they do not simply as the result of

---

[14] Berger and Luckmann, *Reality*, p. 70–84. Berger, *Religion*, pp. 1–37, speaks of the three steps of 'externalization, objectivation and internalization'.

[15] The point is well made by MacDonald, *Pauline Churches*, p. 60.

theological ideas, but also in response to social and economic realities.[16] Holmberg has written:

> What is missing in this type of theologically determined historical reconstruction is an awareness of the continuous dialectic between ideas and social structures. Social life is determined by social factors, including the opinions and consequently the theology of the actors. Paul's theology of *charisma* probably did have an effect on the Corinthian church, but not before it had been formulated and certainly not in any simple, straightforward fashion as if ideas could act directly on social structures.[17]

Elsewhere he has argued that we need to see what Paul says in his letters as an interpretation of how things are, not a simple description of them, so that what Paul says about everybody having a gift of grace tells us how Paul wanted the Corinthians to look at things rather than how the church was actually organized.[18] The absence of established leaders may from this perspective be more apparent than real. They do not feature in Paul's argument because he is here more concerned with attitudes than with constitutional questions.

Turning to the consensus view as exemplified by von Campenhausen, we can see that it has obvious similarities to Weber's idea of *charisma* and its 'routinization' (a view which, as we saw, Weber himself derived from Sohm).[19] According to this theory, the prophetic figure who comes to be seen as the founder of a movement is himself 'a purely individual bearer of *charisma*', understood as a power bestowed by God through a personal call in virtue of which the prophet enters his mission. If his mission is in any way successful, the prophet gathers around himself a body of helpers and followers who have a vested interest in maintaining the benefits of

---

[16] MacDonald, *Pauline Churches*, p. 53. 'His [i.e. von Campenhausen's] comments reflect a common tendency in New Testament interpretation to describe social realities as being the direct result of the application of ideas.'

[17] Holmberg, *Power*, p. 205f.

[18] Holmberg, 'Order', p. 195.

[19] Weber, *Theory*, p. 328, and Haley, 'Sohm', pp. 185ff. Von Campenhausen himself makes no use of Weber.

the ministry after the prophet himself has passed away. The result in the second generation of the movement is the 'routinization of charisma'. Weber explains this as:

> the process whereby either the prophet himself or his disciples secure the permanence of his preaching and the congregational distribution of grace, hence ensuring the economic existence of the enterprise and those who man it, and thereby monopolizing as well the privileges reserved for those charged with religious functions.[20]

According to von Campenhausen this is the process we see at work in the emergence of settled forms of leadership in the New Testament churches, to which the later New Testament documents bear witness. Paul is the prophetic figure and during his lifetime his charisma is shared with and experienced by his churches. On his death his 'staff' provide for the continuation of the experience through the appointment of leaders through whom the charisma will continue to flow. Nothing more clearly indicates the subjection of charisma to routinization than the appointment of elders, who hold office not in virtue of their experience of the Spirit, but because of their age and role as natural leaders. It is implicit with von Campenhausen that this development is to be seen as a decline, a regrettable loss of vision and authenticity.

There is, however, some confusion here. Charisma, for Paul, is a theological interpretation, a value he places on all service rendered to the community, whether exceptional or routine. Weber, on the other hand, uses charisma as the description of a sociological phenomenon — non-routine activity. By confusing the two, scholars like von Campenhausen are able to claim that Paul's charisma teaching excluded the possibility of office, with the result that the (natural) process of routinization is inevitably portrayed as a decline. But if Paul in fact uses charisma language to embrace routine activity, his teaching cannot be used to show that he deliberately avoided recognizing office-holders in his churches, nor should it be used to

---

[20] Weber, *Theory*, pp. 363ff.

suggest that Paul would have deplored the development of routine service into fixed office.[21]

Moreover, Weber has himself been criticized by, for example, Holmberg for underestimating the extent to which the leader himself desires to build a lasting community, and for overestimating the role of personal and financial motives in his immediate successors.[22] It is both likely in theory, and observable in the case of Paul in particular, that the leader would wish to secure his own work and message, and even within his lifetime to provide for his own necessary absences (1 Cor 4:17; 1 Thess 3:1ff.). The process of routinization, while not denied, is accordingly inevitable and present from the start as something with which the founder is fully identified.

As pointed out by Theissen,[23] and MacDonald,[24] Paul is shown by his letters to have been a community organizer. Not in the sense that he had a blueprint for church order in the manner of a John Wesley, but in that the emergence of communities of believers was not a by-product of his preaching, but the goal of it. In consequence Paul cannot have been indifferent to the organization required to facilitate the common life of these congregations. There is no reason to think that Paul was applying 'a kind of well-thought out concept of the relationship of church leaders to their congregations'.[25] The evidence is consistent with the idea that Paul allowed local leadership to emerge in accordance with local realities of power and patronage. Holmberg goes so far as to suggest that there is no such thing as Pauline church order:

> In so far as the Pauline churches have a church order it is not 'Pauline' ... in the sense of 'distinctive' of these churches and planned and given by Paul himself.[26]

---

[21] von Lips, *Glaube*, pp. 196–200.
[22] Holmberg, *Power*, p. 165.
[23] Theissen, *Social Setting*, pp. 27–67.
[24] MacDonald, *Pauline Churches*, p. 53.
[25] MacDonald, *Pauline Churches*, p. 53.
[26] Holmberg, 'Order', p. 199.

But that is not at all to say that Paul had any interest in opposing *charisma* to order in the way that some of his modern interpreters would wish to do. By his personal interventions, through the visits of his accredited representatives and his letters, Paul gave instructions for the good order of the churches:

> Therefore I sent to you Timothy, my beloved and faithful child in the Lord, to remind you of my ways in Christ, as I teach them everywhere in every church. (1 Cor 4:17)

Theissen has shown that a prominent role was played in the Corinthian church by those who had relatively high social status, people who owned a house in which they were able to provide hospitality for the church or whose wealth enabled them to be of service to Paul and the church in other ways.[27] The leadership of the church lay in the hands of such people from the start and in accordance with Paul's deliberate policy, and if they do not feature prominently in the letters it is probably because of 'the personage of Paul himself. The founder has not left the scene, but is fully and energetically active in his church'.[28] Alternatively it may be suggested that at Corinth at least, the leaders are not asked to sort out the church for the very reason that they are themselves implicated in the scandals that beset it.[29]

That distinguished scholars have missed this point in their accounts of the Pauline churches is due to their being guilty of the fallacy of ascribing social realities directly to the application of ideas. Holmberg would have us recognize that passages like 1 Cor 12–14 are 'not primarily a description of reality, but an attempt to change this reality'.[30] In the words of Brockhaus:

> What repeatedly strikes one in all these works, so varied in both theme and theology, is that methodologically they make too little

---

[27] Theissen, *Social Setting*, pp. 73–96.
[28] Holmberg, *Power*, p. 117.
[29] See Chapple, 'Local Leadership', p. 365, Campbell, 'Divisions', pp. 68f., and Clarke, *Leadership*, pp. 112–18.
[30] Holmberg, *Power*, p. 122.

distinction between a reconstruction of church organization in early Christianity, or even just the Pauline churches on the one hand, and the exegesis of passages in which Paul speaks of the Spirit on the other.'[31]

As a result of assuming that, because Paul teaches that something should be the case, it generally *was* the case, many scholars place themselves in the position of having virtually to explain away inconvenient counter-evidence.[32] The resulting picture of Paul and the early church has justly been called 'utopian'.[33]

1 Corinthians: Church Order or Order in Church?

Exegetically the criticism to which the Sohmian view is open is that it has relied too much upon one Pauline letter, and one written to a church where things had manifestly gone wrong. In so doing, it has given too little weight to Paul's purpose in writing.[34] By treating what Paul says in 1 Corinthians 12 as simply a fuller version of what he says in Romans 12, and as if it were intended as a straightforward description of how the churches were organized, we fail to take account of the extent to which what Paul says is influenced by the situation to which he was writing and the precise intention with which he wrote (assuming we can discover these things). We may also fail to ask how much contemporary scholars, and we ourselves, may be influenced by events in the churches of our own day.

After centuries in which a strongly hierarchical pattern of church government prevailed in all the main Christian churches, Lutheran

---

[31] Brockhaus, *Charisma*, p. 93.

[32] See for example the way von Campenhausen works hard to minimize the significance of Phil 1:1, *Authority*, p. 69.

[33] Chapple, 'Local Leadership', p. 58. Cf. von Campenhausen, p. 164.

[34] Holmberg, 'Order', pp. 192f. Chapple puts the general point here as follows: 'This means that we must not only ask, What does Paul say? but also, What does he say it about? (Or what does he say it against?), and, What does he say it for? In other words we must be concerned with the direction of his argument as much as with its position' ('Local Leadership', p. 70).

and Reformed no less than Catholic and Orthodox, these churches have all experienced sweeping changes. In an age impatient of tradition, resistant to authority and confident of the superiority of youth over age, the churches have increasingly felt the need to democratize their structures. The authority of bishops and preachers has been eroded, while the importance of the laity has been stressed. In this situation, the Pauline teaching on the Body and its members has assumed a new prominence, in such a way as to make the democratization of the churches seem no more than the recovery of a lost Christian innocence. In consequence many people have supposed that the changes in the churches have come about solely as the result of a fresh reading of Scripture, unaware of the extent to which the fresh reading of Scripture was itself a response to a changed situation in the churches.

Interpreters of Paul have concerned themselves too little with the purposes for which Paul actually wrote about gifts in 1 Corinthians in particular, and the extent to which the situation he was addressing has slanted the teaching he gives. In consequence, they have supposed Paul to mean that they themselves would mean if they were to give such teaching today, and as if Paul were reacting to the same things that they have been reacting to. Yet in fact there is no reason to think Paul was putting forward his teaching on spiritual gifts in order to promote or preserve democracy in the church. Paul did not share our mistrust of tradition, or of age, and was not contending with entrenched hierarchy in the church. The target in 1 Corinthians is arrogance and disorder. Paul is not appealing to the laity to rise up and realize their long-lost potential, nor to the leadership to relax their grip on the church's life. Rather the reverse! Paul is struggling to regain control of a situation where his authority is being questioned, and where enthusiasts are unwilling to submit to any sort of control.

In such a situation the metaphor of the body and its members is put forward to encourage the Corinthians to value one another. It appears that there were those in Corinth who boasted of their 'pneumatic' power as evidenced particularly in glossolalia. This raises for Paul both practical problems of disorder in the meetings (14:23) and deeper spiritual principles, and, as he does throughout 1

107

Corinthians, Paul tackles the latter first.[35] He insists in the first place that spiritual power is very diverse and does not manifest itself in just one way (12:1–11). All such manifestations of supernatural power are to be seen as God-given gifts, distributed with sovereign freedom, so that no one should boast about them. Moreover the church is Christ's body, and all the members of the church, like the parts of the body, are interdependent and necessary to one another, so that no one should regard himself as superior or despise others (12:12–27).

At the same time, and in some tension with this idea that all are equally necessary, Paul makes clear the precedence of the teaching gifts. Those who bring intelligible speech are more necessary to the church because of their contribution to building up the members in faith and love. For this reason the list of gifts is headed by λόγος σοφίας and λόγος γνώσεως — 'word of wisdom' and 'word of knowledge' respectively (12:8). Despite claims to the contrary,[36] it seems likely that σοφία and γνῶσις refer to the true wisdom and knowledge that Paul himself and other spiritual persons would bring (2:6–16). We should then take λόγος as referring not so much to an isolated 'utterance' as to (a regular activity of) proclamation, instruction or teaching, as it does in 1 Corinthians 1:17–18; 2:4 (cf. 1 Tim 5:17),[37] and so to the contribution of those who instruct the church.

---

[35] So the problem of Paul's own authority, addressed in chapter 4, is approached through the discussion of Wisdom in chapters 1–3, and the problems of dining in temples and eating market food, addressed directly in chapter 10, is approached by way of love for the weaker brother in chapter 8. See further Fee, 1 Corinthians, p. 570.

[36] The fullest discussion of this verse known to me is Dunn, Spirit, pp. 217–21. Dunn believes that σοφία and γνῶσις have been introduced into the discussion in response to the Corinthian valuing of them, but he allows a positive meaning for them here. He interprets them as 'a word spoken under inspiration giving insight into cosmical realities' and 'some charismatic utterance giving an insight, some fresh understanding of God's plan of salvation'. But why should λόγος be taken in this oracular sense? Elsewhere Paul uses it simply to denote his own preaching activity (1 Cor 1:17f.), as in the phrase λόγῳ καὶ ἔργῳ (Rom 15:18). I owe this thought to Dr Paul Fiddes in a popular booklet on Charismatic Renewal published by the Baptist Union of Great Britain in 1980 (see p. 15). He does not elaborate.

[37] There is a good parallel in Acts 13:15, where the synagogue leaders ask the apostles if they have a λόγος παρακλήσεως, explained by BAG as an 'epexegetic gen.'. Although in some places, especially in Luke/Acts, ὁ λόγος is a technical term for the content of the Christian message, in others it simply means the activity of preaching. (Compare Acts 6:4, 8:4, 10:36 with Lk 4:32, 10:39). See BAG, 'λόγος' 1.a.β. and 1.b.β.

Next Paul tells them that, 'God has appointed in the church first apostles, second prophets, third teachers, then workers of miracles ... (12:28). The claims of prophets and teachers are being advanced not against those of overseers or elders, but against those of miracles and glossolalia. The focus is on spiritual gifts, not on church organization, and the 'first, second, third' shows the relative value of the gifts, not the hierarchy of the church.[38] This is confirmed when we turn to chapter 14, whose constant thrust is to promote the claims of intelligible utterance (προφητεία) over those of glossolalia, precisely because of its appeal to the will through the mind (14:3, 13–19).[39]

It is interesting to note that the same thing is true in Ephesians. The concern of the paragraph about gifts of ministry (Eph 4:1–16) is not, of course, with church organization, but with the growth of every member in Christ-likeness and the consequent unity of the whole Body. Every member has a part to play in bringing this about, for each has received 'grace' (4:7).[40] 'Grace' is Paul's way of referring to a person's place in God's redemptive plan (Rom 12:3). The ascended Christ has returned in the Spirit, descended to these 'lower regions' where the church must for the moment live,[41] to give her all that she needs for growth in holiness, and in particular to give certain people to the church who will by their preaching and teaching enable the church to be what it ought to be.[42] These peo-

---

[38] A proper discussion of the terms 'apostles', 'prophets' and 'teachers' is impossible here. By 'apostles' I take it that Paul has in mind mainly himself (so Fee, 1 Cor p. 620). Much speculative ingenuity is spent on distinguishing prophets and teachers and defining their roles in the church, most of it reflecting the ecclesiastical experience or taste of the exegete. My own view is that they are impossible to separate and that they qualify each other: Christian prophecy is didactic and Christian teaching is inspired. Prophecy is *a claim made for* Christian teaching, not a phenomenological description of a kind of 'utterance'. The circle of those who thus served the church is likely to have overlapped substantially with that of προϊστάμενοι, ἐπίσκοποι etc., and to represent different ways of referring to the same people. Alternatively, see Dunn, *Spirit*, pp. 227–38, 272–5.

[39] Fee, 1 Corinthians, p. 652ff.

[40] Unless 'each of us' here refers to the office-bearers of v. 11 among whom the writer numbers himself. So Merklein, *Amt*, pp. 59–62.

[41] So Caird, 'Descent', pp. 535–45.

[42] Lincoln, *Ephesians*, p. 249. I agree with Lincoln, and Merklein (*Amt*, p. 73–5), that τοὺς μὲν ... τοὺς δὲ ... are simply articles belonging with the following nouns, and not as themselves the objects of ἔδωκεν with the nouns acting as predicates. Paul is listing the gifts, not distributing them.

ple are the apostles and prophets of the first generation,[43] corresponding to the evangelists and pastor-teachers of the second and succeeding generations. What is important about them is that they are those that bring God's Word through which the saints will be equipped, the work of the ministry discharged, and the body as a whole built up (4:11–12).[44]

It has been fashionable to link the second of these three, 'the work of the ministry' closely with the first, so as to say that it is 'the saints' who are to do the work of the ministry.[45] This has been shown to be dubious on grammatical and stylistic grounds. The phrase ἔργον διακονίας brings together two words characteristically used by Paul for his own ministry as a preacher of the gospel (2 Cor 3:7–9), and it is likely that this, like the phrase either side of it, refers to something directed *towards* the people of God, not something performed *by* them.[46] The passage needs to be rescued from an anachronistic exegesis according to which its purpose is to teach the 'ministry of the laity'. Every member indeed has a ministry, but special precedence is here given to the 'Word ministries' by which the other ministries are enabled. The passage, whether by Paul or not, accurately captures his concern in 1 Corinthians and restates it in a more general form.

None of what Paul says in either of these letters is put forward in the service of democratic equality, or to exclude regular leadership from the church. *Paul's concern is not so much with 'church order', as with order in church* (14:40), and with the way in which Christians think about themselves and others. That Paul's answer to disorder is not the same as that of Ignatius is not to be denied, but I shall argue that this is a function of the social realities of the situation and not

[43] Grudem helpfully suggests that apostles and prophets are to be identified in Eph 2:20, and I suggest this should be done here too. See Grudem, *Prophecy*, pp. 82–104.

[44] So Barth, *Ephesians*, p. 436, Campbell, 'Evangelist', p. 117–29.

[45] So Barth, *Ephesians*, p. 477–83, 'The Church without Laymen or Priests', and see Lincoln, p. 253 for a list of those defending this view, together with a full discussion of it.

[46] So Merklein, *Amt*, p. 76, Schnackenburg, *Ephesians*, p. 186, Lincoln, *Ephesians*, p. 253, and Collins, *Diakonia*, p. 233f.

of a theological or spiritual principle. Paul's failure to say more about the leaders there were,[47] is more likely to be because their role as household heads was largely unquestioned than because Paul thought them unimportant. Had Paul been advocating a pattern of church life in which the established conventions of society were completely overturned, we should have expected much more mention of the fact. The numerical growth of the churches and the concomitant stresses and strains would demand more organizational structure in the next generation. Meanwhile we see Paul more concerned with Christian attitudes than church government, with humility more than democracy.

Making the Synagogue in our Own Image?

On historical grounds, the consensus is open to criticism for its dependence on a view of the organization of the synagogue which is at best doubtful, and which has in fact often been disputed. We have seen that the 'neo-Sohmians' repeatedly develop their view of Pauline church order in contrast to a Jewish Christianity in which it is supposed the synagogue acted as a model. Elders, it is supposed, were appointed by the Christian churches in imitation of the synagogue, and yet the opinion of those who have made a special study of the ancient synagogue seems very much against this, as we saw in chapter 2. R. J. Banks goes so far as to say:

> In view of the suggestions that the notion of eldership was drawn from the synagogue, it should be noted that there is no evidence whatever for the synagogue having such positions.[48]

To remind the reader of the conclusions reached earlier regarding the government of the synagogue, it appears that the elders as such were not numbered among the officers who ran the synagogue on a day to day basis. When the elders met in council it was

---

[47] See 1 Thess 5:12; 1 Cor 16:15ff.; Phil 1:1. These passages are discussed later in the present chapter, p. 120–126.
[48] Banks, *Community*, p. 149.

not as the elders of the synagogue that they met, but as elders of the Jewish community, as the heads of its noble families and people of honour and influence. In giving place to such people, moreover, we saw that the Jews were in no way unique, since people of this kind were to be found in effective control of most communities in the ancient world, but the synagogues as synagogues are unlikely to have had elders in the sense required, and no one organizing a church in their house in the middle decades of the first century is likely to have thought that they needed to appoint any. Two further points may be made in debate with von Campenhausen.

In the first place, von Campenhausen's argument trades on the ambiguity of the word συναγωγή and of the words 'congregation' and 'community' variously used to translate it. We have seen that, while in many places the Jewish community as a whole had a council to whose members the term 'elders' was indeed applied, this community should be distinguished from congregations gathered for study and prayer, to which the term 'synagogue' most naturally belongs. These latter cannot be shown to have had councils of elders of their own. By using the word 'congregation' (*Gemeinde*) both of the Jewish civil community and the Christian churches, von Campenhausen is able to deduce that if elders make an appearance in Christian congregations they have been taken over from Jewish congregations. But the true point of comparison for the Christian house-meeting should surely by the Jewish meeting for prayer and study, itself often originating in a house, that is to say 'the synagogue'. It cannot be likely that arrangements developed for the government of whole towns, or whole Jewish communities within towns, would have provided a model for emerging Christian house-meetings. Within the meetings for prayer and study, which we call 'the synagogue', the elders do not seem to have formed the sort of body envisaged by von Campenhausen. Administrative decisions appear to have been taken by the appointed officers. Elders were not so much appointed to serve as executives in the modern sense; they existed independently of appointment by virtue of their seniority and social position, and as such were honoured with the chief seats, and their opinion sought first and deferred to.[49] Is it not in fact likely that the picture we have of the Jewish synagogue as an independent congregation meeting for worship under the leadership of its own appointed elders is itself derived from *our* ideas of the Christian churches? It would then be, to coin a phrase, nothing but the reflection of a liberal Protestant congregation seen at the bottom of a deep well!

The second point to note is that von Campenhausen presents the Jewish elders as rabbis or scribes. 'Elders' did indeed become a title of honour for leading older scholars in the Mishnah,[50] but this is hardly evidence for the first century. For von Campenhausen, 'The elders are the professional guardians of the Law and for that reason also leaders of their community'.[51] Surely this is the wrong way round? We have seen that the elders were primarily heads of their families, senior and respected on account of their patriarchal position and relative wealth and power, and therefore were looked to for judicial rulings and decisions. They did not become elders because they guarded the tradition; they guarded the tradition because they were 'elder statesmen'.

Working with the model of the Jewish elder as a scribe enables von Campenhausen to portray the difference between Jewish and Christian elders in purely theological terms:

The Jewish elders, as civic and religious representatives of their community, are entirely bound by law and tradition... . In the Christian Church the situation was from the start entirely different. She was most certainly not living by the Law and by the past, but by her experience in the present of a new sovereignty of God... .[52]

In the light of this, von Campenhausen argues that the Christian elders safeguarded the tradition, but it was the tradition of the gospel, not of the Law. This is surely another example of the idealis-

---

[49] Harvey, 'Elders', p. 331: 'There can be no question of appointing people to be elders: elders exist already.'
[50] Bornkamm, πρέσβυς, *TDNT*, Vol. VI, p. 659f.
[51] Von Campenhausen, *Authority*, p. 78.
[52] Von Campenhausen, ibid.

tic fallacy at work, historical phenomena being ascribed directly to theological ideas. Christian elders are most likely to have differed from jewish elders because of the differing nature of the communities to which they belonged. They would have been honoured spontaneously because of their status, not appointed to guard a tradition. This way of thinking, however, helps to explain why von Campenhausen finds no place for elders in Paul's churches. Elders represent the Law, and the Law is something that 'binds'; for Paul what matters is the new wind of the Spirit. Elders are therefore to be excluded by the gospel itself. The presence of elders in Jewish-Christian churches simply confirms that these churches have not really or fully understood the gospel, and their appearance in Pauline churches can be made to represent a decline in understanding. For the neo-Sohmian tradition the idea of an irreconcilable opposition between Paul and Jerusalem is still very much alive, so that Käsemann can say that, 'Paul's doctrine of the *charismata* is the projection into ecclesiology of the doctrine of justification by faith'.[53]

By contrast, we need to insist that theological concerns should not be allowed to dictate the socio-historical conclusions. The fact that heads of families among the Jews were known as elders and were guardians of the tradition (if indeed that can be shown), does not mean that those whom the Christian called 'the elders' must also have been guardians of tradition, but simply that they were the heads of Christian households and honoured as such.

Present but Peripheral?

What then is the significance of the fact that there is no mention of elders in Paul's letters and yet elders so clearly emerge in his churches in the next generation? If there was not, as the consensus view maintains, a corruption of the Pauline understanding of the church, how do we account first for the silence, and then for the emergence?

One answer is to say that there were (there must have been) elders in Paul's churches from the start; we just do not hear of them

---

[53] Käsemann, 'Ministry', p. 75.

because they were not important. This is the solution offered by J. T. Burtchaell in his book, *From Synagogue to Church*. As the title implies, Burtchaell's thesis is that the earliest churches were modelled from the start on the synagogues from which their first members had come. The likelihood of this, as he sees it, persuades him that where the New Testament record is silent, the pattern of the synagogue can be invoked to fill the gaps. Thus on the subject of the elders he says:

> As soon as early converts in any locale became unwelcome enough in their own synagogues and numerous enough to cluster into a community of their own, *they would require elders.*[54]

Evidence that they did so is derived by Burtchaell from the New Testament as follows:

> Acts refers repeatedly to elders in the Jerusalem community, and mentions them in Lystra, Iconium, Pisidian Antioch (Paul's early foundations) and Ephesus. If the pastoral epistles are indeed directed to Ephesus and Crete, copious references confirm their existence in those communities. Paul addresses elders in Philippi and describes them to the Thessalonians.[55]

This is not really satisfactory for two reasons. First, it rather 'massages' the evidence. Thus, Acts mentions elders in Jerusalem in only three separate narratives (hardly repeatedly). There are only two other references to elders in Acts (Lystra, Iconium and Antioch are the *same* reference!), and the Pastorals mention elders in just three passages (Tit 1:5; 1 Tim 4:14, 1 Tim 5:17–19), hardly 'copiously'. Elders are not mentioned at all in Philippians, and to suggest otherwise is to beg the question. Secondly, as the above quotation shows, the New Testament evidence Burtchaell cites is all arguably post-Pauline. To use it to show that there were elders in the churches from the start is also to beg the question. Burtchaell does not really address the problems of handling evidence from Paul, Acts and the

---

[54] Burtchaell, *Synagogue*, p. 292, my emphasis.
[55] Burtchaell, p. 293.

Pastorals in successive sentences. Instead of taking the biblical witnesses one at a time, as we have sought to do, he assumes they can be harmonized. This is not likely to prove persuasive to the champions of the Sohmian consensus against whom his book is in many ways a welcome counterblast.

But all this is preliminary skirmishing! Even Burtchaell admits that elders are not prominent in Paul (or anywhere else in the New Testament for that matter). *This is not because they did not exist, but because they were not important.*[56] Rather it was the 'charismatics', the apostles, prophets and teachers, who were important. The charismatics led the church; the elders, bishops and deacons merely presided.[57] Only as the Pentecostal fire died down in the church, and the charismatics became a squalid nuisance, did the officers assume the leadership of the church. This seems to me wildly unlikely for three reasons.

In the first place, we may wonder if the distinction between leading and presiding is really tenable. If we have learnt anything about the elders from our study so far, it is that they bear a title of *honour*. In the same way 'overseer' is a title implying *responsibility*. It is one thing to say with the consensus that in the early days no one was so honoured or given such responsibility, but to suggest that there were such people but that their titles did not mean anything is surely incredible.

Secondly, this proposal involves putting a great deal of trust in the Didache, and in a particular interpretation of its evidence made famous by Harnack whereby the evidence of the Didache is crossed with 1 Cor 12:28 to show that the early church knew two kinds of ministry, a translocal charismatic ministry and a settled ministry of bishops and deacons.[58] There are three things to say about this. In the first place, the date and place of origin of the Didache are still

---

[56] Burtchaell, p. 188: 'Both the consensus and its critics have assumed all along that church officers ... would have to be very important, and so they have either affirmed or denied their primitive existence.' He goes on to speak of them as 'a peripheral cadre'.

[57] Burtchaell, p. 350.

[58] This was taken up also by Streeter, *Primitive*, pp. 144–52. I shall say something more about the Didache in Chapter 7.

very uncertain. This makes it precarious to base too much on it, when we do not know who is speaking, to whom, or when, and therefore what about. Secondly, it is doubtful if the Didache witnesses to a threefold order at all. As de Halleux has shown, apostle, prophet and teacher most likely all refer to the same figure, the travelling preacher, or prophet, who is described as an apostle because he travels, and a teacher because he teaches.[59] Thirdly, it is also very doubtful whether 1 Cor 12:28 should be pressed into yielding a charismatic church order. By speaking of apostles, prophets and teachers as 'first, second and third' Paul is concerned to identify himself and other bringers of God's Word as the primary gifts and to subordinate other expressions of enthusiasm and service to them. There is no evidence that any of them, apart from Paul himself, was itinerant, and so the connection with the figure in the Didache fails. This well-worn hypothesis neglects the fact Paul was not merely a charismatic but also a controller, and at times opponent, of charismatics. It illegitimately transfers credit from the account of Paul into that of the bankrupt Didache apostles, and uses the Didache to multiply the number of apostles in Paul's churches![60]

Thirdly, there is good reason to think that it is the household not the synagogue that holds the secret of the early churches' development. Modern interest in the house-church can be dated from Filson's perceptive pre-war article,[61] and the literature on the early Christian house-church is now vast.[62] It is now widely accepted that the household provided Paul and other Christian missionaries with the essential place to meet, that its head provided patronal protection for the

---

[59] de Halleux, 'Ministères', pp. 22–3. See also, Dix, 'Ministry', pp. 140–2.
[60] The matter may be put in the form of a double syllogism, as follows:
The Didache apostles were charismatics;
Paul was an apostle who 'ran' his churches;
Therefore,
Paul was a charismatic (like the Didache apostles),
and apostles (of the Didache type) ran the churches.
[61] Filson, 'Significance', 105–12.
[62] Significant contributions in the last fifteen years include: Banks, *Community*, pp. 33–43; Elliott, *Home*, pp. 165–266; Klauck, *Hausgemeinde, passim*; Meeks, *Urban*, pp. 75–84; Malherbe, *Social Aspects*, pp. 60–91; Stuhlmacher, *Philemon*, pp. 70–5; Gnilka, *Philemon*, pp. 17–31.

new congregation, while his extended family more often than not contributed the core of the congregation and accounted for the rapid numerical growth of the movement. The shape and size of the house greatly influenced the style and size of the meetings that could take place in it, while the patriarchal structure of the family determined to a large extent the leadership structures of the congregation. The references in the New Testament to the 'church that meets in your house' indicate not only the place of meeting but the leader of the church as well.[63] We can no longer reconstruct a Pauline church meeting simply on the basis of Paul's lists of *charismata* without at the same time reckoning with the leading role played by people whose age, wealth, status or education combined to place them in natural ascendancy over other members of the church. This discovery has yet to be fully utilized in understanding the role of the elders in the early churches.

Of course, there are points of similarity between the churches and the synagogues, as between the churches and the associations and clubs that proliferated the Graeco-Roman cities,[64] yet I believe it is to the household that the churches were primarily indebted. In the first place, the household was more than a model; it was the matrix of the new congregation. We are explicitly and repeatedly told of churches' meeting in someone's house.[65] Burtchaell, of course, knows that the Christians used private houses, but he appears to see these simply as buildings, rather than as extended families with built-in authority patterns of their own. Synagogues too may often have started in homes. Excavations have shown that the ancient household provided the meeting place not just for the church, but often also for synagogues and pagan cults as well.[66] By the middle of the

---

[63] The well-known study by Theissen of the people named in 1 Corinthians shows that in almost every case the leading people of the Corinthian church can be shown to have been people of substance and social standing, and this fact must affect our understanding of the Pauline church. Theissen, *Social Setting*, pp. 69–119.

[64] Meeks, *Urban*, pp. 75-84.

[65] The explicit references are 1 Cor 16:19; Rom 16:15; Philem 2, Col 4:15, but there are several references to the household as the meeting place of Christians in Acts.

[66] White, *God's House*, pp. 48, 62. The classic example remains that provided by the excavations at Dura-Europos. See, *The Excavations at Dura-Europos, Final Reports*, Vol. VIII, Parts 1 and 2, C. H. Kraeling, 1956 and 1967.

first century, however, 'In the cities where Paul founded congregations, the Jews had probably already advanced to the stage of possessing buildings used exclusively for the community's functions.'[67]
The synagogue gatherings we meet in Acts would seem to bear this
out.

Secondly, the prominence of the *Haustafeln* in the later Pauline
epistles, and the household language in the Pastorals, witness to the
enduring influence of the household environment on the churches.
At a point in their development where we might have expected the
proliferation of the sort of offices and honours prevalent in synagogue and association, the talk is all of household hierarchy.

For, thirdly, there is a striking absence of the kind of titles of
office that abound in inscriptions from both synagogue and association. Burtchaell, following Frey, lists over ten of these in the synagogue — and then conspicuously fails to find them in the church!
The same is true of the association. Meeks refers to the rich variety
of grand titles found in connection with the association 'which
offered the chance for people who had no chance to participate in
the politics of the city itself to feel important in their own miniature
republics.'[68] We do not find this in the churches, perhaps because it
was foreign to the ethos of the Christian movement, but perhaps
also because the household imposed its own quiet hierarchy on the
proceedings. Finally, we must wonder how likely it is that those
who left synagogues to join the church, and Gentiles who had never
belonged to them, would have wanted to reproduce their structures
when they decisively rejected their whole basis of membership and
initiation. The dependence of the churches on the synagogues is a
large assumption for which little hard evidence can be produced. By
contrast the household matrix of the earliest churches is well attested, and appears to have exercised an enduring influence.

In a fresh attempt to resolve the problem, we shall in this section
begin by directing our attention to the evidence of incipient institutionalization even within Paul's letters. His churches were never

---

[67] Meeks, Urban, p. 80.
[68] Meeks, Urban, p. 31.

without leaders. It will then be argued that the fact that he did not call them 'the elders' owes more to the household structure of the churches and to a peculiarity of the word 'elders' itself than to any deeper theological reasons. Finally we shall see that Paul's own standpoint as a church-planting evangelist led him to use a different vocabulary of leadership to that which developed naturally within the churches themselves.

Local Leadership in Pauline Churches

Paul's letters in fact contain plenty of evidence of the institutionalization latent in Paul's own practice, so that it can fairly be said that the seeds of the later development were sown by Paul himself. To begin with, it is well-established that the earliest churches met in homes, and that Paul, in seeking to establish a church in a city, was dependent on securing the support of someone with a house large enough to provide a place for meetings.[69] This picture is confirmed by a comparison of the stories in Acts with the leadership references in the letters. For example, in his account of the founding of the church at Thessalonica, Luke tells us that the mob attacked the house of Jason because he had 'received' the missionaries (Acts 17:1–9). Jason must be a person of substance since the authorities take security from him to guarantee the good behaviour of the visitors, and it is reasonable to conclude that in receiving them, Jason had actually provided a place for them to preach and gather a congregation and that he had a house large enough for the purpose.[70]

In his letter written to the church at Thessalonica shortly afterwards, Paul refers to a group of people as 'those who labour among you and are over you in the Lord and admonish you' (1 Thess 5:12). 'Labour' renders κοπιῶντας, a word that Paul uses elsewhere

---

[69] Filson, 'Significance', p. 111, Elliott, *Home*, pp. 198–201; Meeks, *Urban*, pp. 75–7, Klauck, *Hausgemeinde, passim*; Stuhlmacher, *Philemon*, pp. 70–5; White, 'Social Authority', pp. 214ff.

[70] Malherbe, *Thessalonians*, pp. 12–17.

to describe his own ministry of preaching and teaching. Chapple has shown that it is a semi-technical word for this.[71] While the right and duty of 'admonishing' was not reserved to a few (5:14), for Paul to speak in this way of 'those who admonish you' is clearly to single out certain people who did this more regularly than others. Labouring and admonishing thus clearly point to a leadership group, as does the remaining word 'those who are over you in the Lord', (τοὺς) προϊσταμένους ὑμῶν ἐν κυρίῳ.

This word occurs again in the list of gifts mentioned in Romans (12:8), as a generic singular, ὁ προϊστάμενος. Most English versions render this by a word for leadership.[72] Some scholars prefer to think of charitable work, because of the immediate context,[73] but others suggest that we do not in fact have to choose between helping and leading, since the help given is patronage, given by a superior to those in his care.[74] Jason provided such help to Paul in the earliest days of the church, according to Acts, and it is reasonable to suppose that he continued to provide it to the church that met in his house. Those in whose houses the church met were people of some standing and they provided not only a place to meet but limited respectability and protection. The same relationship of patronage is probably to be understood in what Paul says elsewhere (Rom 16:2) of Phoebe who is said to have been προστάτις πολλῶν καὶ ἐμοῦ αὐτοῦ — 'helper of many and of myself'. It is natural to suppose that those who thus acted as patrons on behalf of the church in the wider community would also have been looked to for leadership within the life of the church.

Thus in this verse (1 Thess 5:12) with three separate words, κοπιῶντας, προϊσταμένους, νουθετοῦντας, Paul points to a group who were active in teaching, leading and correcting their

---

[71] Chapple, 'Local Leadership', p. 207ff.

[72] 'If you are a leader,' REB; 'If you are put in charge', JB; 'If it is leadership', NIV. The RSV is almost alone in rendering it: 'He who gives aid.'

[73] Cranfield, *Romans*, p. 626, Ziesler, *Romans*, p. 300.

[74] Michel, *Römer*, p. 379, Wilckens, *Römer*, Vol. 3, p. 15, Dunn, *Romans*, p. 731: 'some member of the congregation who by virtue of his or her wealth or social status within the community (city) was able to champion the rights of the little congregation or its socially vulnerable members.'

fellow-members, and calls for recognition of them. We may conclude that from a very early stage in its life, perhaps within a matter
of weeks, there were those who could be called leaders in the church,
whose position rested not on *charisma* in a Weberian sense, but on
the service they performed and the status they enjoyed. Paul would
later teach his churches to regard such people and their contribution as *charismata*, gifts of grace, but that is to use *charisma* in quite
a different sense. Chapple is right to say of these people that their
position was 'neither official nor incompatible with office, but informal and *tending toward office*.'[75] This justifies the conclusion that
some routinization is present form the start of the church.[76]

Similar conclusions can be drawn from the brief reference to the
household of Stephanas at Corinth (1 Cor 16:15). Paul uses three
different verbs to urge the church to respect these people as their
leaders: οἴδατε, ὑποτάσσησθε, and ἐπιγινώσκετε — literally,
'know', 'respect' and 'recognize'.[77] Clearly they enjoy a real, if informal position of leadership in the church, based on a number of
factors. First, they were founder members of the church, a fact
confirmed both by Paul's description of them as ἀπαρχὴ τῆς
Ἀχαΐας — 'the first converts of Asia', and the information that
Paul had himself baptized them (1 Cor 1:16). Secondly, Stephanas
is a householder, implying that he has some status and money and
social standing relative to others. He was not alone in this, since
Paul urges the recognition of 'such people', and the reference to
Gaius who has been host to the whole church (Rom 16:23) very
probably points to one of them. Thirdly, they were active in the
work of the church, like the Thessalonian leaders. Paul says that εἰς
διακονίαν τοῖς ἁγίοις ἔταξαν ἑαυτούς — 'they have devoted
themselves to the service of the saints' (RSV), and then speaks of
παντὶ τῷ συνεργοῦντι καὶ κοπιῶντι — 'to every fellow worker

---

[75] Chapple, Local Leadership, p. Cf. MacDonald, *Pauline Churches*, p. 53.

[76] '*Charisma* does not exist without a charismatic community and consequently *charisma* as a social phenomenon does not exist except in a routinized form.' Holmberg,
Power, p. 176.

[77] I take οἴδατε as an imperative in the light of the meaning of εἰδέναι in 1 Thess
5:12.

and labourer'. This is the distinctive vocabulary of the Pauline mission and implies that Stephanas was prominent in a group of people who were active in preaching and teaching on behalf of the church as a whole. It will not do for Dunn to play down the significance of this by stressing the voluntary nature of Stephanas' service (ἔταξαν ἑαυτούς).[78] From the fact that Paul commends the generosity of Stephanas we cannot conclude that his position lacked regular recognition. Paul's purpose here is to increase the regard in which the Corinthians hold their leaders, and for this reason he emphasizes the willingness of the leaders for which they deserve support. Public office in ancient Greece involved a good deal of generous giving on the part of the office-holder. Volunteering for service is not incompatible with receiving a recognized position as a result, and equally Paul was quite capable of presenting someone's service as a spontaneous act of kindness, even though he had himself expressly requested it.[79] Chapple rightly concludes of the situation in Corinth that although it is premature to speak of 'office' in the Corinthian church at the time this letter was written, office will naturally emerge out of what Paul says here.[80]

The last of these incidental references we shall discuss is the greeting to 'all the saints in Christ Jesus who are at Philippi with the bishops and deacons' (σὺν ἐπισκόποις καὶ διακόνοις) (Phil 1:1). We discuss this last in accordance with the usual view that Philippians was written later than 1 Thessalonians or 1 Corinthians. If so, this provides a convenient progression towards greater institutionalization, but we should remember that the exact date of Philippians is very uncertain and that the mention of such titles of office is itself one of the main indicators of a later date.

Since this is the only reference to ἐπίσκοποι in Paul's letters, we must be cautious in drawing conclusions from it, but some observations may be made with some confidence. First, the people referred to are clearly in some sort of leadership. Second, there are a number

---

[78] Dunn, *Unity*, p. 113.
[79] Allo, *Corinthiens*, p. 465, cites 2 Cor 8:16f., where Paul says in one breath that Titus is coming because Paul asked him to, and by his own choice (αὐθαίρετος).
[80] Chapple, 'Local Leadership', p. 444.

of them, with no single person in overall control. Third, the absence of the definite article suggests that the leaders were not a tightly defined group. Fourth, we cannot be certain that two separate offices are here in view. The words are sufficiently vague to mean no more than 'those who lead and serve', or perhaps, 'those who serve by leading', remembering the way in which Paul is happy to apply the term διάκονος to his own ministry and that of others.[81] The main reason for seeing two offices here lies in the fact that they are clearly distinguished in the Pastorals, but the fact that they later became two offices does not prove that they were so at Philippi at this time. Fifth, they are likely to have included those mentioned by name in the letter: Epaphroditus, Euodia, Syntyche and Clement (2:25–30; 4:2–3).

Although the reference is tantalizingly vague, it seems clear that these people are functionally equivalent to the leaders we have considered at Thessalonica and Corinth. The use of these particular titles could be due to the increased size of the church and the consequent need for a more formalized leadership structure, or might simply reflect a Philippian idiosyncracy that Paul was happy to go along with.[82] ἐπίσκοποι is a very general term in classical Greek and in the Septuagint for those who exercised oversight in a variety of contexts, and, as has often been pointed out, it is an essentially secular term. It was this that led Hatch to the view that the ἐπίσκοποι were financial officers modelled on their counterparts in Greek clubs, and that Paul mentions them here because they were responsible for the Philippians' gift to him. However, since Paul does not mention them in 4:10–20 when he is particularly speaking of the gift, the suggestion has been dropped by most modern commentators. The other thing to be said about this idea is that it presupposes that if a

---

[81] So Collange, *Philippians*, p. 38f., and Hawthorne, *Phillipians*, p. 7f., following Chrysostom; otherwise O'Brien, *Philippians*, p. 48f.

[82] The suggestion of Best (*ATR*, 37, pp. 14–17), based on Paul's omission of the title of apostle in introducing himself, that Paul is gently mocking the Philippians leaders' pretensions, is surely too subtle. Likewise the suggestion of Collange (*Philippians*, p. 41) that Paul mentions them here, with an emphasis on humble service, because he is going to have to rebuke them for the pride that has led them to quarrel.

leader was concerned with finance and welfare, he was not also concerned with spiritual and pastoral matters. Yet the distinction appears to be too modern. The Essene מבקר (*mebaqqer*) (CD 13–14) at any rate appears to have been concerned for both, and it will be suggested in the next chapter that the connection between מבקר and ἐπίσκοπος has been dismissed on inadequate grounds.[83]

Among the commentators who discuss this verse there is a remarkable reluctance to consider the social setting of the oversight implied by these terms. Yet if we ask what it was that the ἐπίσκοποι were in charge of, the best guess is that they were, like Stephanas at Corinth, overseers of the churches that met in their houses. Chapple proposes:

> They are leaders of house churches who formed a 'co-ordinating committee' to provide necessary leadership for the Christian community at Philippi.[84]

He supports this by all that we know of the household context of the Pauline churches, and by noting that Paul here greets not the church but 'the saints', evidence that the church is now too numerous to meet in one house. The overseers then are the hosts of the churches and the 'deacons' assist them.[85] There is then no special significance in there being more than one overseer, except that there is more than one (house-) church in Philippi. The situation may well be the same as that envisaged by Luke's account of Paul addressing the Ephesian leaders (Acts 20:17, 28).

This evidence from three major Pauline letters confirms that the emergence of more formalized leadership was not a development contrary to the Pauline legacy, and that it was inherent from the start in the household setting of the earliest congregations.[86] Their

---

[83] Among recent commentators on Philippians the connection is doubted by Gnilka (*Philipper* p. 37), but viewed more favourably by Hawthorne (p. 8).

[84] Chapple, 'Local Leadership', p. 558.

[85] Roloff also, in an excursus on the development of church office, (*Timotheus*, p. 172f.), sees the emergence of several ερισκοπι as due to the multiplication of house-churches. Cf. also Dassmann, 'Hausgemeinde'.

[86] 'Although it is impossible to speak of fixed offices in the Pauline communities, the formalization or institutionalization of roles is progressing rapidly'. MacDonald, *Pauline Churches*, p. 60.

leaders were the equivalent of elders in all but name, as has often been said.[87] *But the fact remains that Paul did not use the term.* The reason, I now suggest, lies in the connotations of the term 'the elders' itself, as we have seen in earlier chapters.

The Dynamics of the Term 'The Elders'

My proposal is this. *It is the household structure of the earliest churches which is both the factor that makes the calling of people 'the elders' inappropriate in the first generation, and inevitable in the second.*

So long as the local church was confined to one household, the household provided the leadership of the church. The church in the house came with its leadership so to speak 'built-in'. The church that met in someone's house met under that person's presidency. The householder was *ex hypothesi* a person of standing, a patron of others, and the space where the church met was his space, in which he was accustomed to the obedience of slaves and the deference of his wife and children. Those who came into it will have been to a large extent constrained by the norms of hospitality to treat the host as master of ceremonies, especially if he was a person of greater social standing or age than themselves. The table moreover was his table, and if any prayers were to be said, or bread or wine offered, the part was naturally his to play. Dassmann observes:

> Likewise, we may suppose that the host and head of the family was most readily considered for the leadership of the church in his house, on the ground of his natural authority, which gave him independence and influence.[88]

It should be mentioned at this point that the householder could also be a woman, of course.[89] This is known to have been possible

---

[87] See Bruce, *Acts*, p. 280, Bultmann, *Theology*, II, p. 102. Burtchaell says that the passages we have just considered, 'may plausibly imply the kind of responsibility which elders commonly had.' *Synagogue*, p. 293.

[88] Dassmann, 'Hausgemeinde', p. 90.

[89] It was possible for a woman under Roman law (Lex Papia Poppaea, 9 CE) to act χωρὶς κυρίου. *P Oxy* 12, 1467 (263 CE) refers to laws 'which give authority to women

under Roman law, and we meet such women in the New Testament, in the early days of the Pauline churches. Nympha (Col 4:15) appears to be an example of such a person,[90] and perhaps also Lydia (Acts 16:14) and Phoebe (Rom 16:1f.). It is important to bear in mind that there was no one attitude to the place and role of women in the societies of the ancient world. While their freedom was very restricted in traditional Athenian society, wealthy women enjoyed greater freedom in Sparta, and in Macedonia and Asia Minor.[91] While the attitude of the Mishnah towards women is extremely negative,[92] it should not be taken for granted that the same attitudes prevailed in Diaspora Judaism.[93] A number of Jewish inscriptions, admittedly all later than our period, show women holding office in the Jewish communities.[94] There was then probably no one attitude to women in the earliest churches either, and it could change over time in response to changing pressures. Opportunities for women to lead the churches probably did become fewer in the generation after Paul's death, and later in this chapter, I explain why I think this was so.

Meanwhile, a suggestive parallel to the Christian house-church is provided by an inscription from Philadelphia in Lydia and dating from the late second or early first century BCE in which are set out

who are endowed with the right of three children to be independent and to negotiate without a κύριος in the transactions they undertake (ἑαυτῶν κυριεύειν καὶ χωρὶς κυρίου χρηματίζειν). See further Horsley, *New Documents*, Vol, 2, pp. 25–32.

[90] However, the text is disputed. While B reads Νύμφαν καὶ τὴν κατ' οἶκον αὐτῆς ἐκκλησίαν, D reads Νυμφᾶν καὶ τὴν κατ' οἶκον αὐτῆς ἐκκλησίαν, and ℵ, A, C etc. read αὐτῶν. In the first case Nympha is a woman, and the fact that she is hosting the church suggests she is a widow or divorcee. In the second case, Nymphas is a man, while in the third case Nympha, if a woman, is associated with the brothers and presumably not the head of the family. I think the verse is evidence of a woman leading a church in her house, with the textual variations due to the fact that it later became unacceptable.

[91] Witherington, *Earliest*, pp. 5–16. Trebilco, *Communities*, pp. 113–25.

[92] Wegner, *Chattel*, pp. 145–67.

[93] Trebilco, *Communities*, p. 112, nn. 47, 48.

[94] Thus Brooten discusses three inscriptions which refer to women as ἀρχισυνάγωγοι, and six where they are said to be elders. The usual response to this information is to say that the titles are honorific, or that they refer to the wives of men who held these offices. So most recently, Burtchaell, *Synagogue*, pp. 244–6, but Trebilco, *Communities*, pp. 104–26, makes a convincing case for accepting them at face value.

the rules of a Hellenistic cult group meeting in the house of a certain Dionysius.[95] The inscription tells us that Dionysius, in response to a revelation of Zeus received by him in a dream, has opened his house to men and women, free men and slaves so that they can come to engage in worship together. The most relevant parts of it read as follows, in Horsley's translation:

> For health and common salvation and the finest reputation the ordinances given to Dionysius in his sleep were written up, giving access into his *oikos* to men and women, free people and slaves.... .

> To this man Zeus has given ordinances for the performance of the purifications, the cleansings and the mysteries, in accordance with ancestral custom and as has now been written.

> When coming into this *oikos* let men and women, free people and slaves, swear by all the gods neither to know nor make use wittingly of any deceit against a man or woman, neither poison harmful to men, nor harmful spells.... . They are not to refrain in any respect from being well-intentioned towards this *oikos*. If anyone performs or plots any of these things, they are neither to put up with it nor keep silent, but expose it and defend themselves.... .

> At the monthly and annual sacrifices may those men and women who have confidence in themselves touch this inscription on which the ordinances of the god have been written, in order that those who obey these ordinances and those who do not may be manifest.[96]

Here we have a group meeting in someone's home, on the basis of a revelation, for the purpose of worship. It is open to all, and

---

[95] Dittenberger, *Sylloge³*, No. 985. First edited by J. Keil and A. von Premerstein in 1914, it is the subject of an article by S. C. Barton and G. H. R. Horsley, 'A Hellenistic Cult Group and the New Testament Churches', *JAC* 24 (1981), pp. 7–41. It is also discussed briefly by White, *God's House*, p. 45. I am grateful to Dr Bruce Winter for drawing my attention to this.

[96] Barton and Horsley, 'Cult', pp. 9–11.

concerned for moral standards and the maintenance of fellowship. The bulk of the inscription is in fact concerned with the moral requirements that those who come must observe. Barton and Horsley note the absence of reference to hierarchy or offices among the members, but say:

> Is the possibility worth entertaining that, underlying the relations of this cult there is some form of 'household' structure? ... It is consistent with the evidence to conjecture that the text emanates from a cult group, originally comprised of the members of Dionysius' household (including his slaves), now reconstituted on the basis of a new moral code and opened to embrace all-comers and, in particular, other like-minded households.[97]

Here then is a group very much like a Pauline church, founded on the basis of a revelation, open to people of every class, and meeting in a home. There is no hierarchy, and in particular there are no elders, and this, we may think, is because the group is of recent formation, and especially because there is as yet only one such group. No title of office is given to Dionysius, but he is clearly in a dominant position. It is his house, and his dream, and he is laying down the rules. He is presumably the one to offer the sacrifices. Anyone calling him an 'overseer' would not be wide of the mark, but in fact, since there is no apostle speaking into the group from outside, and no other leaders, there is no pressing need to call him anything. Factors that might lead to distinguishing titles would be an increase in the numbers or activities of the group, necessitating a division of labour ('overseers and deacons', for example), or the formation of further groups, making it possible to refer generically or corporately to the various household heads ('elders', perhaps).

In the case of the Pauline churches, as the number of believers meeting in the *atrium* grew, there may well have been need for others to assume responsibility for their care and teaching, and those ready and able to do so. The householder may for this reason

---

[97] Barton and Horsley, 'Cult', p. 23.

have been distinguished from others by the general title of 'over-seer', with other able people as διάκονοι. But no one would think of calling the head of the household 'the elder', for the simple reason that, as we have seen, 'elder' normally occurs in the plural, and 'the elders' would thus be a collective title for the leaders of several leading households acting together. Neither in ancient Israel nor in the Greek or Jewish world of the first century have we found any tendency to use the word in the singular as the title of an office-holder. Of course, most scholars think that the New Testament evidence suggests that already in Paul's lifetime there were several such house-churches in a place like Corinth,[98] but their numbers were apparently still small enough to allow them to assemble for a common meeting in one house.[99]

Links between the various households were probably quite informal at this stage and focused on the apostle himself. As the numbers grew so that it was no longer possible for the whole church to assemble in one place, and with the removal of the apostle and the rising threat of factionalism, the need for a greater degree of local organization would become pressing. The leaders of house-churches would need to relate and act together in a *representative* capacity and at this point nothing could be more natural than to refer to their leaders collectively as 'the elders'. Individually each will have represented his household in the local church, enjoying this honour by reason of his seniority within his own household.

[98] For example, Banks, *Community*, p. 38; Klauck, *Hausgemeinde*, p. 34f.; Meeks, *Urban*, p. 75.

[99] See 1 Cor 11:18, 14:23; Rom 16:23, and the fact that Paul apparently expects the whole church to assemble to hear his letter being read. A different view has been put forward by Gielen 'Formel', pp. 107–25. He argues that the references to ἡ κατ' οἶκον ἐκκλησία are never in fact contrasted in the letters with ἡ ὅλη ἐκκλησία, that they all occur in greetings and in each case refer to the whole church in a certain place meeting in the house of the person referred to. However, in view of what we know of the size of even large houses of the period (Murphy-O'Connor, *Corinth*, p. 156, estimates that the average size of atrium in the house of a wealthy man would hold no more than fifty people, and probably considerably less), the church in a place like Corinth must very soon have outgrown its original meeting place and could only have been confined to one location for a relatively short time. Moreover Gielen ignores the evidence of Acts regarding the meetings of the church κατ' οἶκον. (See Klauck, *Hausgemeinde*, pp. 47–56, Dassmann, 'Hausgemeinde', p. 89 and discussion of this in my next chapter.)

This stage, we suggested earlier, following Chapple, had already been reached at Philippi by the time Paul wrote Philippians. Here the household leaders have apparently acquired the title of overseer, and Paul addresses them collectively as οἱ ἐπίσκοποι. There need be no contradiction here, since we have seen from other contexts that there is nothing to prevent someone applying the term 'the elders' to people all of whom, or some of whom, also have more specific titles of office or function. The title was conveniently vague; it was rooted in the ancient household; and it was readily available, not just in Scripture, but in the contemporary society, being as we have noted in use among both Greeks and Jews, especially in Asia Minor, exactly where our New Testament sources first attest it.

In this way, we believe, Paul's silence about elders finds a ready explanation in the dynamic of the word itself, coupled with the size and character of the churches at the time he wrote. Inappropriate at first, we find the title 'the elders' appearing in the Christian churches just when we might have expected it: not in the first generation, when churches were small, confined to one household, or where, if there were more than one household, organization was fairly *ad hoc* and dependent on Paul himself, but in the second generation, as a ready way of referring to the leadership of several households.

The 'Work' and the Churches

The further reason for Paul's silence about elders may be suggested if we observe a distinction between Paul's team on the one hand and the churches that resulted from it on the other. Paul writes to the churches from outside their life, from the standpoint of his own work and with the perspective of the leader of an itinerant team, and this has coloured the language he uses and sometimes the advice he gives.

The distinction between Paul's mission and his churches has been helpfully made by Banks.[100] Although it was Paul's purpose to plant

---

[100] Banks, *Community*, pp. 152–70: 'Paul's work existed alongisde the local churches founded and supported by it, as a separate entity with a life of its own. But just as Paul's

churches, he did not himself belong to any of these churches, nor after the early days perhaps to any local church. Instead, he lived and worked at the centre, at the head, of a mission with no headquarters and no branches, constantly on the move and dedicated to the single purpose of preaching Christ to the Gentiles. He characteristically speaks of himself as a worker, doing the 'work of Christ'.[101] From this standpoint it is natural for him to speak of those who assisted him as 'fellow-workers',[102] as 'servants',[103] and as 'brothers',[104] and it will be helpful to examine the latter two terms more closely.

Although διάκονος became in time the title of an office in the local church, in its earliest occurrences in the New Testament it is used in fact by Paul to refer to himself and his colleagues. It is important to clarify his meaning since it is possible to exaggerate the lowly significance of this word. According to Beyer's influential article on διάκονος,[105] the fundamental meaning of the verb is to wait at table, and it never loses this sense of service that is at once humble, even despised, and concerned with practical needs. In Beyer's view, Jesus gave a completely new value to such service so that 'the term comes to have the full sense of active Christian love of neighbour'.[106] Even when the word comes to refer to the Christian ministry of preaching the gospel, 'the original meaning is reflected in this phrase'.[107] Similar views have been expressed by E. Schweizer,[108] and by C. E. B. Cranfield,[109] and may be regarded as a consensus view.

---

apostolic career has a history which is independent of the communities fathered by him, the reverse is also substantially true. His communities tended to move away from close dependence on Paul. In fact, clear differences existed between the mission and the churches at the level of the principles upon which they operated.' (p. 161)

[101] E.g. 1 Cor 3:9, 13–15, 9:1, 16:10.

[102] E.g. Rom 16:3; 1 Cor 3:9; 2 Cor 1:24; Phil 2:25, 4:2–3; 1 Thess 3:2. He also characteristically refers to Christian work with the verb κοπιάω.

[103] E.g. 1 Cor 3:5; 4:1; 2 Cor 4:2. Cf Eph 3:7.

[104] From many references see especially Gal 1:2.

[105] Beyer, διακονέω (κτλ), *TDNT*, Vol. II, pp. 81–93.

[106] Beyer, ibid., p.85.

[107] Beyer, ibid., p. 87.

[108] Schweizer, *Order*, pp. 174–7.

[109] Cranfield, *Diakonia*, p. 70.

It has not quite gone unchallenged. D. Georgi argued that διάκονος could also mean 'trusted representative', and that in the New Testament it normally meant 'preacher', but the fact that his discussion was quite brief and contained in a book about 2 Corinthians, which additionally was not translated into English for twenty years, has restricted the influence of his view.[110] Recently, however, J. N. Collins has subjected the word διακονία to a fresh examination in the light of its meaning in secular Greek, and has demonstrated conclusively, in my opinion, that the word basically means 'agent'.[111] As such it contains no necessary sense of waiting at table, but was widely used to mean 'go-between', 'messenger', 'representative' in a wide range of contexts with no disparaging overtones. Even when it was used of servants at table, Collins shows that the occasion described is usually that of a formal, ceremonial or elaborate meal where it might be an honour to serve, so that διάκονος may have been more of a literary than an everyday word for such a responsibility.[112]

In the New Testament also, Collins argues, the basic meaning must be that of 'agent' rather than that of 'table-waiter'.[113] So when Paul declares that he and Apollos are 'servants through whom you believed' (1 Cor 3:5), he is declaring his authority as a messenger of God. It is this which makes inappropriate the Corinthians' attempts to declare in favour of one against another. To be a servant of the New Covenant is to possess 'sufficiency' from God (2 Cor 3:6). Similarly when Paul's opponents called themselves 'servants of Christ' (2 Cor 11:23), it is plainly a term that established their credentials, not an expression of their lowly position.[114] When Paul declares that he became a διάκονος, first of the gospel and then of the church (Col

[110] Georgi, *Opponents*, pp. 27–32, but see also Ellis, 'Co-workers', pp. 441–5.
[111] Collins, *Diakonia*, p. 146.
[112] Collins, *Diakonia*, p. 151.
[113] 'The words do not necessarily involve the idea of being "at the service of" one's fellow-men with what that phrase implies of benevolence' (p. 194).
[114] The same point is made by Martin, *Slavery*, p. 58, in relation to Paul's use of the phrase 'slave of Christ': 'One does not, in the end, relativize the authority of Peter, James, Jude or Paul or by thinking of them as slave agents of Christ. Rather, one ties what they say more firmly to the unquestioned authority of the founder whom they represent.'

1:23, 25), he is not so much implying his own humble status as putting forward his credentials and that of the gospel he preaches. When in the same letter Paul commends Epaphras as a 'faithful διάκονος, he is, says Collins, 'paying him a weighty tribute'.[115]

The origins of the term διάκονος for a subordinate leader in the church lie not in the lowliness or loving kindness of the task performed, but in the idea of trust and responsibility. Paul speaks of taking the collection up to Jerusalem as διακονία not because it was an act of charity, but because in doing so he was acting as the churches' representative (Rom 15:25, 2 Cor 9:1). The sense of 'trusted representative', or 'spokesman', is present in other references too. Paul wanted to use Onesimus not as 'butler to the gaoled apostle' but as an active member of the mission team (Philem 13). Tychicus is a faithful διάκονος precisely as the bearer of Paul's letter and greetings to the Colossians (Col 4:7). In the same way those who first undertook to care for the church in Paul's absence undertook a διακονία on his behalf (Col 4:17), and in due course they had those who assisted them in the same way (Phil 1:1). In this way, as agents, representatives and subordinates of others, διάκονοι appear alongside overseers (1 Tim 3:8ff.). In relation to those they assist, διάκονοι are subordinate, but in relation to others they share in the authority of the one whose assistants they are, whether of God, the gospel, the church, the apostle, or in due course the bishop.[116]

Collins has provided a much needed corrective to our understanding of the word διάκονος, but we should not therefore go to the other extreme. In comparison to the titles of honour known to us from, say, the synagogue inscriptions, διάκονος surely points away from any desire to glory in rank. Paul may have been conscious of the honour involved in being a servant of Christ and steward of the mysteries of God (1 Cor 4:1), but he uses the expression in the course of deflating Corinthian pride. He is hardly using

[115] Collins, *Diakonia*, p. 201.
[116] Collins shows that this understanding makes good sense of references to deacons in the letters of Ignatius too. See e.g. *Philad* 10:1, where the church is to appoint a διάκονος to go as an ambassador to Antioch.

the phrase to compel obedience. In the same way, in the gospel tradition, Jesus is recorded as having enjoined the idea of διακονία on his disciples, and to have done so while explicitly rejecting the vocabulary of rank and dominance (Mt 23:8–12; Mk 10:42–44; Lk 22:25–27). So, although the 'menial' significance of διακονία has been exaggerated, the Christian use of it does point away from the sort of titles of honour beloved elsewhere.[117] In the Pauline letters, however, the point to note is that it is nearly always used by Paul of himself or of those who will in some significant way assist the work to which he is committed.

This is still more true of ἀδελφοί, which, while being in general use in the New Testament, as elsewhere, for 'co-religionists',[118] is in fact Paul's preferred vocabulary for Christian leadership. This understanding of ἀδελφοί has been persuasively demonstrated by Ellis,[119] on the basis of phrases like: 'The churches of Asia send greetings. Aquila and Prisca, together with the church in their house, send you hearty greetings in the Lord. All the brethren send greetings' (1 Cor 16:19). If 'all the brethren' is not to be seen as mere repetition after 'the churches of Asia', then we have a clear and intelligible sequence here: all the Asian Christians, one particular church and its leaders, and finally all the members of Paul's team. Similarly, when we read, 'The brethren who are with me greet you. All the saints greet you' (Phil 4:21f.), the brothers can best be seen as members of Paul's team of workers, distinguished from the church members in general. Ellis concludes:

> When used in the plural with an article, 'the brothers' in the Pauline literature fairly consistently refers to a relatively limited group of workers, some of whom have the Christian mission and/or ministry as their primary occupation.[120]

---

[117] We may also notice the distinction Martin draws between 'slave of Christ' and 'slave of all', *Slavery*, pp. 117ff. While 'slave of Christ' is a claim to authority, 'slave of all' is a rejection of the ranking system persisting among the Corinthian Christians.

[118] Günther, ἀδελφός, *NIDNTT*, Vol. I, pp. 254–8, and von Soden, ἀδελφός, *TDNT*, Vol. I, pp. 144–6.

[119] Ellis, 'Co-workers', pp. 437–52.

[120] Ellis, 'Co-workers', pp. 446ff.

This must make us suspect that in at least some of the places where Paul uses 'brothers' *as a form of address*, the intention is actually to target the local resident leadership in particular, and not just the congregation in general.[121]

In Acts also 'the brothers' appears on occasion to refer to the leadership of local churches.[122] It is 'the brothers' who commend Timothy (16:1) and Apollos (18:27) and vouch for their reputation. Where we might have expected a reference to 'James and the elders', we in fact find a reference to 'James and the brothers' (12:17). When Paul and Silas leave Antioch on what is traditionally called the second missionary journey, they are commended to the grace of God by 'the brothers', a phrase which clearly echoes and parallels what happened at the start of the first missionary journey when Paul and Barnabas were commended to the grace of God (14:26) by the prophets and teachers (13:1–3), that is by the leaders of the Antioch church. It is reasonable to suppose that Acts is here being faithful to the spirit and vocabulary of the Pauline mission.

'Brothers' and 'servants' is, then, the way Paul speaks of himself and his companions. Between the team members themselves it speaks of a fundamental equality — there are no elders here. When those who opened their houses for the work of the gospel and hosted the churches that came into being are also called 'fellow workers' (Philem 1) and 'servants' (Rom 16:1), this is a compliment, a recognition of their involvement in the same work, as it is when Paul applies the term to those who are not directly on his staff (Rom 16:3). These local people are reckoned part of the team. The origin of this language lies in Paul's conception of himself and his work, and it is this perspective rather than a conscious desire to avoid titles of honour, or a determination to exclude the idea of office, that accounts for the absence of talk about elders.

For the churches themselves, things were obviously different, especially as they developed. Here all were not precisely equal.[123] Some

---

[121] This was argued by Farrer, 'Ministry in the NT', pp. 153–6.

[122] Ellis, 'Co-workers', pp. 447–8.

[123] 'The early Christian use of household language is one bit of evidence that there was no egalitarian stage of early Christianity followed by a hierarchical stage.' Martin, *Slavery*, p. 59.

exercised regular functions of leadership and presidency as heads of the houses where the churches met. They could be distinguished from others by the functional title of ἐπίσκοπος. These people may have been 'fellow-workers' and 'brothers' to Paul, but to those who came to Christ through their witness and were nurtured through their teaching, they would more naturally come to be seen as the elders of the community. If that is so, it suggests that Paul's silence with regard to elders may be due not solely to the situation in the churches when he wrote, but also to a difference in standpoint between the author and his readers.

In support, we may think that a similar difference of perspective contributes to the ambiguous attitude of Paul towards marriage, and the contradictory evidence on the position of women in the New Testament documents. In the first place, Paul, while agreeing that marriage is no sin and insisting on the rights and responsibilities of those who are married, also wishes that others were single and affirms that those who do not marry will 'do better'.[124] How can this be reconciled with a local church structure based in and around the household? We may compare the insistence of the Pastorals on the overseer being a married man.[125] Without going into the many disputed points of interpretation in 1 Corinthians 7, we should consider the possibility that Paul is writing from the perspective of his ἔργον, or apostolic work. He is not thinking here about the future or constitution of the church,[126] but about the pressing need to accomplish the 'work'. Men and women who are free of marriage are free to be fellow-workers. When Paul says that he wishes everyone was like himself but that each person has his gift, the gift is probably not simply marriage or singleness as such. Paul's own gift was that of apostle to the Gentiles, for which it was necessary for him to be single, and anyone who was unencumbered

---

[124] 1 Cor 7:1–6, but also v. 7 and vv. 25–38.
[125] 1 Tim 3:1–7; Tit 1:5–9.
[126] If indeed he thought it had much future in this world (1 Cor 7:25–31). The question of whether Paul was expecting an imminent end to the world as he knew it is highly disputed.

might be similarly gifted.[127] If someone had asked Paul whether if he stayed single he was not disqualified from becoming a church-leader, Paul would presumably have replied, 'Each person has their own gift — whether as church leader or missionary.'[128]

The same difference of perspective may help to account for the way in which women feature prominently in the Pauline mission but are thereafter apparently excluded from leadership. There is no need to rehearse the evidence from women among Paul's fellow-workers: Priscilla, Mary, Tryphaena and Tryphosa, Euodia and Syntyche.[129] Women are found enabling the mission of the church by opening their homes, like Lydia at Philippi and Nympha at Colossae, and Phoebe is commended as a διάκονος of the church at Cenchreae and as someone who had given Paul significant help and protection.[130] There is no reason to doubt that such women were able to 'contribute significantly to the spread of Christianity in the early years of its expansion', or that Paul's approach in this matter was deliberate, unusual, and 'resulted in the elevation of women to a place in religious work for which we have little contemporary parallel.'[131]

Yet it may have been easier for Paul to act in this way within the parameters of his 'work'. Without in any way detracting from the boldness of his policy in this matter, it is surely likely that it was easier for a woman to gain recognition for her contribution to the mission, especially if she was a well-to-do widow with a house to offer, than it would be for the growing churches to accept leader-ship from such women, or others like them. 1 Corinthians provides evidence that Paul's attitude may have led to conflicts when applied in the local setting, so that Paul himself needed to try to regulate

[127] Vermes explains the singleness of Jesus in terms of prophetic celibacy (*Jesus the Jew*, pp. 99–102), and I suggest the same constraint may well have been felt by Paul, who elsewhere speaks of himself in prophetic terms (Gal 1:15f.).
[128] Of course, there were missionary couples (Rom 16:3, 7, 1 Cor 9:5), as Fiorenza reminds us (*Memory*, p. 226). Paul was under no obligation to think such a double calling ideal!
[129] Acts 18:18; Rom 16:1–16; Phil 4:2–3.
[130] Acts 16:13–15; Col 4:15; Rom 16:1–2.
[131] Banks, *Community*, p. 157, 160.

the situation.[132] In the Pastorals, women are apparently excluded from leadership altogether.[133] The difference between Paul and the Pastorals in this respect, it may be suggested, is due to the same difference of perspective. Paul writes with the freedom and urgency of his missionary work, but the Pastorals have in mind the need for the Christian community not to attract unfavourable publicity.[134] It was one thing for Paul to make use of women in his work and to acknowledge no distinctions, but those who had to build and guard the churches in the midst of a suspicious and hostile society may well not have felt so free. The same situation that made it natural to speak of the elders, also made it unnatural to recognize women leaders, and the Pastorals are separated from Paul not only in time but also in being written from within the local church setting rather than from outside it.[135]

Conclusions

Anyone who sets out to study the role of the elders in earliest Christianity must explain why they nowhere appear in the earlier Pauline letters, but are found universally in the New Testament documents written in the generation after his death. In this chapter, we have seen that the consensus explanation, according to which elders are excluded from Paul's churches by the apostle's charismatic understanding of ministry in the Body of Christ, is open to serious criticism. Equally to be rejected is Burtchaell's attempt to hold on to both the *charismata* and the elders by arguing that the latter, though present from the start, were unimportant.

---

[132] 1 Cor 11:2–16, 14:33–34. The lack of clarity in these passages may perhaps be due to the fact that Paul is seeking to restrain a freedom he has himself in some measure encouraged. The tension between freedom and tradition identified by Witherington, *Earliest*, p. 125–6, may be a tension between the 'work' and the churches.

[133] 1 Tim 2:9–15. I see no virtue in trying to avoid this conclusion by an exegetical *tour de force*. It seems better to admit it, and attribute it to the cultural context.

[134] See Witherington, *Earliest*, pp. 212–5.

[135] A further discussion of the role of women leaders in the earliest churches and the significance of this for today will be found towards the end of Chapter 8, p.255–257.

A better synthesis can be obtained if we remember what we have learnt from our study of the Jewish and Greek background, that 'the elders' is *more a way of speaking about leaders, than an office of leadership itself.* Its emergence in the Pauline churches was not contrary to Paul's mind, since the seeds of such thinking can be seen in the scattered references to local leadership in Paul's letters. Nevertheless it was not a form of speaking about the local leaders that we find Paul using, and this is not surprising.

In the first place it belongs naturally to a stage in the development of the churches when local leaders must act together as representatives on behalf of a number of house-churches, and this stage was only just being reached when Paul left the scene. In the second place, Paul writes into the local churches from the outside as one concerned with the work of evangelization rather than with church order. Accordingly, he thinks of people as fellow-workers, brothers, and servants of God, rather than as elders of the community. It was the same standpoint that inclined him to see marriage as second-best, and enabled him to make use of women in the work of the gospel with a freedom the churches found difficult to preserve.

Chapter Five

The Elders in Acts

The letters of Paul are the earliest Christian documents known to us, documents moreover that are contemporary with the church situations to which they refer, written by a leading participant in the development of those churches. For this reason our investigation of the elders in the New Testament started there. But the Christian church, of course, did not originate with Paul! As much as twenty years of growth and development separate the earliest Pauline letter from the church's beginnings in Jerusalem, during which time the Christian faith gained adherents at least in Samaria (Acts 8:4–25), Damascus (Acts 9:2), Phoenicia, Cyprus and Antioch (Acts 11:19), as well as no doubt a wide range of places about which our only source is silent. For much of this time Paul was a member, leader (but not the senior leader), and finally commissioned representative ('apostle') of the Antioch church, which was itself in close relationship with the church in Jerusalem.[1] As a Christian and as an evangelist, Paul was not therefore like Melchizedek 'without father or mother or genealogy', nor were his churches without direct antecedents.

Apart from a few allusions in Paul's letters, our only source of information for this early period comes from Acts; and for the years of Paul's independent missionary work also, Acts provides an essential framework without which we have no means of locating his letters within his career. Yet the historical reliability of Acts is a matter of controversy, and without entering into a full discussion of

[1] In a recent study, Nicholas Taylor has argued that we misunderstand Paul's career if we neglect the importance of his relationship to the church at Antioch. See, *Paul*, pp. 88–95.

all the issues involved, some assessment of the reliability of Acts as a witness needs to be made, as a basis for discussing its contribution to our knowledge of the church of the first two generations. This will involve a brief look at the identity of the author, the date at which he wrote, the sources he may have used and the aims and interests with which he worked.

Acts as Evidence

1. *The authorship of Acts.* Ancient tradition identified the author of the anonymous two-volume work, Luke/Acts, with the Luke who is mentioned three times in Pauline letters (Philem 24; Col 4:14; 2 Tim 4:11). What is important for our purposes is that this involves a claim that the author was, at least for part of the time, a companion of Paul. This is a claim to which the book of Acts itself gives support through those passages where the writer uses the pronoun 'we' (16:10–17, 20:5–21:18, 27:1–28:16) in a way which gives the impression that the author was an eyewitness for part of the story. The implication that the author (whom I shall from now on call 'Luke' without seeking to prejudge the issue) was a member of the Pauline circle continues to be taken seriously by a significant number of modern scholars.[2]

Others, however, believe that Luke did not know Paul and that the 'we' references are a literary device intended to give just that impression. They base this on the perceived theological differences between Paul and the author of Acts, and the differences between the portrait of Paul in Acts and the Paul known to us from his own letters. Vielhauer identified four main theological differences.[3] In Christology, Luke was pre-Pauline, with Jesus a man exalted by God to Sonship at the resurrection, whose death on the cross was without effect as atonement. Paul's speech on the Areopagus (Acts

---

[2] Bruce, *Acts* (1990), pp. 3–5; Hengel, *Acts*, pp. 66–7; Fitzmyer, *Luke*, pp. 47–51; Hemer, *Setting*, pp. 308–21; Marshall, *Acts*, pp. 44f.

[3] Vielhauer, 'Paulinism', pp. 33–50.

17:22–31) expounds a natural theology foreign to Paul's thought. The Paul of Luke-Acts is loyal to the Law and never speaks of freedom from it, while the hope of the Second Coming, so important for Paul, has become muted. Haenchen further argues that Luke is wrong about Paul himself. He portrays Paul as a worker of miracles and impressive speaker, but denies him the title of apostle, whereas Paul himself is dubious about oratory and miracles, but bases his whole ministry on his claim to be an apostle.[4] For these reasons many scholars deny to the author of Acts any personal knowledge of Paul.[5]

It will be seen that this difference of opinion depends on a different assessment of the same evidence. For the scholars of the first group, the 'we' passages represent a datum of hard fact in a sea of speculation, and they take precedence over theological differences, which are largely in the eye of the beholder. They are by nature inclined to resolve apparent disagreements between biblical writers. Scholars of the second group judge Acts adversely by the standard of Pauline theology, and dispose rather summarily of matters of historical detail. They are by inclination and training more ready to see disagreement than harmony between biblical writers.

The present writer is more impressed by the methods and arguments of the first group. In the first place, some of the alleged differences of theology seem exaggerated and contrived. It is not obvious that the Areopagus speech differs profoundly in theology from Romans 1:18–32, or that the Christology of Acts is so different from that of Romans 1:3–4. Justification by faith may not feature prominently in Acts, but it is there (13:39), while the 'new perspective' on Paul must make us ask whether Luke is being unfairly compared to a Lutheran caricature of the apostle to the Gentiles. But, second, even if we agree that Acts differs from Paul's thought in some respects, this hardly proves that it was not written by someone who knew and revered Paul. Luke in common with many ancient historians centres his work on heroes, in this case

---

[4] Haenchen, *Acts*, pp. 112–16.
[5] Conzelmann, *Acts*, pp. xxxviii–ix; Pesch, *Apostelgeschichte*, pp. 25–7; Schneider, *Apostelgeschichte*, pp. 108–111.

Peter and Paul, who are presented for the edification of the reader. With such an outlook and purpose, Luke would be likely to stress Paul's powers as a speaker and charismatic. If he has failed fully to appreciate the depths of Paul's thought, this is not uncommon in disciples! Thirdly, the suggestion that the 'we' passages are a literary device, or a deliberate attempt to deceive, cannot answer the question why the author uses it so sporadically and so inconspicuously. They should rather be accepted as evidence that the writer was, *for part of the time*, a participant in the events he describes. They do not prove that his name was Luke, but, as has often been pointed out, if the ascription of Luke–Acts is legendary, why did the legend attach itself to such an obscure figure?

2. *The date of Acts.* The date of Acts is closely bound up with the question of authorship, since, if we accept that the author was for part of the time a companion of Paul, then a date much after 80 CE becomes unlikely, whereas if on theological grounds we think that Luke shows little knowledge of Paul, then a later date would help to explain this.

The range of possible dates suggested for Acts is impressive. Hemer lists over fifty suggestions made in the last hundred years, ranging from 57–59 CE to 135 CE, but in practice concludes that they form three groups: those who argue for a date before 70 CE; those who place Acts shortly before or after 80 CE; and those who believe that Acts should be placed at the end of the first century or later.[6] The third option is commonly advanced by those who on theological grounds deny any acquaintance of Luke with Paul, and is obviously not a view open to those who take the evidence of the 'we' passages seriously.

Those who date Acts in the 60s tend to rely on arguments from silence. Acts does not mention the Jewish War or the fall of Jerusalem; it does not tell us about the death of James in 62 CE or the Neronian persecution and the death of Peter in the middle of the decade; it shows no knowledge of Paul's letters (which is a real problem for a date at the end of the century when a collection of

---

[6] Hemer, *Acts*, pp. 366–76.

Paul's letters is usually thought to have been circulating in the churches). Above all Acts fails to tell us what happened to Paul, whether execution or release, and this, it is argued, is best explained by supposing that Acts was written when the outcome of Paul's case was still in doubt. The other omissions too would be easily explained, if in fact Luke wrote before these events had occurred.[7]

Attractive as it is to date Acts so early and so precisely, such a date is not in my judgement sufficiently secure to build on. When Luke has been as selective as he has throughout his book, failing to tell us, for example, how Christianity came to Rome in the first place, we can hardly conclude from his silence about an event that he did not know of it, or that it had not happened. Luke's selection is governed by his purpose of showing how the gospel was carried to the ends of the earth, particularly through the labours of first Peter and then Paul. It is not hard to see why many of his 'omissions' fall outside that purpose. As to the fate of Paul, Hemer, who is an advocate of a date in the early 60s, and believes that Paul was released for a further period of apostolic activity, to which the Pastorals belong, explains Luke's failure to mention Paul's release as due to the need of discretion: Paul still had powerful enemies.[8] The same argument, however, might be thought to stand if in fact Paul had been executed. The young church also had powerful enemies, and advertising the disgraceful or depressing end of his hero will have formed no part of Luke's purpose.

To place Acts before 62 CE, presumably means placing the third Gospel also before that date. Yet it seems nearly certain that the third Gospel *does* show some knowledge of the fall of Jerusalem.[9] It also means supposing a date in the late 50s for Mark, whom Luke is generally thought to have used. All of these difficulties can be overcome, but the feeling persists that the evidential base is rather narrow in relation to the number of hypotheses it is asked to support.

---

[7] Hemer, *Acts*, pp. 376–410.

[8] Hemer, *Acts*, pp. 406–8. 'If Paul was released, Luke was not at pains to advertise the fact.'

[9] Luke 21:20–24 not only appears to show knowledge of the events themselves, it also appears to have edited Mark's account.

Moreover, Luke gives the impression that he writes from the perspective of one looking back some years after the events. It is this that makes possible Luke's well-known penchant for minimizing conflicts and reconciling positions, in contrast to Paul who writes in the heat of the dispute. It is noteworthy that Bruce, who had previously advocated a date in the 60s, in the later editions of his two commentaries on Acts inclines to a somewhat later date for just these reasons. His conclusion, with which we may agree, is:

> The most that can be said with reasonable confidence is that Acts was written not more than twenty years after its last recorded event.... . If then a date in the late 70s or early 80s is assigned to Acts, most of the evidence will be satisfied.[10]

3. *Sources.* If Acts was written by a member of the Pauline circle not more than twenty years after the Apostle's death, then we need to ask how Luke knew about the things he records, and with what confidence we can use his account to trace the development of church organization. It will be convenient to work backwards through the book of Acts, from the events nearest in time to the date of writing to those furthest away.

From what we have argued so far it follows that for some parts of his narrative, the 'we' sections, Luke needed no sources, since he was an eyewitness of the events he describes. He will also have known personally many of Paul's co-workers, whose names he mentions in his book, and there is no difficulty in supposing that for the whole of the period covered by what are commonly called the 'second and third missionary journeys' (Acts 15:36–21:16), Luke was in a position to know or to find out what had happened.

There is a well-established tradition linking Luke with Antioch,[11] and Bruce has pointed out how the witness of church tradition agrees with the way in which Luke is able to report events at Antioch

---

[10] Bruce, *Acts* (1988), p. 12; Bruce, *Acts* (1990), p. 18. Cf. Bruce, *Acts* (1954), p. 22.

[11] This is found in Eus *HE* 3.4.6; Jerome, *De Vir* III, 7 and also in the anti-Marcionite prologue to the Gospel of Luke, which in the judgement of Heard (*JTS* 6 (1955), p. 10f.) dates in its present form from the third century but contains valuable early tradition.

THE ELDERS IN ACTS

in some detail, and shows a special interest in people associated with Antioch (Nicolas, Acts 6:5, and Barnabas, 4:36, 11:22ff., 13:1ff.).[12] It has long been thought that Luke uses an Antiochene source (probably from 6:1 onwards), but if the tradition is accurate, he may himself have been that source, or have been well-placed to ask questions of those who had been present. The story of Acts may be said to centre on Antioch from 6:1–15:35, since the story of Stephen and the Hellenists with which it beings, though taking place in Jerusalem, is likely to have been treasured in Antioch (11:19). Into this section, Luke has inserted a block of material about the exploits of Peter, which is probably of different origin (9:32–11:18).

It is for the story of the church's earliest days in Jerusalem (Acts 1–5) that Luke shows the least signs of being well informed. The story is constructed around a very few incidents, in which some scholars have detected duplicate narratives. A larger proportion of the story is given over to speeches (which, of course, Luke composed) and summary statements of the church's life and progress that invest the story with a somewhat ideal quality. The account has a slightly Old Testament feel to it, like the birth narratives at the start of Luke's Gospel. One is reminded of Dorothy Sayers' characterization of the 'stained-glass window decorum' with which the gospel story used to be presented in church:

Sacred personages, living in a far-off land and time, using dignified rhythms of speech, making from time to time restrained gestures symbolic of brutality. They mocked Him and railed on Him and smote Him, they scourged and crucified Him. Well, they were people very remote from ourselves, and no doubt it was all done in the noblest and most beautiful manner. We should not like to think otherwise.[13]

This does not mean that these chapters are without historical worth, but it does mean that extra caution will have to be exercised when deriving historical information from them. Not only was Luke

---

[12] Bruce, *Acts* (1990), p. 8.
[13] D. L. Sayers, *The Man Born to be King*, p. 22.

not present at the events they describe, but for his informants also they lay at least thirty years before.

Beyond that it is not really possible to be more precise about the sources of Luke's information. The search for written sources is less fashionable today than it was, due mainly to the lack of agreed results, and it seems more likely that Luke's sources were people rather than documents. On the other hand, if we ask what use Luke may have made of his opportunities of finding out the facts, we may say that Luke has been shown to compare favourably with the best historiography of his time, which knew the difference between pious legend and historical fact.[14] Ancient historians from Herodotus to Polybius certainly thought it important to visit the 'scene of the crime' and to talk to people who had been present,[15] and if we take seriously Luke's claim to be writing an orderly and reliable account, based where possible on the testimony of eye-witnesses and personal reminiscence,[16] we may well believe that at the core of each of Luke's vivid narratives lies some element of authentic testimony, however much Luke may have written it up in his own style and for his own purposes.[17] It has also been shown from the detailed knowledge of local conditions which he displays that Luke is a careful and well-informed writer.[18] None of this proves the truth of any individual statement in Acts, but it creates an initial presumption that Luke knows what he is talking about.

4. *Purposes.* Finally, we may ask what interests and purposes have controlled Luke's selection and presentation of the stories he records. From the preface to Luke's first volume, we may conclude that he was concerned to provide reliable information about the church's beginnings (Lk 1:1–4), and from the opening sentences of Acts we learn that Luke understood these beginnings as a continuation of

[14] Hengel, *Acts*, pp. 1–34; Hemer, *Acts*, pp. 63–100.

[15] Hemer, *Acts*, p. 67–70.

[16] There is a debate over the precise connotation of κἀμοὶ παρηκολουθηκότι ἄνωθεν πᾶσιν, Lk 1:3. Cadbury argued that it implied a claim to personal participation (Cadbury, *NTS* 3 (1956–7), pp. 128–32). Hemer (Acts, p. 322ff.) is more cautious.

[17] Hemer devotes a long section to showing the 'feasibility in principle' of such an approach, and especially of Luke's possible dependence on Peter, pp. 335–64.

[18] Hemer, *Acts*, pp. 101–220; Sherwin-White, *Roman Society*, pp. 71–98.

the activity of Jesus (Acts 1:1). It is made plain that Jesus is now operating in the world through the Holy Spirit (1:5, 2:1, 33), and accordingly Luke is concerned to show that the spread of the church 'to the ends of the earth' (1:8) is directed and empowered by the Spirit. The Spirit is needed to confirm the conversion of the Samaritans (8:15–16); the Spirit prompts Peter to visit the Gentile Cornelius (11:12). The Holy Spirit directs the church at Antioch to send out missionaries into Gentile lands (13:1–3), and leads the church at Jerusalem to approve the admission of the Gentiles without the necessity of circumcision (15:28). It is the Holy Spirit who makes people overseers in the church and so provides for the church's continuing life (20:28). Through his stories of miracle and revelation, Luke makes it clear that the progress of the church is the work of the Spirit.[19]

It is probable that in recording the spread of the church through the power of the Spirit, Luke has an apologetic purpose within the church of his own day. Like Paul before him, he is concerned to vindicate the Gentile mission against its detractors, and to promote the unity of Jews and Gentiles in the one church. This is made plain both by the attribution of the Gentile mission to the purpose and power of God, as we have just seen, but also by the space given to the conversion of Peter to this point of view and his subsequent acceptance of Gentile hospitality (10:1–11:18); to the pivotal Council of Jerusalem where the principle of Gentile inclusion is laid down (15:1–35); to the trials of Paul (22:1–26:35); and by the final speech of Paul to the Jews in Rome with its closing declaration, 'Let it be known to you then that this salvation of God has been sent to the Gentiles; they will listen.' (28:29).

Haenchen suggests that, while Luke and Paul shared a common purpose in this respect, their answers to the problem are quite different. While Paul justified the Gentile mission on 'internal evidence', by showing that the Law leads to sin, and that Christ is the end of the Law, Luke justifies it form without by showing through miracles and revelations that God has willed it.[20] It is extraordinary

---

[19] Kee, *Good News*, pp. 28–41.
[20] Haenchen, *Acts*, p. 112f.

that these two approaches should be seen as incompatible rather than complementary! The difference between them grows even less if we allow Romans 14:1–15:13 to indicate the overriding purpose of Romans, which is not to present justification by faith for the individual so much as to promote the mutual acceptance of Jews and Gentiles at one table in the church (Rom 15:7ff.).[21] Luke seeks to accomplish the same reconciling purpose by presenting the Pauline understanding of the gospel as something believed by all the principal figures in the church. Accordingly he allows us to see the importance of the Jerusalem church in the church's beginnings, and presents Peter and Paul as joint initiators of the Gentile mission.[22]

No doubt Luke had other purposes, such as the presentation of the church as a lawful religion, and Christians as loyal citizens of the empire. What is of interest to our present purpose, however, is to note what does *not* appear to have been among Luke's purposes. He does not seem to have any doctrine of the church, or to be concerned to promote any particular form of church organization. This is generally admitted.[23] Luke includes a number of references to the church's leaders at different stages of its development, but he never attempts to relate these or reconcile them. Similarly, Luke presents no doctrine of the sacraments, and there is no consistent pattern in Acts according to which people become Christians.[24] This does not mean that the search for the forms of the earliest Christian churches is hopeless, but it does mean that if we seek to reconstruct the history of the development of the ministry using the scattered and unsystematic references in Acts, we shall be using Luke's writing in a way incidental to his purpose. This, so far from being illegitimate, should give us all the more confidence, since, if we

---

[21] Watson, *Paul,* pp. 94–8.

[22] Bruce, *Acts,* (1990), pp. 21–27.

[23] Haenchen, *Acts,* p. 93; Barrett, *Church,* 'If among the purposes he had in mind for his second volume Luke intended to include an account of the origin, authorization and functions of the Christian ministry, he was singularly unsuccessful in carrying out his intention' pp. 49ff.

[24] This makes the term *frühkatholisch* inappropriate to describe Luke's theology, and raises serious doubts about a late date for *Acts.* See Marshall, 'Early Catholicism', pp. 217–31; Barrett, *Church,* p. 79.

are able to glean any information and discern any pattern, we shall know that we are not merely finding what Luke intended us to find, or arriving at conclusions dictated by Luke's theological interests.

The House-Churches of Jerusalem

Even though our information about the earlier days of the church in Jerusalem is sparse, it does enable us to see that the church met in houses. This is a neglected feature of the study of the church in Acts. Most of the discussion of early Christian house-churches has concentrated on Paul. This is not surprising. Although the references to 'the church in the house' in Paul's letters are relatively few,[25] they are primary evidence for the household setting of the churches, which cannot be doubted and which both interprets, and is interpreted by, the situations addressed by the letters in which they stand.[26] But in fact the household church was not unique to the Pauline mission, nor is there any reason to think that Paul was its inventor. The household setting features prominently in Acts from the very beginning,[27] but the implications of this for the study of church order and leadership have not always been seen.

The evidence for house-churches in Acts may be set out as follows.[28] In the first chapter of Acts the disciples assemble in an upper room of a Jerusalem house (τὸ ὑπερῷον, Acts 1:13). This word was in general use in the Hellenistic period to refer to the upstairs room of a house.[29] Only large houses would have such a room available where twelve or more people might meet for prayer, and the presence in the background of a well-disposed person of means may be suspected.[30] The word occurs again in the Dorcas story

[25] Rom 16:5; 1 Cor 16:19; Col 4:15; Philem 2.

[26] So, for example, the existence of different house-churches will have contributed to the disunity in Corinth and elsewhere. See Dassmann, 'Hausgemeinde', p. 88.

[27] 'We should envisage the believing community in Jerusalem as organized in a number of household groups.' Bruce, 'Jerusalem', p. 649.

[28] Klauck, *Hausgemeinde*, pp. 48–51. Rordorf, 'Gottesdienstsräume, pp. 110–28.

[29] *BAG*, p. 842; Thurston, ὑπερῷον, p. 21.

[30] Thurston (see note 29) argues that it was a room built into the wall of the temple, on the ground that no private house would be able to hold 120 persons (Acts 1:5). The

(9:36ff.), where the owner is a woman 'full of good works and acts of charity', which suggests again that she was a person of means, able to provide for widows and perhaps host the church there (9:41).

In his summary statement at the end of chapter 2, Luke tells us that the believers worshipped daily in the temple and broke bread κατ᾽ οἶκον (2:46). Although this occurs in a Lukan summary passage, there is no reason to doubt its truth or to think that it belongs to any idealizing tendency.[31] Lake and Cadbury say that this does not imply one meeting place but separate meeting places.[32] The formula is repeated in 5:42, and should be understood to imply regular meetings in different centres, and not, for instance, to casual visits to one another's homes.[33] Household gatherings are a feature of the Lukan account, both for the Jerusalem church (4:31, 8:3, 12:12), and for the Pauline mission (17:5, 20:7ff., 20:20, 21:16, 28:30). The mention of Saul persecuting the church κατὰ τοὺς οἴκους is particularly important, indicating as it does that Saul was raiding the houses where the church was meeting to catch the believers *in flagrante delicto*.[34] Most of the time Luke writes so as to emphasize the unity of the earliest community and the central role of the Twelve, but the existence of separate groups and scattered meetings is still discernible through his account. It is implied, for example, by the vast numbers of believers Luke mentions (2:41,

reference to 120, however, belongs to a separate story and is not necessarily the same place. It cannot be likely that the sect of the Nazarenes enjoyed good relations with the temple authorities, and, if we have to choose, it is more likely that Luke has exaggerated the Christians' attendance at the temple than fabricated their meetings in homes.

[31] Indeed, if any part of Luke's statement is to be suspected of idealism, it is surely his stress on the early Christians' continued links with the temple.

[32] 'Luke's fondness for the distributive use of κατά together with his variation κατ᾽ οἴκους (8:3) leads to the presumption that his idea is rather 'in separate houses' (*domatim*)' Jackson and Lake, *Beginnings*, IV, p. 29.

[33] White comments: 'The phrase κατ᾽ οἶκον in Acts is regularly rendered 'from house to house', more or less at random, a sense that is traceable to the Vulgate (*circa domos*). It would be more consistent with the inferred customary action in Acts 12:12 as well as with the Pauline usage simply to render it 'at home' (cf. 1 Cor 16:19 and esp. Philemon 2). This seems to be more in keeping with the distinction being made in Acts between the private gathering 'at home' versus the public worship 'in the Temple', *God's House*, p. 188, n. 7.

[34] Rordorf, 'Gottesdiensträume', p. 114.

4:4),[35] by the Hebrew/Hellenist conflict of chapter 6, and by the meeting in the house of Mary in chapter 12, which, as Klauck notes, implies the existence of groups other than itself (12:17).[36]

In the second half of Acts we have the independent evidence of the Pauline letters to show that Luke is right about the church meeting in houses. The Pauline formula ἡ κατ᾽ οἰκίαν ἐκκλησία finds an echo in Luke's references to 'so and so and his house' (Acts 16:15, 31–34, 18:8; cf. 1 Cor 1:14–16). Klauck rightly observes that the significance of these references has been obscured by the debate about infant baptism. All the evidence is that the earliest churches, Palestinian no less than Gentile, met in homes, as indeed did the Pharisaic *haburoth*. In the Diaspora many of the synagogues must at least have started as house-meetings, and in the last chapter we saw that houses could provide a meeting place for pagan cults as well. By no means all religion in the ancient world went on in temples, and the Jerusalem temple would not have been a suitable place for the Christian breaking of bread.

But *if the earliest Christians met in homes, then they also had leaders at the household level, leaders provided by the household structure itself.* Not every citizen had a home in which he could show this sort of hospitality. We have already seen in the case of Corinth that only comparatively well-off people owned the kind of house that is presupposed there, and that it was such people who gave to those who assembled leadership that was patronal as well as pastoral in character. Those who were converted joined what were already small communities, extended families containing relatives, slaves and possibly clients as well. The leadership role of the householder was not something that had to be invented from scratch. It was already well-established, sanctioned by custom, and understood both by those who exercised it and those who benefited from it. The traditional Jewish household did not differ in this respect from the Graeco-Roman household,[37] so there is no reason to doubt that the same

[35] These numbers, if they are not to be taken literally, are not to be dismissed as sheer fiction. They surely preserve the memory that the church quite rapidly outgrew the capacity of a single meeting-place.

[36] Klauck, *Hausgemeinde*, p. 49.

[37] Verner, *Household*, p. 44–7.

patterns prevailed in the house-churches of Jerusalem as we have seen in the house-churches around the Aegean.

E. S. Fiorenza also stresses the importance of the household in the development of the earliest churches.

> House churches were a decisive factor in the missionary movement insofar as they provided space, support, and actual leadership for the community.[38]

Yet she believes on the basis of Galatians 3:28 that the early Christian missionary movement practised a radical egalitarianism, so that, 'the customary rules of behaviour no longer applied'.[39] She reconciles these statements by appealing to the way in which within Graeco-Roman society, the household was the woman's proper sphere of authority. The way was thus open for women to be leaders in the house-churches.

There is surely some contradiction here. On the one hand normal rules did not apply, so women could be leaders, and on the other hand the household was the normal sphere of women's authority, so the rules applied after all! Both arguments need to be treated with caution. A woman had authority within the household over other women and slaves, hardly over her husband and other men who came into the house as his guests or clients. It must be doubtful if in a mixed meeting of a household-church it was normal for women to preside (though they were surely active). The most we should say is that where women were already heads of their households, as a result of being widowed or divorced, this probably provided women leaders in the churches, at least in the early days.

As to the idea that normal rules did not apply, this seems both unproven and unlikely. The prominence of men in the New Testament records, together with the fact that this revolutionary position seems not to have needed to be argued for, suggests that the household with its structures of authority in which people for the most part felt comfortable and secure exercised an unquestioned influ-

---

[38] Fiorenza, *Memory*, p. 177.
[39] Fiorenza, *Memory*, p. 176.

ence within which the egalitarianism of earliest Christianity was interpreted and lived out.

Acts does not tell us by what title these leaders were called individually. In the Pauline churches, we have argued, the household leader was known as the ἐπίσκοπος. We do not know what he was called in the churches of Judaea, but if we examine the parallel provided by the contemporary Essene communities, we may hazard a reasonable guess.

The attempt to show that the origins of the Christian ἐπίσκοπος lie in the מבקר (*mebaqqer*) known to us from the Damascus Rule (CD) and the Qumran Community Rule (1QS) is not new,[40] but in recent years has tended to be dismissed.[41] It is, however, worth reconsidering in the present context. The Damascus Rule provides for communities of Essenes living not in Qumran but in towns and cities outside. These groups it refers to as 'camps', and at the head of each camp is a Guardian (*mebaqqer*). This man is to be between thirty and fifty years of age, a scribe able to interpret the Law. He has the responsibility of examining postulants and admitting them to the community, He is to care for the members like a shepherd, and he receives and distributes money given for charity. The key passage reads as follows:

> He shall instruct the Congregation in the works of God. He shall cause them to consider His mighty deeds and shall recount all the happenings of eternity to them. He shall love them as a father loves his children, and shall carry them in all their distress like a shepherd his sheep. He shall loosen all the fetters which bind them that in his Congregation there may be none that are oppressed or broken. He shall examine every man entering his Congregation with regard to his deeds, understanding, strength, ability and possessions, and shall inscribe him in his place according to his rank in the lot of Light. (CD 13:9–10)

---

[40] Jeremias, *Jerusalem*, pp. 259–62; Nauck, 'Probleme', pp. 443–52; Goppelt, *Apostolic*, pp. 188f.; Thiering, 'Mebaqqer', pp. 59–74.

[41] Braun, *Qumran*, B.2, pp. 329–31; Fitzmyer, 'Jewish Christianity', p. 293ff.; Merklein, *Amt*, p. 376ff.; Hainz, 'Anfänge', pp. 98–102, Lohse, 'Entstehung', pp. 70–3.

There are some striking similarities with the role of the Christian ἐπίσκοπος, especially as it appears in 1 Peter:

> Tend the flock of God that is in your charge ... not as domineering over those in your charge but being examples to the flock. (5:1–5)

It also finds an echo in the prayer for the ordination of a Bishop in the *Apostolic Tradition* of Hippolytus, early in the third century:

> to feed your holy flock ... to loose every bond according to the power which you gave to the apostles. (AT 3)

It has been objected that the Septuagint uses words of the ἐπισκεπτ- group to translate the Hebrew פקד (*paqad*) not בקר (*baqar*),[42] and that the role of the *mebaqqer* in The Damascus Rule is too authoritarian to serve as a model for any Christian office known to us from the first century. Merklein doubts whether the Christian ἐπίσκοπος examined and admitted new members, and considers that the picture provided by The Damascus Rule rather resembles a monastic abbot.[43] Braun calls him a 'theological jurist', and notes that the *mebaqqer* always appears in the singular, whereas on their first appearance Christian ἐπίσκοποι are plural (it is remarkable how much weight one verse of one letter of Paul can be made to bear!). Not until Ignatius, it is argued, do we find anything like that in the church.[44]

First, however, as Nauck has pointed out, the linguistic argument is not very impressive since the Community Rule (1QS) itself equates the offices of *mebaqqer* and *paqid*,[45] and in the Septuagint ἐπισκέπτεσθαι is used to translate *baqar* in Ezek 34:11, the very shepherd passage that probably lies behind the picture of the *mebaqqer* in the first place.[46] Jeremias considers the linguistic correspondence exact.[47]

[42] Goetz, 'מבקר', pp. 89–93.
[43] Merklein, *Amt*, p. 376.
[44] Braun, *Qumran*, B. 2., p. 330f.
[45] Nauck, 'Probleme', p. 447.
[46] Goppelt, *Apostolic*, p. 188, also, *Petrusbrief*, p. 325, Thiering, 'Mebaqqer', p. 70.
[47] Jeremias, *Jerusalem*, p. 259ff.

Second, Nauck is surely right to draw attention to the way in which the ordination prayer for the Bishop in Hippolytus echoes the role description of the *mebaqqer* in The Damascus Rule, especially in the phrase, 'he shall loosen all the fetters' (CD), or, 'to loose every bond' (AT 3). Both derive ultimately from Isaiah 58:6.

Is not this the fast that I choose: to loose the bonds of wickedness, to undo the thongs of the yoke, to let the oppressed go free, and to break every yoke?

But since that passage of Isaiah is not about ordination or the role of officers or leaders of any kind, Nauck thinks it too much of a coincidence for Essene and Christian sources to have drawn on Isaiah independently. Influence of Qumran on Christian thought and practice at some point seems likely, in which case it is much more likely to have come through Jewish- than Hellenistic-Christian channels.

Third, we may say that it is not suggested that the early Christians went to Qumran to ask how to organize a community, or read the Damascus Rule and appointed overseers accordingly. Jeremias in fact thinks that any similarity of office may have been mediated to the church through the Pharisaic groups, but even if this is so, we are talking about the Christians adopting *a word*. What would make it likely that they would do so would be if they had a role to be filled for which this would be a suitable title. The house-meetings provide such a role. This is the neglected point. The tendency has been to associate ἐπίσκοποι with the Gentile church on the fragile grounds that the word is Greek and is first found in a Christian document in Phil 1:1. It then comes to be called 'the Pauline model', and is no longer associated with Jerusalem. Alternatively, the interest has been in apostles and we have asked whether the *mebaqqer* provides a model for the apostles, but since the two are not close the search has quickly ended. But in the house-meetings, which we have seen to have been part of the Jewish-Christian churches no less than the Greek, we have a setting that cried out for leaders to do the things the *mebaqqer* did. The Christian groups must have had a close functional resemblance to the 'camps', small sectarian groups living in the midst of an unsympathetic society, using wilderness

157

terminology to define themselves as the true Israel — and *someone* must have examined and enrolled catechumens!

It is not necessary to show that Christian leaders did everything that Essene leaders did, or did it in the same way, or for the same reasons. Certainly they did not. But to deny a connection between the two on theological grounds, is another example of the fallacy of idealism, and would be like saying that the role of the Protestant pastor is not derived from that of the Roman Catholic priest because some of the things they do are different and their reasons for doing them (their theology) differs also. This is of course true, but sociologically we should have to say that they are more similar than different.

It is not possible to prove that the term ἐπίσκοπος entered the vocabulary of the Christian churches by this route, but we may think that the possibility has been too quickly dismissed. The κατ' οἶκον references in Acts suggest that the Jerusalem church was not one monolithic congregation, even though Luke's interest is in presenting it as such. Furthermore, Paul refers to 'the churches of God which are in Judaea' (1 Thess 2:14; cf. Gal 1:22), a reminder of the existence of congregations which, if they came under Jerusalem's authority, nevertheless assembled separately. All these congregations would have needed their own 'overseers', people to do the very things that the Damascus Rule shows the *mebaqqer* doing. Like ἐπίσκοπος, *mebaqqer* is a functional word, devoid of priestly connotations, already in use in the immediate environment of the earliest churches and in the Essene communities that the earliest congregations might have been expected to encounter.

To summarize the argument so far: if the earliest churches, from Jerusalem onwards, met in houses, as Acts suggests, then those house-churches will have had leaders form the start, whatever they may have been called. In Aramaic-speaking areas they may have acquired the functional title of *mebaqqer*. In Greek-speaking churches, this would translate naturally into ἐπίσκοπος. The Christian ἐπισκοπή would then be seen to have originated informally in the earliest Jewish period of Christianity, rather than to have been adopted by the Pauline churches in some kind of dependence on Greek clubs and societies. It is in favour of this that the shepherd metaphor, which became the dominant image of the ἐπίσκοπος, is not found in secular Greek in association with words of the ἐπισκεπτ- group,[48] though of course it was readily available in the Old Testament tradition, and had already been used by the Damascus Rule.

The Jerusalem Elders in Acts

This reconstruction makes the best sense of Luke's references to the elders in connection with the church at Jerusalem. Luke mentions them in just three contexts. They appear first without explanation in a brief notice that when the church at Antioch collected money for the relief of famine in Jerusalem it sent it 'to the elders by the hand of Barnabas and Saul' (11:30).[49] Next they appear several times in the account of the Jerusalem conference, where the word is always linked to the apostles in the phrase 'the apostles and the elders' (15:2, 4, 6, 22, 23, 16:4). This phrase is quite distinctive and occurs nowhere else. Finally there is a mention of them receiving Paul on his final visit to Jerusalem: 'Paul went in with us to James and all the elders were present' (21:18). The first two of these passages come from Luke's 'Antiochene' material and the third is in a 'we' passage.

The usual view of the place of these elders within the history of the Jerusalem church has been as follows. The earliest leaders of the church were the Twelve,[50] whom Luke calls 'the apostles'. At some

---

[48] Nauck, 'Problem', p. 452. Merklein admits this, *Amt*, p. 377.

[49] Some scholars believe that Luke has misplaced the reference here. The phrase about Paul delivering gifts to the elders originally belonged to the visit described in Acts 21, where we are told all the elders were present, and Luke has relocated it to avoid having to tell us that the elders rejected the collection. (Achtemeier, *Quest*, p. 46, Taylor, *Paul*, p. 52). This has the merit of removing a discrepancy between Galatians and Acts on the number of Paul's visits to Jerusalem, but doesn't explain why Luke needed to do anything so clumsy. He could either have left it out altogether, or retained it without saying anything about how the elders responded. After all, he does not say anything about the elders' response in 11:30.

[50] Most modern scholars do not follow Luke in identifying the apostles with the Twelve, but they accept that Jesus called twelve men to serve as a symbol of the eschatologically restored Israel, and that these men led the primitive church. See, for example, Conzelmann, Acts p. 12; Roloff, *Apostelgeschichte*, p. 35; Lohfink, *Community*, pp. 9–12, 75–81; Meyer, *Aims*, p. 153; Sanders, *Jesus*, p. 98–106.

point in the first ten or fifteen years of the church's existence an office of elder was created similar to that of the Jewish synagogue, either to succeed the Twelve, whose members began to leave Jerusalem in order to preach the gospel, or as assistants to the apostles in the administration of the church.[51] James replaced Peter as the leader of the church and the elders took the place of the apostles. This was the origin of the office of elder as we find it in other documents of the apostolic and post-apostolic age. This view was held by Lightfoot in the nineteenth century,[52] and continues to be held, with variations, among modern scholars.[53]

It is open to question in the light of the way 'the elders' was used in the ancient world. We have seen that among the Jews the term elders usually connoted respect rather than office. We have seen that among the Greeks the same thing applies. 'Elders' serves as a collective title for those with most honour in the community, among whom the holders of various offices would be included, so that 'elders' is an imprecise term in comparison to terms denoting the holders of definite office. Insofar as Jewish elders formed a council, the evidence suggests that this was a civil body to govern the community as a whole, and that it is unlikely that synagogues, as individual congregations, had boards of elders. In short 'the elders' is not so much a defined office or rank, but more a way of referring quite generally to those who held office or possessed rank and to whom respect was due on account of their seniority.

That 'the synagogue did not have an office of elder in the sense often assumed has not gone unnoticed, as we have already noted,[54]

---

[51] Lindsay, *Church*; Farrer, 'Ministry', pp. 133–42; Bruce, Acts (1988) p. 231, n. 44.

[52] Lightfoot, *Philippians*, pp. 179ff.

[53] Pesch, *Apostelgeschichte*, p. 357: 'Die Ältesten sind ein Leitungsgremium zunächst der Jerusalemer, dann auch anderer Ortsgemeinden, gebildet vermutlich aus bewährten Gemeindemitgliedern nach Analogie der judischen Synagoenvorstanden.' See also Schneider, *Apostelgeschichte*; Roloff, *Apostelgeschichte*.

[54] Harvey, 'Elders', p. 318–32; Sobosan, 'Presbyter', p. 129–46; Powell, 'Ordo', p. 290–328. Bornkamm, πρέσβυς, p. 660f., on the contrary speaks of the communal order of the Jewish community being 'continued in the constitution of the synagogue', where the title πρεσβύτεροι refers to 'the leaders of the community and disciplinary body of the synagogue. cf. Lk 7:3'. Yet even so Bornkamm notes the comparative rarity of the term and the honorary nature of the title.

although this fact has not usually been brought to bear on the elders of the Jerusalem church. In a recent article, however, Martin Karrer acknowledges this difficulty,[55] and he argues that the early church derived its eldership not from contemporary models but from the account in Numbers 11 of the seventy elders on whom the Spirit rested. A reference in an apocalyptic passage of Isaiah to the LORD manifesting his glory to the elders in Jerusalem shows, according to Karrer, that this was part of Jewish expectation for the last days.[56] Believing as they did that they were living in the last days, that they were witnessing the eschatological ingathering of Israel, the early church will have developed an office of eldership to care for the daily needs of the people and to rule on the application of the Law in the new conditions of the last days. This we see the Jerusalem elders doing in Acts 11:30 and 15:1–35.[57]

The first weakness of this otherwise attractive view is its assumption that the occurrences of the word 'elders' must denote a definite office with distinct functions. But we have seen that 'the elders' tends to be an imprecise title of honour for whatever leaders there may be, while in fact the two functions assigned by Karrer to the elders are weakly anchored both in Numbers and in Acts. The story of the appointment of the elders in Numbers is certainly closely connected with a story about the miraculous provision of quails to satisfy the people's hunger, but nothing is said about the elders distributing this food, while to see the elders of Acts 11 as almoners reads too much into a text which surely intends us to see the gifts from Antioch being received by the church's *leaders*. Equally, while the elders in Israel gave rulings in cases of civil law, there is nothing about this in the Numbers story, and while the apostles and elders are certainly giving a ruling about the applicability of the Law in Acts 15, and doing so with the help of the Holy Spirit (Acts 15:28), everything that is said of the elders is said also of the apostles, so

[55]Karrer, 'Ältestenamt', p. 159. He says that the most we can say of the elders of the synagogue is that they were 'nur eine Sitzordnung nach Alter'.
[56] Isaiah 24:23, 'for the LORD of hosts will reign on Mount Zion and in Jerusalem and before his elders he will manifest his glory'.
[57] Karrer, 'Ältestenamt', p. 166–70.

that it is inappropriate for Karrer to single out the elders and call them 'lawyers'.[58]

The second weakness is the way that Karrer supposes that theological ideas were responsible for shaping the organization of the primitive church, to the neglect of social realities, in this case the household churches and the prestige enjoyed by those who led them. I suggest that, if the elders of Numbers •11 and Isaiah 24 played some part in the thinking of the Jerusalem church, it will not have been the case that the Jerusalem leaders read these passages and concluded that they needed to appoint elders, but rather that they read these passages and *saw themselves to be the elders*, Scripture being understood in the light of present experience, rather than present reality of the church being shaped to conform to Scripture.

If, then, the way the term 'the elders' was used in the world of that time suggests that we should not be looking for a separate group of officials who bore this title, we need to ask who there was in the church of Jerusalem to whom this honorific might naturally be applied. In the case of the Pauline churches, I have argued that 'the elders' was a natural way of referring collectively to the household leaders, the ἐπίσκοποι, when they were acting together in a representative capacity. Jerusalem too had its household-churches, and their leaders, I have suggested, were designated individually by the term *mebaqqer*. Collectively, it would have been natural to refer to them as *zaqenim* — πρεσβύτεροι — and this, I think, will go a long way to explaining Luke's references to the elders in Jerusalem also. But there is something else to be said.

Jerusalem, of course, was unique in having within it a body of twelve men who exercised leadership in virtue of their special commissioning by Jesus to be the nucleus of the eschatologically restored Israel. It is uncertain what became of this group, whether they left Jerusalem on missionary service, or died out, or whether they continued in leadership up to the time of the Jewish War, their number being made up as necessary by others to maintain the

[58] Karrer, 'Ältestenamt', p. 170.

symbolic significance of Twelve.[59] Luke's evidence is most commonly understood, as we have seen, to mean that the elders succeeded the apostles in the leadership of the church. Recently, for example, Bauckham has suggested that, as the number of the original Twelve dwindled, a new body was formed under the leadership of James, with any surviving apostles forming part of it, and it is this body whom Luke calls 'the elders'.[60] But if in fact the Twelve, as an institution, continued for any length of time in Jerusalem, then the term 'the elders' would naturally have been applied to them, especially if, as is likely, that body included members of the original group, those whom Luke calls 'the apostles'.[61]

This makes good sense of the three places where Luke mentions the Jerusalem elders. In Acts 11:30 Luke surely intends us to understand that the gifts from Antioch were received by *the church's leaders* rather than by subordinate officials. Similarly in 21:18 the stress is on all the leaders being present. In Acts 15 the cumbersome phrase 'the apostles and elders' also means to show that this historic decision was taken by the whole leadership of the church, including both the Twelve and those who led the meetings κατ' οἶκον, titles being heaped up in the way we saw was common in Septuagintal Greek.

'From Jerusalem Round to Illyricum'

As a final step, I shall argue that it is possible to use the evidence provided in incidental fashion by Luke in Acts to trace a line of

---

[59] We are regularly assured that this did not happen, that when James bar Zebedee was executed his place was not filled, but can we be sure of this, given the selectiveness of Luke's account? The symbolic importance of the Twelve, together with the space Luke gives to describing Matthias's appointment, might suggest the opposite: the number was maintained, and this is how it was done.

[60] Bauckham, *Relatives*, p. 75. Bauckham presents evidence to suggest that the list of bishops of Jerusalem, preserved independently by Eusebius and Epiphanius, should in reality be seen as a list of the new eldership surrounding James, pp. 70–9.

[61] That 'the elders' refers to the apostles in this sense was suggested by Jackson and Lake, *Beginnings*, I.5, p. 56, and I have myself suggested the same thing, proposing that in the phrase 'the apostles and elders' (15:2ff.) the καί is epexegetic. See Campbell, 'Elders', pp. 526ff.

development between this reconstruction of the church at Jerusalem and the churches known to us from the Pauline and post-Pauline letters.[62] This means that we shall look next to the church at Antioch.

It has often been suggested that at Antioch a different pattern developed, that of 'prophets and teachers',[63] but the evidence for this is really very weak. According to Luke,

> Now in the church at Antioch there were prophets and teachers, Barnabas, Symeon who was called Niger, Lucius of Cyrene, Manaen a member of the court of Herod the tetrarch, and Saul. (Acts 13:1)

There is no doubt that Luke here means to describe the leaders of the church at Antioch, but no reason to think that he means us to understand that they held offices of prophet and teacher in contra-distinction to elders or whatever. In the first place, it seems likely that prophets and teachers are not being clearly distinguished here.[64] Luke is very interested in the activity of prophets, hardly in the office of prophet. Prophets are a sign that the Spirit is poured out on the church, empowering its messengers and guiding its decisions. 'Teachers inspired by the Holy Spirit' probably catches his meaning. Second, there is nothing to prevent us supposing that a man could be both an overseer/elder and also a prophet/teacher. Those who provided the earliest churches with its meeting-places and its leaders were the sort of people who were assumed (in Sanders' phrase) 'to know things and run things'.[65] Such people were looked to for teaching, and so were teachers, and their teaching was received as a word from God, and so they were acclaimed prophets.

---

[62] Of course this must not be taken to imply that we can claim to have a picture of the whole of early Christian development. We are limited by Luke's account to just the geographical sweep is covered by Paul's career (Rom 15:19). We know nothing of the church's eastward or southward spread, or of the life of churches in rural areas.

[63] Streeter, *Primitive*, p. 75. Roloff, *Apostelgeschichte*, p. 193.

[64] So Haenchen, *Acts*, p. 395, Marshall, *Acts*, p. 215, Schneider, *Apostelgeschichte*, p. 113.

[65] Sanders, *Law*, p. 79. Sanders is arguing for the influence of members of the priest-hood within the synagogues, as evidenced by Josephus. He writes: 'This simply shows how strong was the assumption that priests and men of property knew things and ran things; the two went together, and not everyone was well educated.'

Luke's purpose in this particular story is not to describe the constitution of the church but to attribute the Gentile mission to the leading of the Holy Spirit. This is seen by the following verse. In justification of his claim that the leaders of the Antioch church were prophets and teachers, he portrays them receiving the guidance of the Holy Spirit in setting apart Barnabas and Saul for missionary service. Clearly we have here a theological interpretation of a corporate decision in which the church's leaders played a prominent part.

We may suppose that the church at Antioch met in homes and consisted by this time of several such house-churches; that is to say, it assembled, as the Jerusalem church assembled, κατ 'οἶκον. If we apply to its leaders the criteria used by Theissen to categorize the prominent people in the Corinthian church, we notice that Manaen at least enjoyed high social status, and that Barnabas was or had been a man of property (Acts 4:37). Paul was a Roman citizen. Of Simeon and Lucius nothing is known except that they appear to originate from North Africa. They could well have come to Antioch in the course of trade and belong to the same class as Lydia (Acts 16:14). In the absence of other evidence, we should assume that they were men of standing, since named individuals in Acts are generally people of this kind.[66]

In this passage, however, we are told that the prophets and teachers were κατὰ τὴν οὖσαν ἐκκλησίαν.[67] This phrase, which is similar to that used by Paul when addressing the whole church, τῆ ἐκκλησίᾳ τοῦ θεοῦ τῆ οὔσῃ ἐν Κορίνθῳ, strongly suggests that a reference to the whole Antiochene church is intended in Acts 13 also. This makes it likely that these men enjoyed some sort of recognition by the church as a whole. If so, then the church at Antioch has moved beyond the first stage of being a single house-church, or of several such groups without any organization. It is a

---

[66] Theissen, *Social Setting*, p. 179f.

[67] The use of the present participle in this way is a Lukan peculiarity, cf. Acts 5:17, 11:22, 28:17. No completely satisfactory explanation seems to have been established (see Bruce, *Acts* (1990), p. 292). I suggest a certain formality or recognized standing is meant, similar to the addition of ὑπερεχούσαις in Rom 13:1 which gave rise to the English expression 'the powers that be'.

The elders.

reasonable guess that these men were the leaders of churches that met κατ᾽ οἶκον, and that they together formed the leadership when the believers met κατ᾽ ἐκκλησίαν. Individually, and κατ᾽ οἶκον, they functioned as ἐπίσκοποι. Corporately, and κατ᾽ ἐκκλησίαν, they could correctly have been called οἱ πρεσβύτεροι.

This prepares the way for a correct understanding of the notorious Acts 14.23:

> And when they had appointed elders for them in every church, with prayer and fasting they committed them to the Lord in whom they believed.

The key words are: χειροτονήσαντες δὲ αὐτοῖς κατ᾽ ἐκκλησίαν πρεσβυτέρους. Luke has often been accused of reading elders back into the narrative from the church order of his own day, since Paul, as we have seen, called no one 'elder'.[68] However, we have seen reason to doubt whether the absence of elders in Paul's letters reflects a deep theological aversion to them. There were always leaders in Paul's churches to whom the term 'the elders' would sooner or later be applied, so that,

> the most we can deduce from these facts is that Luke has used a term current in his own time to refer to leaders who may possibly have been known by other designations in the earlier period.[69]

Once again, it is a case of many terms, one concept.

In any case, if we accept the basic historicity of the journey being described in Acts 13–14, the point may not be relevant, since the event described took place not in the high-noon of the Pauline mission, after he had broken with the church at Antioch and launched out on his own, but while he and Barnabas were missionaries of the Antioch church, and Barnabas was the senior partner.[70] It is natural to suppose that Barnabas and Paul will have reproduced in the churches they founded the organization prevailing in the church

---

[68] So Conzelmann, *Acts*, p. 112; Haenchen, *Acts*, p. 436; Lüdemann, *Early*, p. 163; Roloff, *Apostelgeschichte*, p. 220 among many others.

[69] Marshall, *Acts*, p. 241. The same point is made by Bruce, *Acts* (1990), p. 326.

[70] Taylor, *Paul*, pp. 88–95.

from which they had been sent out. At all events, it seems clear that Luke himself thought they did so, since he is at pains to make the accounts in 13:1–3 and 14:21–23 resemble each other, as we shall presently see.

But it may be asked, if the elders are the leaders of the houses where the church met, and as such are in place from the start, why do they need to be 'appointed'?[71] The answer to this lies in the meaning of the verb χειροτονεῖν as Luke has used it in this verse. In classical Greek the word meant 'choose' or 'elect', originally by raising the hand, but in time the derivation was forgotten, and the 'hand' element became as much a dead metaphor as it is in the English terms 'hand down' or 'hand-pick'.[72] It is not found in the Septuagint, but it is used by Jewish authors, sometimes with God as the subject, to mean simply 'choose' or 'appoint to office'.[73] In the New Testament the churches appoint Titus to travel with Paul (2 Cor 8:19). There is an important occurrence of the word in the Didache, where the churches appoint bishops and deacons (15:1) and Ignatius uses it three times of the churches appointing official envoys.[74] On the other hand, in Patristic Greek it came to mean 'ordain with the laying on of hands', reviving the literal sense of 'hands'.[75] It is regularly asserted that here in Acts it simply has the meaning of 'choose' or 'appoint', most of the discussion being over whether a vote of the congregation was involved. Any thought of the laying of hands is, we are told, excluded.[76]

In arguing the opposite, I wish to draw attention to the striking similarities of language between this passage and other Lukan 'ordination' passages, a similarity which is even more impressive when the Pastorals are brought into the picture, as they should be.[77] When

---

[71] The same question arises with Tit 1:5, which will be discussed in the next chapter.

[72] *BAG*, p. 889.

[73] In Philo, *Praem*, 52, *Mos* I, 198 and Josephus *AJ*, 6.312, it is God who appoints. In Philo *De Jos* 248; *Flacc* 109; Josephus *AJ*, 13.45, a ruler makes an appointment.

[74] Ignatius, *Philad* 10.1, *Smyrn* 11.2, *Pol* 7.2.

[75] For example: *Apost Can* 1; *Apost Const* 2.2.3, 3.20.1; Lampe, *PGL*, p. 1523.

[76] Lohse, *Ordination*, pp. 67–8; Prast, *Presbyter*, p. 217.

[77] Wilson, *Luke and the Pastoral Epistles*. The chapter on 'Church and Ministry' (pp. 53–68) is one of the most impressive arguments for Acts and the Pastorals having at the least come from the same circle.

the passages are set side by side as in the table opposite it will be seen that one vocabulary of ordination unites Acts and the Pastorals, and that the resemblance is closest between Acts 13:3 and Acts 14:23. The account of the sending out of Barnabas and Saul mentions fasting, prayer and the laying on of hands (Acts 13:3, νηστεύσαντες καὶ προσευξάμενοι καὶ ἐπιθέντες τὰς χεῖρας), and Luke supplies his own interpretation of the whole event when he recalls that the missionaries had been 'commended to the grace of God' (Acts 14:26). The Lycaonian elders are likewise 'committed to the Lord', and the story mentions hands, prayer and fasting (χειροτονήσαντες ... προσευξάμενοι μετὰ νηστειῶν). In the light of this, I think we should agree with Johnson that 'Luke uses it [sc. χειροτονεῖν] synonymously with "laying on of hands".'[78] It is then the first appearance of what came to be its normal Christian meaning.

If then Luke used χειροτονεῖν to mean 'the laying on of hands', what did he understand by it? The short answer is 'blessing', as Everett Ferguson has made plain.[79] His argument is as follows.

The development of ordination both in Christianity and Rabbinic Judaism was greatly influenced by two Old Testament passages, the ordination of the Levites (Num 8:5–13) and the appointment of Joshua (Num 27:15–23), although Christians and Jews used the tradition in different ways. David Daube was right to draw attention to the difference between the Hebrew סמך (samakh), meaning 'to lean upon' (so as to create a substitute), and שׂים (s'im) which refers to the hands lightly resting on someone as a sign of blessing. However, Ferguson argues against Daube that all Christian occurrences of the laying on of hands (including those relating to an act of commissioning) are to be understood in the latter sense of blessing and not as equivalent to the rabbinic samakh for two reasons.

---

[78] Johnson, Acts, p. 254. He does not, however, elaborate. The same point is made by Spicq, Pastorals, p. 727 in an excursus on ordination. Ferguson, 'Ordination', p. 39, leaves the matter open, but he stresses the connection between the two passages.

[79] Ferguson, 'Jewish and Christian Ordination', HTR 56 (1963), pp. 13–20; 'Laying on of Hands; Its Significance for Ordination', JTS 26 (1975), pp. 1–12; 'Ordain, Ordination', ABD, Vol. 5 (1992), pp. 37–40.

Acts 6:1-6	Acts 13:1-3	Acts 14:21-23	1 Tim 4:14	2 Tim 1:6	Tit. 1:5
ἐπισκέψασθε	ἀφορίσατε	—	—	—	—
καταστήσομεν	—	—	—	—	καταστήσῃς
ἐξελέξατο	—	—	—	—	—
—	νηστεύσαντες	μετὰ νηστειῶν	—	—	—
προσευξάμενοι	προσευξάμενοι	προσευξάμενοι	—	—	—
ἐπέθηκαν τὰς χεῖρας	ἐπιθέντες τὰς χεῖρας	χειροτονήσαντες	μετὰ ἐπιθέσεως τῶν χειρῶν	διὰ τῆς ἐπιθέσεως τῶν χειρῶν	—
		παρέθετο τῷ κυρίῳ (cf. 20.32)	διὰ προφητείας cf. 1.18		
		παραδεδομένοι τῇ χάριτι τοῦ θεοῦ (14.26)		τὴν παραθήκην μου cf. v. 14, 2.2	

First, rabbinic ordination of the kind referred to emerged in the years 70–135 CE, and cannot be shown to have existed earlier. Second, the Christian laying on of hands, unlike the rabbinic ordination, is always accompanied in the New Testament by prayer (as the rabbinic rite was not), making it not so much the creating of a substitute as a simple prayer for God's blessing, whether in healing or equipping for service. Ferguson argues that the immediate root of this Christian practice is the often recorded practice of Jesus.[80] Prayer for blessing rather than enthronement remained at the heart of Christian ordination as it developed, and the sense of this prayer is captured by Luke in Acts 14:23 by the phrase, 'committed them to the Lord'. The Lycaonian elders, like Saul and Barnabas before them, and the Ephesian elders after them (20:32) were entrusted to God's grace in prayer accompanied by the laying on of hands.

In this way it is possible to see how the elders could be both 'in place' already, as household leaders, and also set apart for their ministry of leadership by the departing missionaries. Like elders everywhere they had emerged rather than been appointed, recognized in virtue of their seniority, status and contribution to the church, rather than appointed *as elders*.[81] But now the apostles were leaving and entrusting the work of the gospel to them, and so, as they themselves had been prayed for and commended to God, so now they committed these others to the grace of God. It was a rite that might easily be repeated (Acts 20:32).[82]

What we should particularly notice is that the elders are appointed κατ' ἐκκλησίαν. While this may mean no more than this

[80] E.g. Mark 10:13–16.

[81] Cf. Harvey, 'Elders', p. 331: 'there need be no question of appointing people as elders: elders exist already'.

[82] Prast, *Presbyter*, pp. 212–22, shows how Acts 14:21–23 functions as a striking parallel to the more extended 20:17–35. He argues that Luke deliberately excludes the idea of ordination by substituting prayer that God will himself equip the elders for their service. But how does prayer that God will equip his servant *exclude* the idea of ordination? Might it not *define* it? However, the parallelism between the two passages is valuable, enabling us to use the later passage to interpret the earlier. As the one is not an appointment, so little is the other. In both a departing missionary *blesses* those who will carry on the work. This may not be Prast's understanding of 'ordination', but I think it is Luke's!

happened in each of the cities they had previously visited, in view of the way Luke has used κατ' οἶκον and κατ' ἐκκλησίαν previously, it must be possible that we should see this κατ' ἐκκλησίαν as similar to the κατὰ τὴν οὖσαν ἐκκλησίαν of Acts 13:1. If so, then Luke, speaking in summary fashion of a development that embraced a whole number of churches, is referring to those who within their own house-churches are overseers, but who, seen collectively and from the outside, can naturally be described as elders. Only in this respect is he guilty of anachronism, since at the very early stage which he is describing, the churches will hardly have multiplied to this extent. Yet he has not imported a foreign concept into the story, but merely telescoped two stages of the churches' life: the initial stage in which the believers gathered κατ' οἶκον, and the situation that his readers were familiar with in which the household heads gathered κατ' ἐκκλησίαν.

This finds support from the only other place that Luke refers to elders or overseers at all. When Paul summons the leaders of the church at Ephesus (Acts 20:17), he is said to summon τοὺς πρεσβυτέρους τῆς ἐκκλησίας. Luke then has him deliver a speech which, by its many deliberate evocations of Paul's style and thought, is intended by Luke to serve as Paul's testament to the churches he will not see again (i.e. the churches of Luke's generation, now bereft of the apostle).[83] Paul reminds the leaders to shepherd 'the church of God which he obtained with his own blood',[84] and in which the Holy Spirit has made them ἐπίσκοπους (20:28).

It has sometimes been thought, as by Barrett,[85] that Luke is here speaking of the worldwide church in a way otherwise unique in Acts.[86] This seems to me very improbable. In the first place, it cannot mean this in v. 17, where Paul summons the elders of the

---

[83] This speech has received an extended discussion by Barrett, 'Address', pp. 107–21.

[84] We need not discuss here the two disputed readings, 'church of the Lord' or 'church of God', and 'his own blood' or 'the blood of his own'.

[85] Barrett, 'Address', p. 114.

[86] The only other possible exception is 9:31, which even Barrett is not very impressed with. The exact text is in any case a matter of dispute and Giles, ʼΕΚΚΛΗΣΙΑ', pp. 137–40, argues that if the singular is read here it refers to the church of Jerusalem scattered through persecution.

church. In the second place, it is not clear how the elders could be said to shepherd the universal church. More important, since everywhere else in Acts ἐκκλησία refers to the local church in a city, and since the phrase 'church of God' is characteristic of Paul,[87] and is linked here with Pauline phrase about the blood of Christ, it seems best to agree with Giles that we have here either a reminiscence of what Paul actually said, or a conscious effort to reproduce what he was known to have thought.[88]

'The church of God' is then used here, as in Paul's letters, of the local congregation, the church at Ephesus, which the elders are to shepherd. We may then envisage the situation as follows. The church at Ephesus has grown to the point where it has a number of ἐπίσκοποι, each, we may suppose, the head of his own house-church. Together they are the elders of the church, and it is a such that Paul summons them and reminds them of their responsibilities. They are the elders of the church because they are the overseers of the household congregations of which it is comprised. Barrett thinks that by crediting their appointment to the Holy Spirit, Luke is speaking polemically against the contemporary institutionalization of the church in his day,[89] and this, if true, might seem to tell against the idea that the overseers owed their position to their social standing. There need be no conflict, however, between a socio-historical and a theological account of the same event. As in 13:1–3, faith may see the hand of God in events for which historical explanations can also be given.[90]

Conclusions

Although, as I said at the start of this chapter, Luke does not have a

---

[87] 1 Cor 1:2, 10:32, 11:22, 15:9, 2 Cor 1:1; Gal 1:13. He also uses it in the plural: 1 Cor 11:16; 1 Thess 2:14.

[88] Giles, 'ΕΚΚΛΗΣΙΑ', pp. 136f.

[89] Barrett, 'Address', p. 118.

[90] Theissen says: 'It is the characteristic trait of the religious tradition that it masks its moorings in human activity, preferring to speak of the gods' activity or to testify to an experienced reality lying beyond sense perception.' *Social Setting*, p. 175f.

special interest in 'church order', and certainly does not write in order to show that a particular pattern was adopted 'everywhere and by all', he has in fact enabled us to trace a fairly clear and constant pattern of development. It is the household pattern of the earliest churches that is the key to this. Thus, in Jerusalem we see the church meeting in homes, and this fact enables us to deduce the existence of household leaders similar to those known to us from the Pauline letters. It is not essential to my argument to accept the verbal link with the Essene communities, and to suppose that in Jerusalem these leaders were called *mebaqqerim*, but the existence of household churches in Jerusalem provides a plausible (and neglected) link between the Essene *mebaqqer* and the ἐπίσκοποι of the Pauline churches.

As Luke's story moves beyond Jerusalem, the same pattern is occasionally visible. The plural leadership of the church at Antioch is best explained by the likelihood that the church there consisted of a number of congregations meeting κατ' οἶκον, whose leaders acted together κατ' ἐκκλήσιαν. Some of the stories of Paul's church-planting work show him operating in and from the homes of well-to-do people, just as his letters also suggest. Three or four years after its founding, we are not surprised to find that the church at Ephesus has a number of leaders, who are described as ἐπίσκοποι (Acts 20:28), exactly like the leaders at Philippi (Phil 1:1). I suggest that these leaders too are the heads of their own house-churches.

Luke does not often use the term 'the elders', but when he does, it is probably not to denote some other order of leaders, but rather as an alternative term for the leaders whom we also meet under other titles. It has long been recognized that he equates 'elders' and 'overseers' in Acts 20:17, 28, and it is reasonable to suppose that in his account of the founding of the churches of Lycaonia (14:23) 'elders' is used simply as an alternative to 'overseers'. I have argued that in Jerusalem also we should not look for any other referent for the term 'the elders' than the leadership of the church there, both the apostles Luke mentions, and the household overseers/ἐπίσκοποι/ *mebaqqerim* whose presence I think we may deduce.

It is regularly said, however, that in speaking of elders Luke is reading back into the story the circumstances of his own time. For

173

example, in a recent article tracing the history of the church at Ephesus from Paul to John, Schnackenburg discounts the story of Paul sending for the Ephesian elders, because, as he says, in Paul's time leadership was exercised by volunteers and a wide range of 'fellow-workers'.[91]

In reply we may say first, that there is no contradiction in referring to volunteers and co-workers as 'elders'. Stephanas, for example, placed his home at Paul's disposal (1 Cor 16:15ff.), and so could be called a 'volunteer'; he shared in the superintendance of the church, and so could be called a 'co-worker'; as one of the first converts (ἀπαρχή) and head of one of the constituent house-churches in Corinth he had a double claim to be numbered among the elders of the church. The belief that the appearance of elders in Acts is anachronistic rests on a view of the Pauline evidence that we have already seen to be wrong.

But, secondly, we must ask, what is there about elders that marks them out as belonging properly to Luke's time? Luke wrote, we suggested, contemporaneously with the Pastorals, and belonged to the same circle as the author of those letters. In the next chapter, I shall argue that one of the Pastorals' concerns is the introduction of the *single overseer*, not with establishing elders (despite Tit 1:5, to be discussed). It is the emergence of the 'monepiskopos' that is the contentious development in the years towards the close of the first century. The term 'elders', where it appears, should be more properly thought of as a survival than a development. If then Luke were concerned to read back the church order of his own day into the story of the church's beginnings (and I do not think he was), he would be much more likely to do as Clement does, and portray the apostles as establishing bishops and deacons (1 Clem 42:4), than as introducing elders. I submit that the information about the development of the church's structures which Luke provides, he provides untendentiously, and that the evidence, though fragmentary, permits us to see a fairly unified pattern of development.

---

[91] Schnackenburg, 'Ephesus', p. 49: 'Lukas trägt die Verhältnisse seiner Zeit an'.

The significance of this reconstruction will be apparent when we turn to the Pastorals. For the view is frequently expressed that the situation addressed by the Pastorals is that of a *Verschmelzung*, a merging, of two church orders that were originally separate: Pauline bishops and deacons have been merged with Jewish elders. Quite apart from whether this fits the evidence of the Pastorals, I have tried to show here that there was no need for a *Verschmelzung*, since the household basis of the churches ensured that similar arrangements had been followed 'from Jerusalem as far round as Illyricum' (Rom 15:19), and that the Pastorals stand not so much at the meeting of two roads, one from Thessalonica, Corinth and Philippi and the other from Jerusalem, but near the end of a single road that Luke enables us to trace from Jerusalem, through Antioch and Lycaonia, to Macedonia and Achaia, and then to the churches of Asia Minor in the last third of the first century CE.

Chapter Six

The Elders and the Bishop in the Pastorals

We turn next to the Pastoral Epistles and consider their evidence separately from that of the other Pauline letters in accordance with the widely held opinion (which I have come to accept) that these letters come from a different hand and from a time later than the apostle's death. This is not the place for a full discussion of the date and provenance of these letters at once so Pauline and so unPauline, but it will be helpful to set out the opinions regarding these questions on which the present discussion of church leadership in the Pastorals is based, opinions which we may think are in turn reinforced by the conclusions to which we shall come.

The case against attributing the Pastorals directly to the hand of Paul, as letters written by him in his lifetime in the same way as *die Hauptbriefe*, is well known and rests on four main kinds of argument: stylistic, theological, historical, and ecclesiastical. The style and vocabulary of the Pastorals have been exhaustively analysed and shown to be markedly different from that of the earlier Pauline epistles.[1] Theologically the Pastorals lack many of the great Pauline themes, or else reproduce them in what might be called a 'routinized' form (1 Tim 1:8–11, 2 Tim 1:9–10; Tit 2:11–14, 3:4–7), in a way rather similar to Luke/Acts (cf Acts 13:38).[2] Historically it has always proved difficult to fit the biographical details of the Pastorals into the framework of Paul's life as we know it from Acts, requiring

---

[1] Harrison, *Problem* and Grayston and Herdan, 'Authorship'.

[2] Barrett, 'Controversies', Trummer, *Paulustradition*. For the view that the author of Luke/Acts was also responsible for the Pastorals, see Moule, 'Problem', pp. 113–32; Wilson, *Luke and PE*; Quinn, 'Last Volume', pp. 62–75.

most supporters of Pauline authorship to posit a further period of missionary activity by Paul after the Roman imprisonment with which Acts closes.[3] Ecclesiastically it is argued that the Pastorals presuppose a degree of development that goes beyond anything known to us from the accepted letters of Paul.[4]

This is not the place for a full consideration of the strength of these various arguments. Individually they can each be countered with more or less satisfactory solutions: the change in style is due to a secretary's freedom, the absence of great Pauline themes is due to the specific purpose of these letters, the apparent historical discrepancies are due to the great gaps in Acts and in our knowledge of Paul's life, while the ecclesiastical differences are based on an understanding of Paul in terms of *charisma* which, as we have seen, many scholars have come to doubt. In this way, some scholars continue to defend the traditional view that the Pastorals are Pauline, though from a later period of his life otherwise unknown to us.[5]

My own view is that while the historical discrepancies can probably be put down to the imperfect state of our knowledge, and the theological differences are very much a matter of opinion, the variations in style and vocabulary are very difficult to explain without recourse to a secretary so independent as to be virtually another author. It seems quite possible that such people existed in the Pauline circle even within his lifetime, accounting for the variations between other letters in the Pauline corpus, but that this circle continued to work after his death or imprisonment, producing the letters we are now considering.[6] The conjecture of Bauckham that the real author

---

[3] Reicke, 'Chronologie', Metzger, *Letzte Reise*; Prior, *Paul*, pp. 83f.; Fee, *Pastorals*, pp. 3–5.

[4] Hanson, *Pastorals*, pp. 31–8.

[5] Among modern commentators, authenticity has been defended by Spicq (1969[4]) and Kelly (1963), by Jeremias (1981[12]), who adopts the 'secretary' hypothesis, and by Fee (1988), though with important reservations (p. 26). The most recent commentator to take this position is Knight, who also inclines to the secretary hypothesis, with Luke as the most likely secretary. Authenticity has been defended in a number of studies, notably Prior, *Paul* (especially for 2 Tim), and Johnson, *Writings*, pp. 255–7, 381–9.

[6] I am indebted to Earle Ellis's demonstration that the Pastorals have been composed in part from blocks of pre-formed tradition, although he uses this to support essentially Pauline authorship. See, Ellis, 'Traditions', pp. 237–53.

might in fact be Timothy himself is attractive, although nothing in the present study depends on it being true.[7]

What may surely be said with confidence is that whether or not the Pastorals were written in the situation after Paul's death, they *presuppose it*. All three letters give instructions that presuppose Paul's absence. Titus has been left in Crete to complete unfinished business (Tit 1:5). Timothy must reckon with the possibility of Paul being delayed (1 Tim 3:15). 2 Timothy takes the form of Paul's last will and testament. Admittedly all three letters speak of reunion (1 Tim 3:14, 2 Tim 4:9ff., Tit 3:12), and this view means seeing these verses as added for the sake of verisimilitude, but all the instructions in the letters, all the action they envisage, will take place *without Paul*. That is to say these letters function in the same way as does Paul's address to the Ephesian elders (Acts 20:17–35), and play a role similar to that of John 14–16. As the upper room discourse provides reassurance and instruction for those who have to live out the faith after Jesus' departure (and not only the disciples but those who 'will believe in me through their word' (17:20), 'those who have not seen and yet believe' (20:29)), so the Pastorals intend to provide guidance for the Pauline churches as they prepare to live in a world from which their founder has been removed. There is much to be said for the suggestion of Meade that the Pastorals provide for the *Vergegenwärtigung* of Paul's message for those who must continue his work in his absence, which is now seen to be permanent.[8]

But if the Pastorals cannot be dated to Paul's lifetime, there is no need to put them very much later, in particular not as late as the beginning of the second century. J. Quinn, who favours 80–85 CE for the letters as we have them, points to the concern of the letters to speak for Paul's good name and office.[9] If we may suppose that Paul's execution in the early 60s was an embarrassment to many in the church, and that the Pauline gospel had still to be fought for in the years immediately after his death, then the Pastorals fit well into that period. The impression given by Clement (1 Clem 5:6) and

---

[7] Bauckham, 'Letters', p. 494.
[8] Meade, *Pseudonymity*, pp. 130–9.
[9] Quinn, *Titus*, p. 19.

Ignatius (Eph 12:2) is that Paul's reputation is by then secure. The opposition faced by church leaders in the Pastorals can most plausibly be seen as Jewish in character (Tit 1:14, 1 Tim 1:8ff.), and to be of a piece with the activities of the Judaizing counter-mission that gave Paul himself such trouble, and which lies behind Colossians and Ephesians too.[10] This, and not Gnosticism, is what posed a threat to the Pauline gospel and it better fits the years immediately after Paul's death than later. Finally, if the Pastorals belong to the period of Clement and Ignatius, we should expect a much clearer and more settled picture of church order, whereas notoriously that is just what commentators on the Pastorals disagree about! For these reasons, we may think that Quinn is being a little cautious, and that there is no solid objection to bringing down the date of the Pastorals to within ten years of Paul's death. Our exegesis of the passages of the Pastorals that deal with elders and overseers may, if accepted, be thought to make this more likely.

Church Leadership in the Pastorals

The Pastorals contain a number of references to people with leading functions in the church. They mention elders three times (1 Tim 4:14, 5:17ff.; Tit 1:5), someone called 'the overseer' twice (1 Tim 3:1–7; Tit 1:7–9),[11] and deacons once (1 Tim 3:8–13). In addition there is an extended passage on widows, some of whom are to be 'enrolled' as such (1 Tim 5:2–16, esp. v. 9ff.), and two references to prophecy, though not to prophets (1 Tim 1:18, 4:14). Finally there are the figures of Timothy and Titus themselves: do these represent for the author the holders of a separate office, or are they, as the (real or supposed) recipients of the letters, simply sitting for the portrait of the overseer(s) and/or elders who are the writer's real concern?

---

[10] Most recently Goulder, 'Visionaries', pp. 15–39, but also Hooker, 'False Teachers', pp. 315–31.

[11] Throughout this chapter, I have translated ἐπίσκοπος by the word 'overseer', rather than 'bishop', in an attempt to avoid anachronistic associations. The only exceptions are the passages that quote or allude to the writings of people who themselves used 'bishop'.

Three passages are of special importance for this study: Titus 1:5–9; 1 Timothy 3:1–13, and 1 Timothy 5:17–25. It will be helpful to draw attention afresh to what they say and the questions they raise.

There are good grounds for thinking that, if these letters were originally produced and circulated as a group, Titus stood first, as Quinn has suggested.[12] The elaborate introduction to this little letter is intelligible as an introduction to the three letters issued together as a single collection. While the very Jewish character of the church scene in Titus, contrasted with the more Hellenistic milieu of 1 Timothy, suggests that the writer may have designed his triptych to speak 'to the Jew first and also to the Greek', before concluding with a moving and personal appeal to all who would follow in Paul's steps. If this is right, then the passage in Titus would have been read first, and the fact that it mentions both elders and the overseer enables us to relate the two terms before going on to passages that mention only one of these offices. Nothing in the following argument depends on this being true, but approaching the Pastorals through Titus rather than through 1 Timothy may enable us to look at the text from a different angle. We shall look at the passages one by one.

1. *Titus 1:5ff.*

> This is why I left you in Crete, that you might amend what was defective (τὰ λείποντα ἐπιδιορθώσῃ) and appoint elders in every town (καὶ καταστήσῃς κατὰ πόλιν πρεσβυτέρους) as I directed you, if any man is blameless, the husband of one wife, and his children are believers and not open to the charge of being profligate or insubordinate. For an overseer, as God's steward, must be blameless (δεῖ γὰρ τὸν ἐπίσκοπον ἀνέγκλητον εἶναι ὡς θεοῦ οἰκονόμον) ...

There follows a further list of five things an overseer ought not to be, and six qualities he should possess, followed by a demand that

---

[12] Quinn, *Titus*, pp. 19f. also Quinn, 'Last Volume', pp. 62–75.

he be an instructed believer able both to teach (παρακαλεῖν) the faithful and refute (ἐλέγχειν) false teachers.[13]

There are questions here that need not detain us. We do not need to discuss whether and when Paul had visited Crete,[14] for example, nor the meaning of 'husband of one wife', nor the question of the source of the list of qualities demanded of the overseer. But we may well wonder at the situation envisaged, and why so elementary a step as the appointment of elders has not already been taken. We may wonder whether elders are senior men who are to be appointed to some office, or are the prospective holders of the office of elder. Above all, we need to know why the writer can move in this way from elders to the overseer, explaining (γάρ) the qualities required for the one by reference to a list of qualities required for the other, so that the two words appear to be identical in meaning. It will be convenient to discuss these questions after looking in the same way at the other two passages.

2. 1 Tim 3:1–8

The saying is sure: If anyone aspires to the office of overseer (ἐπισκοπῆς ὀρέγεται), he desires a noble task. Now an overseer must be above reproach (δεῖ οὖν τον ἐπίσκοπον ἀνεπίλημπτον εἶναι), the husband of one wife, temperate, sensible, dignified, hospitable, an apt teacher (διδακτικόν), no drunkard, not violent, but gentle, not quarrelsome, and no lover of money. He must manage his own household well, keeping his children submissive and respectful in every way; for if a man does not know how to manage his own household, how can he care for God's church? He must not be a recent convert, or he may be puffed up with conceit and fall into the condemnation of the devil; moreover he must be well thought of by outsiders, or he may fall into the reproach and the snare of the devil. Deacons likewise must be serious (Διακόνους ὡσαύτως σεμνούς) ...

---

[13] Miniscule 460 (thirteenth century) adds a note about not ordaining bigamists and other offenders, even as deacons. This late addition, Spicq suggests (p. 306), is an attempt by a scribe to bring the passage into line with the situation of his own day, notably by including the deacons whom *Titus* omits to mention.

[14] Hanson (pp. 22–3) sees no reason to doubt that this preserves an authentic memory.

THE ELDERS

There follows a similar list of the qualities required in deacons. In this context, we do not need to discuss whether the correct reading in v. 1 is πιστός or ἀνθρώπινος, or whether female deacons or the wives of deacons are intended in v. 11. But we notice that the qualities demanded of an overseer are those of a well-to-do householder and wonder what this tells us about the organization of the church. We observe that these two offices are just those that appear in Philippians 1:1 (as also in Did 15:1–2, and 1 Clem 42:4), but that the overseer is again in the singular, and that (in comparison with Titus 1, and the letters of Ignatius) there is no mention of elders.

3. *1 Tim 5:17ff.*

> Let the elders who rule well (οἱ καλῶς προεστῶτες πρεσβύτεροι) be considered worthy of double honour, especially those who labour in preaching and teaching; for the scripture says, 'You shall not muzzle an ox when it is treading out the grain,' and, 'The labourer deserves his wages.' Never admit any charge against an elder except on the evidence of two or three witnesses... .

The passage continues to give instructions about how to deal with elders who persist in sin, and how to avoid the situation in the first place through careful selection. Does οἱ καλῶς προεστῶτες πρεσβύτεποι refer to all the elders, or is this a group within the body of elders? Are those who labour in preaching and teaching a further subset of the elders, or identical with οἱ προεστῶτες, or is this another way of referring to all the elders? With which of these possible groups, if any, is the overseer to be identified? If the 'honour' they are to be paid is financial, in what sense is it to be double? Double *what* exactly?

Overseer and Elders: Some Common Explanations

It will be seen that the central problem, and the one whose answer determines the answers to all the others, is the relationship of the elders and the overseer. Solutions to this puzzle can be said to fall into four groups.

182

1. In the first place there are those that more or less identify the two, and then seek to explain the difficulties. For this approach, the basic datum is the way the writer has expressed himself in Titus, where, as we have seen, he can explain the reason for appointing a certain kind of men to be elders by reference to the qualities required of an overseer. This strongly suggests that they were at this time alternative titles for the same office, a view which gains support from Acts 20:17, 28; 1 Pet 5:1–2, and 1 Clem 44:1, 5. This solution has a long pedigree going back at least to Jerome, who stated: 'Among the ancients, bishops and presbyters are the same, for the one is a term of dignity, the other of age.'[15] It was the view championed by Lightfoot:

> It is a fact now generally recognized by theologians of all shades of opinion, that in the language of the New Testament the same officer in the church is called indifferently 'bishop' (ἐπίσκοπος) and 'elder' or 'presbyter' (πρεσβύτερος).[16]

Facts of that kind have proved to be in short supply in the century since Lightfoot wrote, but his view has continued to be enormously influential, and has generally been followed by those who maintain the Pauline authorship of these letters, although not only by them.

The major objection to this has been the fact that the overseer appears in the singular in the Pastorals and the elders (generally, cf. 1 Tim 5:19) in the plural. Those who maintain the identity of overseers and elders must see the singular as generic.[17] Within this approach there are minor variations. Thus while Kelly says that the two offices are identical, or that they at least overlap, Fee suggests that 'elders' is a comprehensive term including both overseers and deacons.[18] For Spicq, the two are almost but not quite the same, for while the overseer is an elder, the elders are not all overseers, since the overseer is the leading elder, *primus inter pares*.[19] Dibelius and

---

[15] Jerome, *Letter* 59.
[16] Lightfoot, *Philippians*, p. 95.
[17] Kelly, *Pastorals*, p. 13, Fee, *Pastorals*, p. 84.
[18] Fee, *Pastorals*, p. 128.
[19] Spicq, *Pastorals*, p. 450–55.

Conzelmann say that if the passages about the overseer are not interpolations (as they think they may be), then the singular is generic. Overseers were, or became, members of the presbytery, though perhaps only one of the circle of presbyters acted as overseer. Such leading elders are overseers, and οἱ προεστῶτες πρεσβύτεροι are to be seen as πρεσβύτεροι ἐπισκοποῦντες.[20] In any case, they discount the idea that the singular is due to the fact that the Pastorals envisage a 'monepiskopos', since in their opinion this figure is represented by the supposed addressees of the letters, Timothy and Titus themselves.

2. The second kind of solution to the problem involves denying that the elders in the Pastorals are holders of an office of eldership at all. They are simply the honoured older members of the church from whom the overseers would routinely be chosen. In this case there are just two offices in the church of the Pastorals, overseers and deacons, the elders being a class of people who stood high in the esteem and counsels of the churches. We have seen that this was the view of Sohm and Lowrie, and among commentators on the Pastorals its principal champion has been Jeremias. He does not refer to Sohm, but draws our attention to the problem that if 'elder' refers to an office, then 1 Timothy 5:17 appears to suggest that some elders will be paid more than others on the basis of their performance, an idea he does not think probable (and we may agree). We should recognize, he says, 'that the word *presbyteroi* is not so much a description of office, but of age.'[21] In this way the people who are to be given double honour are, 'those older men to whom an office has been entrusted', in other words the overseers. This fits well with the context in 1 Timothy 5, which begins by using πρεσβύτερος in just this sense (v. 1), and which goes on to speak of the support of widows: overseers, in this interpretation, are to receive twice the stipend paid to widows. The absence of elders from the passage dealing with the qualifications of office-holders (1 Tim 3; Tit. 1) is now explained, since the only offices are overseer

---

[20] Dibelius and Conzelmann, *Pastorals*, pp. 54–7.
[21] Jeremias, *Pastorals*, p. 41, also Harvey, 'Elders', p. 330.

and deacon, exactly as in Philippians.' Ἐπίσκοπος (Tit 1:7) 'is the name of the office that those selected assume.'[22]

The major difficulty with this view, which has in other ways much to commend it, being very much in agreement with the understanding of 'elder' which we have seen to be correct, is that it involves taking καταστήσῃς (Tit 1:5) in an absolute sense, similar to the use of the English word 'ordain' which in certain contexts can be used to mean 'ordain to the priesthood', the office to which a person is ordained being left understood. Jeremias does not seem to be aware of the problem.[23]

Καθίσταναι is regularly found in both classical and biblical Greek with the sense of appointing someone to office. *BAG* list two relevant uses: in the first, καθίσταναι is followed by an accusative for the person appointed, and ἐπί and genitive for the responsibility. For example, 'Who then is the faithful and wise servant, whom his master has set over his household (ὃν κατέστησεν ὁ κύριος ἐπὶ τῆς οἰκετείας), to give them their food at the proper time?' (Matt 24:45). In the second group, καθίσταναι is followed by an accusative for the office-holder appointed, as in 1 Macc 3:55: 'And after this Judas ordained captains over the people (κατέστησεν ἡγουμένους)', or by a double accusative, as in: 'Who made me judge or divider over you [τίς με κατέστησεν κριτὴν]?' (Luke 12:14).

In none of these cases are we left to infer the office to which the appointment is made. The nearest example of this seems to be provided by 1 Clement. In 42:4, Clement says that the apostles appointed their first fruits to be bishops and deacons (καθίστανον τὰς ἀπαρχὰς αὐτῶν ... εἰς ἐπισκόπους). Here the result of the appointment is made plain in the words εἰς ἐπισκόπους and we are not left to infer this in the way being proposed for Tit 1:5. However, he does use κατέστησαν absolutely a few lines further on.

And what wonder is it if those who were in Christ, and were entrusted by God with such a duty, established those who have

---

[22] Jeremias, *Pastorals*, p. 69.
[23] Nor does Harvey, 'Elders', p. 329f.

been mentioned (κατέστησαν τοὺς προειρημένους)?' (43:1); and,

> For this cause, therefore, since they had received perfect fore-knowledge, they appointed those who have already been mentioned (κατέστησαν τοὺς προειρημένους) (44:2).

Here clearly the office to which the aforementioned people were appointed is left to be understood, exactly as is suggested for Tit 1:5, but we may well think that it is implied by the context and by the use of προειρημένους. For a writer to begin a letter by using καθίσταναι in this absolute sense, leaving the office of appointment to be understood or deduced from the occurrence of 'overseer' two verses later, is very unlikely, unless there was a tacit understanding among his readers of which we otherwise have no evidence.[24]

Finally, we may note one other passage where Clement may be thought to provide support for this view. In 54:2, he says:

> Only let the flock of Christ have peace with the presbyters set over it (μετὰ τῶν καθεσταμένων πρεσβυτέρων).

This led Sohm to claim that 'die bestellten Alten ... sind die Bischöfe',[25] and certainly these references go some way to establishing Sohm's case and providing support for Jeremias' view, but perhaps they do not go quite far enough. We have spent a good deal of space on this interpretation both because it has been rejected too quickly, and because we shall see there is a way in which it might be resurrected in a better form.

3. What we may call the third group of solutions to the problems presented by the references to leadership in the Pastorals considers that the Pastorals come from a time when a single overseer has emerged from the ranks of the presbyters as head of the local church

---

[24] Cf. the English use of ordain in the sentence, 'The Church needs to ordain more graduates', where graduates are the people from whom the ordinands are to be drawn (like elders for Jeremias), not the office to which they are ordained (which is understood by everybody to be the priesthood). Harvey's case is rejected on these grounds by Roberts, 'Elders', p. 404.

[25] Sohm, *Kirchenrecht*, p. 96.

on the pattern that we find in the letters of Ignatius. A. T. Hanson provides a well worked out version of this view.[26] According to him, elders and overseers originally had a different origin. Elders originated in the Jewish-Christian churches following the model of the synagogue, while ἐπίσκοποι first appeared among Gentile-Christians who used a general Greek term for 'anyone who had authority to oversee or inspect anything or anyone else'.[27] In time, and certainly before the time the Pastorals were written, these terms became interchangeable and referred to the same local church leaders. The Pastorals, however, are concerned with a later development, the ministry of the single overseer, or monarchical overseer, who is to be found in the Pastorals modelled by 'Timothy' and 'Titus'.

It is in reality the monarchical episkopos who under the guise of the apostolic delegate is being addressed and reminded of his duties.[28]

This is the writer's real concern, to provide a handbook for such leaders and to encourage the churches to accept them. The ambiguity regarding overseers and elders is deliberate,[29] since the writer wishes to claim the authority of Paul for this ministry, yet knows that church order in Paul's day had been much less developed and there had been no single overseer in charge of the local church.

According to Hanson, 'the strongest evidence for this lies in the extent of the authority which the fictional Timothy and Titus are expected to exercise'. They ordain clergy, choose whom they like as church officers, and exercise discipline with 'very much the authority which we find Ignatius ascribing to the bishops of his day'.[30] This seems to be going too far, however. Ignatius may make extravagant claims for the importance of the overseer's presence and presidency, but we do not, in fact, hear of a single thing that he

---

[26] Hanson, *Pastorals*, p. 31–38.
[27] Hanson, *Pastorals*, p. 32.
[28] Käsemann, *Essays*, p. 87. Also Bornkamm, πρέσβυς, p. 667.
[29] Streeter, *Primitive*, p. 108–10.
[30] Hanson, *Pastorals*, p. 33.

actually *does*, and certainly not of his 'ordaining clergy'.[31] He twice
speaks of the appointment of deacons to travel to Antioch as the
church's representatives (*Smyrn* 11:2, *Philad* 101), but it is clear
that even such lowly appointments are made by the congregation as
a whole, and not on the authority of the overseer alone. So far from
the Ignatian overseer appointing elders, he was himself elected from
their number,[32] a picture that gains support from other early texts.[33]
On the other hand it is Paul himself, as we know from letters, who
speaks as one conscious of authority in his churches, and who exercises it by visit, by letter and on occasion by accredited representative.[34] If the Pastorals are really from long after Paul's death, it
seems likely that they are drawing on the authoritative image Paul
and his delegates were remembered to have had as a way of urging
what they have to say upon the churches. The congregations who
heard these letters being read are urged to accord a like authority to
their own leaders (1 Tim 4:12). Accordingly, we should reject the
view that the Pastorals simply provide a handbook for the guidance
of 'monepiskopoi', and move to consider another view.

4. Within the Sohmian tradition, as identified in the
introduction,the tendency is to see the Pastorals as concerned with
bringing together two different types of church order originating
within diverse streams of Christian tradition. J. D. G. Dunn puts it
as follows:

> Perhaps the best explanation for this form of ministry and church
> organization is that the Pastorals represent the fruit of a growing
> rapprochement between the more formal structures which Jewish
> Christianity took over from the synagogue and the more dy-
> namic charismatic structure of the Pauline churches after Paul's
> death.'[35]

---

[31] Lohse notes that ordination is not even mentioned by the Apostolic Fathers, *Ordi-nation*, p. 68.

[32] Jay, 'Presbyter', p. 141.

[33] According to Clement the overseer/elders who have been overthrown were ap-pointed with the consent of the whole church (44:3), while the Didache directs the readers to 'appoint for yourselves' bishops and deacons.

[34] See further Best, 'Authority', and *Convert*, and Holmberg *Power*, pp. 79–81.

[35] Dunn, *Unity*, p. 115.

In his recent commentary, H. Merkel writes:

> If in the Pastorals we find in the leading position now the elders, now the bishop, then we shall agree with the widespread hypothesis that two conceptions of diverse origin have been combined (*verschmolzen*).[36]

A curious variation on the theme is found in Quinn, who sees the explanation for the appointment of elders in Tit 1:5 as follows:

> To such Jewish-Christian churches the Pauline missionary experience is proposed, the vanguard of which will be a body of new presbyters on the Pauline model, '*as I myself commanded you*'.[37]

The suggestion is normally made in terms of the introduction of a Pauline order of overseers and deacons, rather than of elders, as by Roloff who speaks of the 'reconciliation' (*Angleichung*) of the presbyteral and episcopal constitutions.[38]

Roloff presents us with the fullest version of this view in an excursus in his commentary on 1 Timothy,[39] and it will be worth summarizing and commenting on what he says. The presbyteral constitution, he believes, came into the Christian church by the adaptation of Jewish models. Contemporary Judaism knew of elders both in the government of the community and the synagogue, and what qualified a person for eldership, beside advanced age (which in ancient society served as evidence of maturity and experience), was esteem and good public reputation. Jewish-Christian congregations probably adopted this model very early on. Paul, on the other hand, never mentions elders, because for him leadership derives from *charisma*, on the basis of which various people are acknowledged to have certain functions in the church (including the ἀντιλήμψεις and κυβερνήσεις of 1 Cor 12:28). The overseers and deacons (Phil

---

[36] Merkel, *Pastoral*, pp. 91f.
[37] Quinn, *Titus*, p. 84. He speaks elsewhere of 'the more archaic, Jewish-Christian congregations of the Christian movement being updated according to the Pauline model' (p. 16).
[38] Roloff, *Timotheus*, p. 170.
[39] Roloff, *Timotheus*, pp. 169–89.

1:1) are a natural development of that, fully reconcilable with the idea of *charisma,* as leadership based on age and esteem is not.[40] In this idea of eldership, opposed in principle to leadership based on *charisma,* we recognize the neo-Sohmian view as mediated by von Campenhausen.[41]

Roloff sees that the overseers of the Pauline churches were those who from the start opened their homes for meetings of the congregations,[42] and the multiplication of house-churches led naturally to the multiplication of the overseers — hence the plural form in Phil 1:1. These men were heads of their houses and would usually have presided over the Lord's Supper in their homes.[43] In the Pastorals, we see the Pastor attempting to marry these two systems of church government together, the household overseers and the council of elders, as can be seen from the fact that overseers and elders are never mentioned in one and the same passage. 1 Timothy 3 reads as if there were only overseers and deacons; 1 Timothy 5 as if there were only elders. Only Titus 1 mentions both together in an awkward juxtaposition whose purpose is to move the church from one to the other. In another passage (1 Tim 5:17), he singles out the active elders and calls them to function as overseers by preaching and teaching.[44] By so doing he is trying to bring it about that the office of overseer, which until now has been limited to individual households, is now extended to the local church as a whole. The occurrence of overseer in the singular shows that the author's purpose is that henceforth the whole local church should be structured as a household of God (1 Tim 3:15) under one overseer, as the house-churches had been up to now.

There is much in this analysis with which we may readily agree. The recognition that the overseers were those who opened their homes for congregational use is very welcome, explaining as it does both the emergence of several overseers in one place and the silence

---

[40] Roloff, *Timotheos,* p. 171.
[41] Though Roloff is careful to distance himself from extreme expressions of this view and acknowledges the impact of Holmberg, p. 172, no 315.
[42] Roloff, *Timotheos,* p. 172.
[43] It will be recalled that we have argued for this conclusion in chapter 4.
[44] Roloff, *Timotheos,* p. 175.

of Paul's letters on such questions as who is to preside. It must be recognized, however, that this damages the idea of *charisma* as the determining factor of church leadership more than Roloff allows. As heads of families, the overseers will have brought with them to their leadership unspoken assumptions of their own fitness to lead, and those who joined them will have shared these. If the overseers enjoyed status in the church and surrounding society based at least in part on seniority and property, then their position in the church did not depend only on the functions they performed, still less on *charisma* in any sociological sense, however much Paul might want them to be seen as the fruit of God's gracious giving. People of whom this is true can rightly be described, especially from the outside and as a body, as the elders of the church.

This should lead us to question the whole notion of *Verschmelzung* to which Roloff and others subscribe. In the first place, we are always being told that the 'system' of overseers and deacons is the Pauline order as it emerged in his churches, something which others, such as the churches of the Pastorals or the Didache, could be asked to take into their system. This is a lot to build on one otherwise unexplained reference in a single Pauline letter. How do we know that the appearance of ἐπίσκοποι and διάκονοι in Philippi does not represent the adoption by a Pauline church of titles developed elsewhere? We have already seen reason to believe that the role of ἐπίσκοπος as leader of a household church stems from the earliest days of the church.

Second, Roloff speaks of 'the invasion (*das Eindringen*) of eldership into the Pauline churches'.[45] This presupposes a rather complicated history for the church of Ephesus. First, Paul founds the church without *ex hypothesi* installing elders, and apparently without appointing overseers and deacons either. Then for some reason elders 'invade' the church. Then the Pastor attempts to persuade the church to convert its elders (back?) into overseers and deacons by the curious device of having Paul tell Titus to appoint elders! We wonder

---

[45] Roloff, *Timotheos*, p. 175.

why a Pauline church did not have overseers and deacons in the first place, or how and why it lost them, and how and why this invasion of elders took place.

Merkel and Quinn avoid some of these questions by presupposing that the Pastorals are written to *Jewish*-Christian churches for the purpose of bringing them into line with the Pauline model, but in that case we may ask why these (fictitious) letters are explicitly addressed to *Pauline* churches, as Ephesus at any rate was well known to be. We may also wonder why a writer wanting to lead a church from elders to overseers should begin by saying that the purpose of the letter is that the addressee should appoint elders. Would we not expect him to lend the authority of the absent apostle to the installing of overseers, especially if, as is claimed, everyone knew that it was overseers and not elders that had been the Pauline model?

Third, we may wonder why the author needed to make such a meal of reconciling these two 'systems'. No one else seems to have had any difficulty in simply equating the two offices. Luke simply has Paul appoint elders (Acts 14:23) and then call them overseers (20:28). 1 Peter, written to churches in areas first evangelized by Paul, speaks without difficulty of elders acting as overseers (1 Pet 5:2).[46] Clement similarly uses overseer and elder interchangeably (1 Clem. 44). Elders and overseers, we may feel, did not need to be reconciled; they could simply be equated, seen to be a merely verbal distinction without a difference. The apparently clumsy alternations of singular and plural in the Pastorals, and their failure to name overseers, presbyters and deacons together on the Ignatian pattern demand an alternative solution.

A further variant is put forward by H. Merklein, who speaks of the Palestinian '*Ältesten-verfassung*' being 'superimposed'

---

[46] I follow Selwyn, Kelly, Goppelt and Michaels in accepting as authentic the longer text, reading ἐπισκοποῦντες, bracketed by UBS³ and N/A²⁶. This is the reading of the majority of MSS, including p^{72}, ℵ², A, P, Ψ, but is omitted by ℵ* and B. The likeliest explanation for its omission is that a scribe was offended by the idea of presbyters operating as bishops, while there seems no special reason why anyone should have included it in a text that lacked it.

THE ELDERS AND THE BISHOP IN THE PASTORALS

(*Überlagerung*) on the '*Episkopen-Verfassung*'. The end of the first century saw the disappearance of the first *post-apostolic* generation and this led to a crisis of confidence in which the church turned to its elders to provide authoritative tradition. Overseers were increasingly recruited from the ranks of the honoured older people with the result that,

> 'from πρεσβύτερος, which originally had been a title of honour connected with age, in the end there emerges a purely ecclesiastical title of honour, which independently of age guarantees its bearer a place of high regard in the church.[47]

There appears to be some contradiction here, since first we are told that the church turned to its older members to provide its overseers, and then that as a result the term elder lost its association with age. In other words, as the overseers got older, the elders got younger! It is difficult to see how this can be squared with the evidence of Ignatius, which would come only a few years after the development that Merklein describes, nor does he explain where the emergence of the 'monepiskopos' fits in.

None of these solutions seems fully satisfactory, because they all neglect to take seriously the household setting of the churches, and its effect on the development of the ministry. In particular, our conclusions so far have already gone some way to undermine the *Verschmelzung* idea by showing that there did not exist two opposed forms of church government needing to be reconciled. Paul, the Jew, whose ideas on church-planting had originally been developed with Jewish colleagues in Antioch, had no urge to set up a new kind of church order. From Jerusalem to Corinth, the churches were nurtured in homes, received oversight from their familial ἐπίσκοποι, who were naturally known by the collective title of πρεσβύτεροι. Is there then a better explanation for the Pastorals speaking of the various offices of church leadership in just the way they do? We shall see that there is.

[47] Merklein, *Amt*, pp. 386–7.

Overseer and Elders: A Fresh Explanation

At the close of his illuminating study of local leadership in Pauline churches, A. L. Chapple states as one of his conclusions:

> Our findings suggest that there is room for a reappraisal of the evidence of the Pastorals, to see whether it portrays a quite different situation and outlook than is evident in Paul (as the consensus view maintains), or whether it represents only a more developed version of what is evident in 1 Thessalonians; 1 Corinthians and Philippians. (as our conclusions may suggest).[48]

Exactly so! In particular it seems that the household context, which has proved so fruitful for the reinterpretation of the church in the earlier Pauline epistles has still not been allowed to play its full part in understanding the Pastorals, despite the important study by D. Verner devoted to this subject.[49]

That the *Sitz im Leben* of the Pastorals is the household church familiar to us from the earlier Paulines can be seen from the following evidence.[50] Household language and imagery are used to describe the church itself. It is the household of God (οἶκος θεοῦ, 1 Tim 3:15), the great house (μεγάλη οἰκία 2 Tim 2:20), of which the overseer can be called the steward (θεοῦ οἰκονόμος Tit 1:7). H. von Lips writes:

> The expression οἶκος θεοῦ is not merely metaphorical. Rather, the structure of the congregation is actually modelled on the underlying constitution of the household.[51]

The life of the Christian community is to be advanced by the application of a code of household relationships: Christians relate to one another as members of households, and Verner shows such codes to have influenced the terms in which the overseers and dea-

---

[48] Chapple, 'Local Leadership', p. 621.

[49] Verner, *Household.*

[50] A valuable summary of this appears in Maier, *Social Setting*, p. 44ff. He goes on to show this holds good well into the second century.

[51] von Lips, *Glaube*, p. 142.

cons are described.[52] The church of the Pastorals has comparatively wealthy people within it (1 Tim 2:9, 1 Tim 6:1–2, 9–10, 17–19), and the evidence is that the church leaders were among them. They are warned against being φιλάργυρος (1 Tim 3:3), and are called rather to be φιλόξενος (v. 2). It is widely agreed today that this does not just refer to hospitality extended to Christian travellers, but also to the hosting of the church meeting (cf. Rom 16:23).[53] They can be encouraged to aspire to leadership on the grounds that it is a καλόν ἔργον, a phrase that was also used to describe the public benefactions expected of the well-to-do.[54] One such leader is probably the figure of Onesiphorus (2 Tim 1:16–18), whom Paul commends in terms reminiscent of the commendation of Stephanas (1 Cor 16:15ff.). Onesiphorus is well-known for his service to the church at Ephesus, has the means to travel and to 'refresh' Paul, and is leader of a household, probably a house-church, that is greeted in this letter.[55] (In the light of this understanding, the widespread view that Onesiphorus' household is mentioned because he himself is dead must be seen as questionable.) In the light of this evidence, Malherbe is surely being over-cautious in saying that the Pastorals cannot be pressed to yield information on the house-church.[56]

The most significant development in the ordering of these churches in the period after the death of Paul is the emergence of a single ἐπίσκοπος over the church in a certain place. This appears to have taken place not all at once but at different times in different places. The way that Ignatius can assume that the churches of Asia Minor have 'monepiskopoi' over them is also evidence that Antioch had such an office, and it is likely that James, at the head of the Twelve, had long ago occupied this position in Jerusalem. Clement, on the other hand, makes no reference to such a person in Corinth in 96

---

[52] Verner, *Household*, pp. 91ff. Cf. von Lips, *Glaube*, p. 141: 'Die Rolle des Hausvaters/ Erziehers ist für die Gemeinde übernommen, da sie als adäquat für die Lehr - und Leitungsaufgabe angesehen wird. Sie wird von Männern übertragen, denen von Haus aus diese Rolle zukommt und die dar in bewährt sind.'
[53] White, *God's House*, pp. 103ff.
[54] Verner, *Household*, p. 151.
[55] Klauck, *Hausgemeinde*, p. 68.
[56] Malherbe, *Social*, pp. 98ff.

CE, and the silence of Hermas and of Ignatius (in his letter to the Romans) is often taken to suggest that there was no 'monepiskopos' in Rome when they wrote. But the situation of the churches of the second generation, consisting of households and led by a group of household ἐπίσκοποι known as the elders, was a situation that tended towards the emergence of a single leader. The role played by Paul himself created such an expectation. Paul wrote to his churches as a father to his children, and exercised authority among them by visit, letter and through accredited representatives.[57] When the apostle himself was no longer able to visit, or not able to visit often enough, whether because of death, imprisonment, or the sheer multiplication of churches, and the increasing complexity of their problems, the need arose for some oversight within the local churches, and for a leader to emerge among the overseers of the various house-churches (or elders). Moreover, as Dassmann has argued, the metaphorical use of the 'house of God' to describe the church would lead naturally to the thought of a head over the house.[58] We need to locate the Pastorals in relation to this development.

My proposal is that the *Pastoral Epistles are written, not to effect an amalgamation of overseers and elders, but to legitimate the authority of the new overseer.* Not so much to enable the Pauline churches to take elders into their system, or the Jewish-Christian churches to embrace overseers and deacons, but to enable them to adopt a single shepherd, with the title of ἐπίσκοπος, as leader of those who as ἐπίσκοποι in their own households were already known as the elders in relation to the local church as a whole. This will be seen to make sense of the ambiguities that we noted earlier in the various passages of the Pastorals that refer to 'the overseer', 'the deacons' and 'the elders'.

1. We have already seen reason to accept that Titus is the first of the Pastorals, either, in the case that it enjoyed individual circulation, because it describes a situation apparently less well developed than 1 Timothy, or, if the three letters were published together,

---

[57] Best, 'Authority', pp. 12ff. and *Converts*, pp. 29ff., 73ff. Holmberg, *Power*, pp. 79ff.

[58] Dassmann, 'Hausgemeinde', pp. 95f.

because its impressive introduction fits it to stand first in the collection. Assuming the second to be correct, the first passage the reader comes to is Titus 1:5–9, which speaks of the appointment of elders κατὰ πόλιν. This phrase is well-attested in contemporary literature and may mean no more than 'in all the cities' or 'from city to city', but in view of the way we have seen κατά used by Luke in the phrases κατ' οἶκον and κατ' ἐκκλησίαν I think we are justified in seeing here a reference to the level at which those appointed were to operate. When the church met κατ' οἶκον there were those who gave leadership to it, the heads of houses, like Stephanas (1 Cor 16:15), who acted as ἐπίσκοποι καὶ διάκονοι (Phil 1:1). When these men met together or were considered together κατ' ἐκκλησίαν they were known οἱ πρεσβύτεροι exactly as Luke says (Acts 14:23). Here in Titus 1:5 we find the expression κατὰ πόλιν used with πρεσβύτεροι. Now this may, of course, simply be a variant of κατ' ἐκκλησίαν, but in view of the fact that the letter immediately goes on to speak of ὁ ἐπίσκοπος (in the singular), it is tempting to think that what is going on here is the elevation of one of the πρεσβύτεροι to be ἐπίσκοπος at city level — κατὰ πόλιν. The title πρεσβύτεροι would still apply to such ἐπίσκοποι when considered collectively, just as it had to the household ἐπίσκοποι. Both κατ' οἶκον and κατὰ πόλιν, the individual leader is ὁ ἐπίσκοπος. Viewed together the several leaders are οἱ πρεσβύτεροι.

This would make sense of the situation of the churches presupposed by the letter. The writer speaks of Titus being left in Crete to 'amend what is defective'. Assuming the letter to be pseudonymous, it is reasonable to suppose that the writer had a particular need in mind, and, as this is the beginning of the body of the letter, that this is central to his purpose in writing. The need can hardly be to appoint leaders of the various household churches, since these men as heads of the various houses, senior men among the first believers, will have been there from the start. It is not conceivable that Paul will have left any church or group of churches without that most basic kind of leadership, and still less that a disciple of Paul writing a generation later will have thought such leadership to be lacking, nor, in the event that the founding of the Cretan churches is a post-Pauline development contemporaneous with the letter, that the evangelists had left behind them isolated converts but no communities. But it is conceivable that this letter will have been written in this way to legitimate the appointment of elders κατὰ πόλιν, to whom the title of ἐπίσκοπος is being given. These people will carry out the work that had previously been the responsibility of the apostle or his delegates, and by the device of addressing Titus as a model for the 'city-elders' (sc. ἐπίσκοποι) whom he is to appoint, the writer tells the new leaders what sort of people they are to be – they are to model themselves on Titus, and Paul, of course.

2. This may explain the curious way in which the further instruction on the kind of people overseers and deacons should be opens by quoting a saying to the effect that, 'If anyone aspires to the office of bishop, he desires a noble task' (1 Tim 3:1). The writer is clearly encouraging people to be willing to serve in this capacity, but, if we are right in our analysis so far, the first bearers of the title ἐπίσκοπος will hardly have been candidates for a position that came to them by virtue of being 'first-fruits' and household leaders. We can hardly imagine that anyone needed to be encouraged to aspire to be an *elder*, since being an elder is largely a matter of being recognized as what one already is. But one can see why a person might need encouragement to stand out from among the other house-leaders and elders of the church to assume the role of city ἐπίσκοπος, and why a traditional saying about public service should be thought applicable to such an aspirant, since there is to be for the first time an obvious analogy between the leadership of the church with that of the city in which it finds itself.[59]

If we read the Pastorals in the order proposed, the next place we encounter the overseer, first introduced in Titus 1, is 1 Tim 3:1–13. Accordingly he is now called 'the overseer' *tout court*, without mention of the elders to whom he belongs, and the accent falls on the kind of man he should be and the qualities he should show. His

---

[59] I think the saying is a piece of traditional wisdom, although the reading πιστός is to be preferred, ἀνθρώπινος being an attempt to make this clear. I suggest that the words πιστὸς ὁ λόγος in 1 Tim 3:1 originally referred to something else (3:16, for example), and that the pre-formed piece about the qualities of leaders has been inserted after it. See Campbell, 'Sayings', pp. 80–4.

fitness to lead the wider church is to be seen in his leadership of his own house (1 Tim 3:4–5).[60] He is to be without reproach, a person with a good reputation based on his personal life as a well-respected family man, who displays the qualities expected of such a person by pagans and Christians alike. As host to the church, he will need to be φιλόξενος; as administrator of the church's gifts, he will need to be ἀφιλάργυρος; as one who shepherds the flock with the Word, he will need to be διδάκτικος, a word which may fairly be seen to be explained by Tit 1:9: 'He must hold firm to the sure word as taught, so that he may be able to give instruction in sound doctrine, and also to confute those who contradict it.'

The list of qualities has the appearance of being a pre-formed tradition inserted into the argument at this point,[61] and I suggest that it was developed originally for the formation of those who as heads of household were called to lead the church in their house. Here it is being applied, probably with some developments, to the new overseer. Accordingly, the overseer is someone who has proved himself at household level, τοῦ ἰδίου οἴκου προϊστάμενος (1 Tim 3:4, cf. 1 Thess 5:12), but is now called to something bigger, the care of the church of God (v. 5). The 'household of God' (1 Tim 3:15) in the Pastorals is something bigger than an individual house-church, but is a development from it. Whereas in the first generation the church and the house were identical, the head of the family being the overseer of the church that met in his house, in this second generation, the local church in the town is seen as the household of God, a 'great house' (2 Tim 2:20), and the person who oversees it is seen quite naturally as the steward of God's house (Tit 1:7).

Of the διάκονοι (1 Tim 3:8–13) little needs to be or can be said, except that they are *overseer's* διάκονοι, Διάκονος like ἐπίσκοπος itself is a neutral, functional word, dependent for its content on the context. It is a word that expresses a relationship of subordination and agency on behalf of someone else.[62] We cannot assume for the

[60] Klauck, *Hausgemeinde*, p. 67.
[61] Ellis, 'Traditions', p. 245, and Dibelius/Conzelmann, *Pastorals*, p. 132.
[62] Collins, *Diakonia*, passim. Linton, *Problem*, p. 107, speaks of '*ein inhaltleeres Beziehungswort*'.

διάκονοι of the Pastorals the duties performed by deacons in the church of the next century. In default of other evidence, we should assume that a διάκονος assists his principal in whatever business he has, and this finds support in the present passage where much the same qualifications are demanded of the deacons as of the overseer.

It is disputed whether the deacons teach. On the one hand, they are not said to be διδάκτικος; on the other, they have to hold the mystery of the faith with a good conscience, which rather suggests that they did teach. What is striking is that they too appear to be householders and heads of families. Accordingly, the possibility must exist that διάκονοι is how the author of the Pastorals chooses to style those household overseers, or elders, who are *not* going to be καλῶς προεστῶτες, who will assist the overseer by continuing to lead their own household churches. If that is so, and it is only a suggestion, then we should have to say that it did not catch on. By the time of Ignatius, such people were called elders and sat with the overseer at the Table, while διάκονοι referred to those who served in humbler ways.

3. It is fully in accordance with this that when overseers as a class are in view that they should be referred to as 'the elders', as we may think they are in 1 Tim 5:17. Here we meet people called, οἱ καλῶς προεστῶτες πρεσβύτεροι ... μάλιστα οἱ κοπιῶντες ἐν λόγῳ καὶ διδασκαλίᾳ. It is theoretically possible to find here four groups of people: elders, elders who rule, elders who rule well, and elders who preach and teach, but in the first place the situation is considerably simplified if we understand the phrase about preaching and teaching as referring to and further defining the persons under discussion in the first half of the verse. This means taking the word μάλιστα expexegetically in the sense of 'that is to say' or 'I mean'. That this is possible has been shown to general satisfaction by Skeat in relation to 2 Tim 4:13,[63] but it makes good sense to understand it in this way wherever it occurs in the Pastorals,[64] as Hanson suggests.[65] The second phrase then further defines the refer-

[63] Skeat, 'Parchments', pp. 173–7.
[64] 1 Tim 4:10, 5:8, 5:17, 2 Tim 4:13; Tit 1:10.
[65] Hanson, *Pastorals*, pp. 92, 101, 175.

ent and gives the grounds on which 'double honour' is appropriate. Secondly, there is no distinction intended between those who lead and those who lead *well*, as if what was being proposed was a sort of productivity bonus. καλῶς is an echo of καλόν ἔργον (1 Tim 3:1) and belongs to the language of compliment (as 'Honourable Members' refers to all members). 'Honour' is doubly due to those who lead the church in this excellent way. We may conclude then that just one group of people is referred to in this verse. Who are they?

From what we have seen so far about the way the word 'elders' was used, the reference here might either be to the household ἐπίσκοποι, or to the new 'monepiskopoi' with whose introduction it is proposed the Pastorals are concerned. In some ways, the present context might seem to favour the first of these alternatives. The previous paragraphs have been about relationships in the household of God (as promised in 1 Tim 3:15) and there is a natural progression from discussing older men in general (5:1) and widows (5:3–16) to discussing those older men who lead the churches through their preaching and teaching. It is also in favour of this that the passage goes on to speak of the discipline and appointment of elders and could be read as instructions *to* the new ἐπίσκοπος rather than *about* him. However, in the first place there is no reason to think that at the end of the first century the overseer appointed elders at all. There is no trace of this in Ignatius,[66] and the likelihood is that on the contrary the elders appointed one of their number to be overseer,[67] the elders owing their position to their role as household leaders.[68] Secondly, the fact that the passage almost certainly concerns the stipend paid to the 'well-presiding elders' suggests that it is with the new post of ἐπίσκοπος κατὰ πόλιν that the instruction is concerned. It must be doubtful whether the ἐπίσκοποι in the primary sense of household leaders needed or received a stipend.

---

[66] *pace* Hanson, *Pastorals*, p. 33, who speaks of the Ignatian bishop ordaining clergy. But where do we find the Ignatian bishop doing any such thing? Contrast Dassmann, 'Hausgemeinde', p. 91, who brings out the essential equality of bishop and elders in Ignatius.

[67] Jay, 'Presbyter', p. 141.

[68] Dassmann, 'Hausgemeinde', pp. 88–94.

They were *ex hypothesi* well-to-do people. Patrons received loyalty from their clients, but hardly money.[69] On the other hand ἐπισκοπή in the new sense may well have been a full-time job which even a well-to-do person might hesitate to take on for nothing. I conclude that it is more likely that 1 Tim 5:17ff. refers to those who will occupy the new post of 'monepiskopos' in the various town churches.

What is demanded on behalf of these new ἐπίσκοποι is 'double honour'. Τιμή is the governing thought of the whole passage, from 5:1 to 6:2, being the ethical currency in which all relationships within the household are expressed. Just as all have a certain measure of seniority, so all are owed an appropriate measure of τιμή. Respect is to be paid to those to whom it is due (Rom 13:7). Three applications of this principle are made here: the honour and support of widows (vv. 3–16), the honour and support of leaders (vv. 17–25), and the extent to which the respect due from slave to master is modified in the household of God (6:1–2). 'Honour' is thus a flexible concept and means giving to everyone his due, including where appropriate financial honoraria.

The meaning of 'double honour' can be understood against this background. It seems plain that finance is involved, first because it clearly is in the case of widows (v. 3), and second because of the citations in verse 18 that are used to support the giving of this double honour. The maxim about the threshing ox had already been used in this sense by Paul (1 Cor 9:9), while the second appears to be a reference to the teaching of Jesus to which Paul also alludes (1 Cor 9:14). But it is surely unnecessary, as it seems inherently implausible, to suppose with Kelly that all elders receive something and presiding elders receive double the amount; or with Jeremias that all older people received some sort of dole, the overseers receiving twice as much. The latter suggestion is surely ruled out by the requirement that only needy widows should be supported. 'Double honour' need not be understood arithmetically. Rather the letter directs that while all elders should be honoured, the new overseers who are giving their time (κοπιῶντες) to preaching and

[69] On Gal 6:6, see Kirk, 'Salary', p. 106.

teaching are *doubly worthy* of honour, receiving not only obedience but financial support.

Before leaving the Pastorals, we may take note once again of the very different view of the development of church office taken by J. T. Butchaell in his book, *From Synagogue to Church*. Rather than seeking to account for the emergence of a 'monepiskopos' and relate the Pastorals to this development, Burtchaell maintains there was always such a person in the local church, only he was eclipsed by the prominence of 'charismatics'. Burtchaell bases this conclusion on the belief that the earliest churches were breakaway synagogues, which replicated all the offices of the synagogue from the start. This he regards as 'an antecedent likelihood'.[70] The ἐπίσκοπος is thus the Christian ἀρχισυνάγωγος, whom Burtchaell calls 'the Community Leader'.[71]

There are two problems with this view. In the first place, Burtchaell never really addresses the problem of the relationship of the overseer and elders in the Pastorals which suggests that, except in Jerusalem, the position of 'monepiskopos' emerged *later*. As we have already said, he places too much reliance instead on the Didache, and on a particular interpretation of its evidence, to which we shall return in the next chapter.

More fundamentally, Burtchaell neglects the household setting of the churches, which our sources attest, in favour of a synagogue pattern, of which our sources say nothing. Although he refers from time to time to the churches meeting in houses, he seems to have in mind only the physical setting that the houses provided for the churches, rather than the community structure provided by the household.

It might be thought that if the churches and synagogues both originated in private houses, as it appears they did, that their development would be similar and that it is legitimate to transfer to the account of the churches the various officers found in the synagogues. This neglects an important difference. The synagogues were older and more developed than the churches. Burtchaell's list of synagogue officers is taken from Frey's *Corpus Inscriptionum Judaicarum*, and this evidence, as well as being entirely epigraphic, is also for the most part later by some centuries than the period of

[70] Burtchaell, *Synagogue*, p. 274.
[71] Burtchaell, *Synagogue*, p. 283.

earliest Christianity. When a community is able to put up expensive inscriptions to honour its dead it has moved a long way from its household origins. Even in Judaea at the time of the New Testament, the synagogues have been there some time, enjoy official recognition, and have the opportunity of constructing buildings. It is unlikely that the whole elaborate pattern of office and honour on which Burtchaell relies would have been appropriate to the earliest Christians, or even at that time available for their imitation.

Conclusions

We may think of the development of the leadership of the church in three stages, designated respectively as κατ' οἶκον, κατ' ἐκκλησίαν, and κατὰ πόλιν. At the first stage, when the apostle is still exercising oversight, and the numbers of believers and households are small, the local leaders are called, at least by some people in some places, ἐπίσκοποι. At the second stage, where the households are multiplying and the various household leaders are having to act collectively, they are called πρεσβύτεροι. While at the third stage, with the churches bereft of apostolic oversight and threatened with disunity and dissent, ἐπίσκοπος comes to refer to the overall leader of a group of house-churches in a town. The diagram opposite may make clear my meaning.

To put it another way, the words ἐπίσκοποι and πρεσβύτεροι are flexible with changing referents during our period. Ἐπίσκοπος first refers to the leader of a house-church, but then to the leader of a town-church. οἱ πρεσβύτεροι is first a way of referring to the house-church leaders considered together and acting corporately, but then denotes those leaders in the town-church who are precisely *not* the overseer or bishop. This is fully in accordance with the way the word behaves in its Greek and Jewish background where we have seen that it is an imprecise term of honour rather than the title of any specific office.[72]

---

[72] Recalling Linton's description of διάκονος as 'ein inhaltleeres Beziehungswort', we might perhaps term πρεσβύτερος as 'ein inhaltleeres Verehrungswort'!

Stage 1 κατ' οἶκον	Stage 2 κατ' ἐκκλησίαν	Stage 3 κατὰ πόλιν
e.g. 1 Thess 1 Cor	Acts 13:1–3 Acts 20:17ff.	Pastorals Ignatius
ἐπίσκοπος = house-church leader	ἐπίσκοποι = house-church leaders	ἐπίσκοπος = town-church leader
few households	households multiply to pull apart	households tending
apostle able to input	apostle less able to input	apostle in prison or dead
no one called πρεσβύτεροι collectively	πρεσβύτεροι denotes leaders acting *under* ἐπίσκοπος	πρεσβ. denotes house-leaders

Appendix to Chapter Six
The Elders in the Rest of the New Testament

Nothing in the non-Pauline letters of the New Testament contradicts any of these conclusions, though one must admit that the references are either so brief or unclear that they could probably be made to agree with any scheme arrived at independently of them. It is almost impossible to say anything very definite about the elders in James (Jas 5:14), since the letter has no interest in church structures or offices. The elders are envisaged as able to assemble together at the house of the sick person and at his invitation. This suggests that they all live in one town or belong to one church. They may simply be the sort of senior men mentioned in 1 Tim 5:1, or they may be the leaders of the various house-churches, the various ἐπίσκοποι, who are collectively οἱ πρεσβύτεροι, and who are to act together in response to a serious threat to the life of one of the members.

The elders in 1 Peter are clearly at least older men, since they are contrasted with νεώτεροι, but they are also leaders and office-holders, since each has a κλῆρος to look after. Efforts have been made to show that νεώτεροι refers either to deacons,[73] or the newly baptized,[74] but it seems best to see the word as referring simply to those who were not elders, that is to say all the other church members.[75] The κλήροι are best interpreted by reference to the flock of God. The duties of these leaders are entirely expressed in terms of the shepherd metaphor, which, as we have seen, originates in the Old Testament and is found in CD 13, Acts 20:28, and Ephesians 4:11

---

[73] Stählin, *Apostelgeschichte*, p. 84, referring to Acts 5:6.
[74] Elliott, 'Ministry', p. 379ff.
[75] Michaels, *1 Peter*, p. 288f.; Goppelt, *Petrusbrief*, p. 330f.; Davids, *1 Peter*, p. 183.

before becoming quite general in early Christian literature. The qualities demanded of them agree closely with the requirements for the overseer in the Pastorals. If this is a picture of the whole church, then the κλῆροι will be the individual congregations over which the elders preside, the lot being a metaphor to express the idea of divine appointment. On the other hand, since the letter is being sent to a number of different churches, the elders may be the 'monepiskopoi' of those scattered churches, once again quite naturally styled by the collective term 'elders'. We can hardly say more without knowing the date and authorship of the letter.

If we believe that the letter is by Peter himself, and so written not later than the mid-60s, then we shall probably see the elders as leaders of house-churches within their respective local churches. Peter, in that case, presumably calls himself a 'fellow-elder' as a way of identifying himself with those to whom he writes. If however we think that Peter is not the author, and that the letter belongs to the post-apostolic generation (as I suppose), being contemporary with the Pastorals, then we should probably see the elders as the sort of town-overseers as we have seen in Titus 1:5–9, and that one of their number has assumed the authority of Peter to address them. It is then likely, but not capable of proof, that the writer is himself the 'monepiskopos' of his church, who for the same reasons of courtesy, wishes to identify himself with those to whom he writes. The opening greeting in Polycarp's letter to the Philippians provides a possible parallel: 'Polycarp and the elders with him.'

When we turn to the Johannine Epistles we find the same distinction between older and younger believers as in 1 Peter. John addresses the older men as 'fathers', in contrast to the 'young men', and refers surely to the elders of the church (1 John 2:13f.).[76] But then the Greeting of 2 and 3 John presents us with the most puzzling use of πρεσβύτερος in the New Testament: 'The Elder to the Elect Lady ...', 'The Elder to the beloved Gaius ...'. As we have

---

[76] I take it that 'little children' refers to all believers, and that they are then divided into two groups, as in 1 Peter 5, 'fathers' and 'young men'. So Talbert, *Reading John*, p. 24.

seen, the term is nearly always used in the plural, and for an individual either to be given, or claim, the title, 'The Elder', breaks all the rules! Judith Lieu says that the expression 'has yet to find a satisfactory explanation',[77] and reaches no conclusion. R. E. Brown lists five possible solutions.[78] If we discount the idea that the term is here a nickname, or term of affection, these five break down into two kinds of answer: those which see it as the title of an office, and those who see it as a claim to authoritative tradition, whether of an apostle, a disciple of the apostles or a second generation witness. It is impossible to be certain, but perhaps the first has been too quickly dismissed by Brown and Lieu.

It is objected that, if he is merely *an* elder, why does he call himself *the* elder? If he is the overseer, why does he call himself the elder? And why does he address another church? However, when we remember the flexible nature of the term 'elder', which could often refer to those who held other offices or were known by more precise titles, it seems to me there is no problem in an overseer calling himself an elder. The author of 1 Peter effectively does this, as we have seen. So long as we think of him addressing a church in another town in the manner of a diocesan bishop, or metropolitan, this is bound to seem inappropriate or anachronistic. But if 'The Elect Lady' is *his own church*, of which perhaps Diotrephes, and even Gaius and Demetrius, are household leaders, then it seems quite possible that the writer is indeed the 'monepiskopos', and that he adopts this style for the same reason that Peter calls himself your 'fellow elder'. If so, the Johannine letters and 1 Peter provide us with the first examples of the change which the Pastorals were written to effect.

Finally, and for the sake of completeness, it remains to say a word about the twenty-four elders in the Book of Revelation (Rev. 4:4). Commentaries on Revelation discuss who these figures are, and what they symbolize. Are they angels,[79] or the saints of the Old Testament,[80]

---

[77] Lieu, *Letters*, p. 52.
[78] Brown, *Epistles*, pp. 648–51.
[79] Beasley-Murray, *Revelation*, p. 114.
[80] Prigent, *L'Apocalypse*, p. 84.

or do they symbolize the patriarchs and apostles?[81] It is not necessary here to pursue these questions. The question for us is why they are called 'elders' at all. It is an old and attractive suggestion that John has pictured the heavenly worship in terms of the earthly worship familiar to his readers, so that the heavenly elders sit around the throne of God as the earthly elders sat with the overseer at the Eucharist. It is probably safer to say simply that kings, high priests, and overseers tended to have about them a cluster of distinguished persons, for whom 'the elders' was a readily available term of honour, and John, in picturing the heavenly throne room, has furnished it in the traditional manner.

Much more might be said about these passages. What is offered here consists of no more than suggestions, for the purpose of showing what the proposed solution for the problems of the Pastorals might look like when applied to the problems of other nearly contemporary documents.

[81] Caird, *Revelation*, p. 63.

Chapter Seven
Beyond the New Testament

The most important development in the leadership of the churches in the post-apostolic generation (60–90 CE) was the emergence of monepiscopacy, such as we find later in the letters of Ignatius. In the previous chapter, it was argued that the Pastorals stand at the beginning of this development, being themselves written to promote it in the Pauline churches. While the letters ascribed to Peter and John can best be understood to presuppose an early form of monepiscopacy, written by those who were conscious of their authority as the leaders of their churches following the deaths of their apostles.

Certainty in these matters is, of course, impossible, because the documents themselves cannot be precisely dated, nor their addressees identified. There is, then, always a danger of circular argument: the letters are dated by reference to a pattern of development that itself rests in part on the dates assigned to the letters. No reconstruction therefore can be better than plausible.

The plausibility of the present reconstruction will in part depend on how well it agrees with the evidence provided by the earliest documents outside the New Testament canon, and how much light it throws on the problems they raise. In particular, we need to ask how far our understanding of the elders in the New Testament agrees with the later development of the office of presbyter, and explains the later history of that word. Accordingly, this chapter will begin by looking at the two most important sources of information from beyond the New Testament, 1 Clement and the letters of Ignatius, before sketching the later development of the presbyterate.

Clement of Rome

The letter from the church at Rome to the church at Corinth, known as 1 Clement, is usually dated to 96 CE, though the arguments for such a precise date are extremely weak.[1] It was written in response to a crisis in the church at Corinth caused by the removal from office of certain elders (44:6). Exactly what has happened and why has always been unclear, and we shall return to it. Meanwhile, we note that Clement writes to secure their reinstatement and to restore the unity and good order of the church. For this purpose, he draws on traditional ideas of respect owed by the young to the old and by the led to the leaders, and it is plain that for Clement the two largely overlap. He recalls their former good order when they 'walked in the laws of God, obedient to your rulers, and paying all fitting honour to the older among you' (1:3), and castigates their present unrest.

> Thus the worthless rose up against those who were in honour, those of no reputation against the renowned, the foolish against the prudent, the young against the old' (3:3)

For Clement, good order means respecting those who rule us, honouring the older ones, instructing the young in the fear of God and leading our wives to that which is good (21:6). At the end of the letter, he gives a description of the delegation sent by the church at Rome that serves as a picture of what it means to be an elder in the church:

> We have sent faithful and prudent men, who have lived among us without blame from youth to old age. (63:3)

---

[1] The case rests on two planks: the belief that the phrase διὰ τὰς αἰφιδνίους καὶ ἐπαλλήλους γενομένας ἡμῖν συμπορὰς καὶ περιπτώσεις (1 Clem 1:1) refers to persecution; and the acceptance of the tradition preserved by Tertullian and Eusebius that there was a persecution of the church by Domitian, with which these words are then identified. This interpretation has become traditional since Lightfoot (*AF*, I.1, pp. 346–58), but Welborn ('Date', pp. 35–54) points out that the words of 1 Clem 1:1 are extremely vague, that the tradition of Domitian's persecution is widely doubted, and that 1 Clement conforms to the type of ancient letters written to promote harmony and concord, which regularly began with a reference to the author's difficulties as an excuse for not writing earlier.

In all of this, Clement faithfully reflects the traditional values and attitudes regarding age and respect which we have seen in his contemporary, Plutarch.[2]

Church leaders are described by Clement as being appointed by 'other eminent men, with the consent of the whole church' (44:3, cf. 57:2).[3] The phrase ἐλλόγιμοι ἄνδρες exactly describes the kind of people 'elders' were held to be, and the kind of people who became leaders of churches. The process by which Clement says they were appointed is that which Linton describes as 'a non-egalitarian, legislative assembly',[4] in which the members as a whole follow what the ἐλλόγιμοι propose. Such ἐλλόγιμοι are not merely eminent in faith or in terms of church office, but are most probably eminent through their social position and age as well. As H.O. Maier says:

> It is plausible to assume a situation in 1 Clement in which Christians meet in the homes of well-to-do leaders.[5]

Church leaders are variously called by Clement οἱ ἡγούμενοι (1:3), οἱ προηγούμενοι (21:6), and οἱ ἐπίσκοποι (42:4). He also refers to οἱ καθεσταμένοι πρεσβύτεροι — 'appointed elders' (54:2). From the way in which Clement can talk about rejecting πρεσβύτεροι from the ἐπισκόπη (44:4–5), it seems plain that he equates elders and overseers and draws no clear distinction between them. This is usually taken as evidence that there is *as yet* no distinction in Corinth and/or in Rome, but it may simply be, as we shall see, that it does not suit Clement to recognize a distinction. Clement knows that Paul had appointed leaders from among his first converts (ἀπαρχαί 42:4. Cf. 1 Cor 16:15). He further claims

---

[2] See above chapter 3, p. 77–79, 86.

[3] Dix, 'Ministry', pp. 253–63, argues that 'eminent men' refer to 'apostolic men', but Jay, 'Presbyter', pp. 133–5, follows Lightfoot in preferring a more general reference, and I agree. Whether or not the 'other eminent men' are other than the apostles or other than the first generation of 'presbyter-bishops', ἐλλόγιμος will not bear Dix's special interpretation of 'apostolic'. It is something of a favourite with Clement, being used by him at 57:2, 58:2, and 62:3 as a term of honour, not to say mild flattery.

[4] 'eine beschliessende ungleichmässige Versammlung', Linton, *Problem*, p. 189f.

[5] Maier, *Social Setting*, p. 93; Countryman, *Rich Christian*, p. 167.

apostolic authority for the succession of 'other approved men' when the first generation of leaders died (Cf. 2 Tim 2:2). Whether or not the apostles made this provision, there is no reason to doubt that Clement is referring to what actually happened — other approved men did succeed them.

What we do not find in 1 Clement is any recognition of a single bishop in overall charge of the church. Again, this may simply be because there was no such person, and that the development envisaged by the Pastorals is not yet known in Corinth (or presumably in Rome). But there may be more to it than that. The exact cause of the dispute in Corinth is never made clear and has been the source of a good deal of speculation. G. E. Bowe has suggested the arrival in Corinth of visiting itinerant missionaries claiming superior spiritual status,[6] but there does not seem to be any evidence that the dispute was about doctrines or ideas, whether charismatic or Gnostic. Maier prefers to think that the problem concerns,

> a division within one or two of the Corinthian house-churches which has resulted in the creation of an alternative meeting place, the exodus of members who are sympathetic with these persons and, presumably, the exclusion of members who are opposed to them.[7]

This has in its favour the references to the proper *place* for worship to be offered (40:2, 41:2), but Clement does not seem to follow up this point and for the most part presents the dispute very much in terms of the removal of *leaders*.

More convincing is the suggestion of R. M. Grant that the situation involved, 'a presbyter-bishop who achieved some sort of primacy only by deposing other presbyter-bishops'.[8] This agrees with the way Clement in 53:4 appeals to the example of Moses, who prayed that he himself might be blotted out of God's book if only the people as a whole might be spared, as the basis for urging some person, presumably a leader, to accept voluntary exile for the sake of the community.

Who then among you is noble, who is compassionate, who is

---

[6] Bowe, *Crisis*, p. 153.
[7] Maier, *Social Setting*, p. 93.
[8] Grant, *Fathers*, p. 164.

filled with love? Let him cry: 'If sedition and strife and divisions have arisen on my account, I will depart, I will go away whithersoever you will, and I will obey the commands of the people; only let the flock of Christ have peace with the presbyters set over it.' (54:1–2)

If the dispute, in fact, centres on one man, whom Clement for reasons for delicacy avoids naming, it begins to look very much as if the problem has less to do with a group of 'young Turks', or an ungovernable church meeting, and more to do with an attempt to introduce monepiscopacy in the manner recommended by the pastorals! The bishop has sought to be more than a chairman of the presbyters, and has sought to centralize the worship of the church under his own presidency in the way later to be advocated by Ignatius. The result is the *de facto* demotion of the other presbyters, who have until now led the churches in their own homes, and perhaps shared in the leading of any meetings the church has had all together. Now they are reduced to sitting with the bishop in the one meeting, and are forbidden to hold their own meetings. This could conceivably have been represented, either by them or by Clement, as removing the elders from their office (ἐπισκοπή, 44:4) and being disloyal to the presbyters (47:6).

This, as Grant says, would explain why Clement does not follow through his analogy of Christian ministry with Old Testament orders (40:5) by comparing the high priest to the bishop. It also does justice to Clement's remark that the apostles knew that there would be 'strife for the title of bishop' (44:1), which would be an odd phrase if the dispute was about replacing one group of elders by another, but perfectly appropriate if the dispute was about how many people should bear the title of ἐπίσκοπος. Clement might still present it in terms of a failure to give due respect to those who are the elders, but the dispute is really about episcopacy and its relationship to the elders. Clement wants to preserve the identification of elders and overseers that he knows belongs to the time of the apostles (as indeed we have seen that it did), but some unnamed person has sought to promote his own episcopacy at the expense of the other house-church ἐπίσκοποι.

214

This seems more likely than the view put forward by L.W. Countryman, which in other respects has much to commend it.[9] Countryman notes the churches' indebtedness to their wealthy members, who provided places for the church to meet, places to bury their dead, and much of the money needed to sustain the churches' charitable work. In the early days this led to the churches' leaders being the very people who thus opened their homes, as we see from the case of Stephanas (1 Cor 16:15ff.) and the qualifications for the bishop in the Pastorals (1 Tim 3:1–7), and the same pattern continued into the second century when many of the bishops known to us by name appear to have been people of status and means.[10] As the churches grew in size, however, it would obviously be impossible for all well-to-do people to be leaders, with the result that there were an increasing number of wealthy people in the churches who found themselves disappointed of the kind of rewards for committed membership that were normally enjoyed by such people in clubs and societies of the time. From this rich potential for conflict, Countryman argues, comes the churches' ambiguous attitude towards the rich. They needed them, yet increasingly feared them, while the rich either threw their weight around or withdrew into heresy or apathy. He suggests that this helps to explain the problem at Corinth. The troublemakers are rich believers who have refused to accept the authority of the churches' leaders.

That the strains and tensions at Corinth arise from the disappointment of socially powerful people seems to me very likely, but we may think that Countryman is wrong about the identity of the elders. He calls them 'the clergy', and thinks Clement is writing to defend them against the insurrection of wealthy members. However, it is misleading to speak at this stage of 'clergy', and to think of the elders as clerical. On the contrary, the elders who have been ousted are not the victims of the well-to-do; they *are* the well-to-do, who have been robbed of their former status and influence by the advent of a bishop who is centralizing power in the church, presum-

---

[9] Countryman, 'Patrons', pp. 135–43, and *Rich Christian*, pp. 149–82.
[10] Countryman, *Rich Christian*, p. 181, n. 43.

ably with the support of a majority of the members, which is why Clement can speak of *the church* rising up against its elders 'for the sake of one or two persons' (47:6). If this is right, Clement would not be so much on the side of the 'clergy' against the wealthy, but on the side of the wealthy against a much more restricted leadership that has robbed them, not just of the influence they might have expected, but of the influence they actually used to enjoy as leaders of their own house-churches.

All attempts to identify the cause of the trouble in 1 Clement must, of course, be somewhat speculative, but that the problem is fundamentally social rather than doctrinal seems extremely likely, and Countryman's picture of the frustration of the well-to-do person excluded from the church's leadership is convincing. If, in addition, we remember the household basis of the churches up to this time, and see that the elders as house-leaders were among these well-to-do people, it does not require much imagination to see that the elevation of one of their number to be bishop could not be without loss of independence and status for others. To present the advent of monepiscopacy as simply a step taken by the elders for their own convenience (providing the group with a chairman, for example) is unrealistic. Clement calls these house-church leaders 'the elders', both because, as we have seen, it was a natural way of referring to leaders collectively, and because it enables him to present their deposition as an act of impiety, a denial of honour to those to whom by definition honour was due.

Ignatius of Antioch

Ignatius went to his martyrdom in the reign of Trajan, between 98 and 117 CE. It is not possible to be more precise, but there is a consensus from Lightfoot,[11] to Koester,[12] that places the date of the letters around the year 110 CE, perhaps as much as twenty years after Clement. These letters are the first Christian documents to

[11] Lightfoot, *AF*, II.1, p. 30.
[12] Koester, *Introduction*, Vol. 2, p. 281.

name overseer and elders together in a way that clearly distinguishes them. Earlier writers either refer only to overseers and deacons but not elders (Did 15:1–2; 1 Tim 3:1–13), or move between the terms overseer(s) and elders in a way that appears to equate them (Acts 20; Tit 1:5–9; 1 Pet 5:1–5; 1 Clem 44).

As is well known, Ignatius repeatedly calls for obedience to the overseer, the elders and the deacons, yet makes clear the overseer's supremacy. We should, however, be cautious about speaking of a 'threefold order' in the churches of Asia Minor in Ignatius' day. In the first place, it has often been remarked that the very strength with which Ignatius has to insist on the supremacy of the bishop suggests that others did not share his view and may not have been conforming to his expectations. In the second place, simply because Ignatius provided the terms in which the church of later centuries defined its ministry and order it is easy for us to read into Ignatius the situation of later times. In fact, Ignatius' true interest is not so much a 'threefold order' as the supremacy of the bishop. Most modern interpreters have shared Ignatius' interest in bishops and have been inclined to accept Ignatius' portrayal of church order as a simple description of how things were. Remembering the social status and importance of the elders within the church hitherto, we need to ask what Ignatius' prescription means for them. When we do, we shall notice the curious fact that Ignatius mentions the elders so frequently, yet says so little about them.

Ignatius is a man facing a crisis, not simply the obvious crisis of his own impending martyrdom, but a crisis in the church. Although the details are not clear to us, it seems to have taken the form of the spread of what Ignatius saw as false teaching. Whether this teaching was one error or two need not detain us here, but it appears to have been promoted by Jewish Christians,[13] or by Christians who appealed to the Old Testament and perhaps employed a sophisticated

---

[13] See especially Mag, 8–10; Philad 5–9. There is a good case for maintaining that this was the source of the problems encountered by the authors of Col., Eph., and the Pastorals also, what Goulder has called a Jewish-Christian counter-mission ('Visionaries', p. 17).

interpretation of it (Philad 8:2), and the effect in the opinion of Ignatius was to deny the real incarnation of Christ.

It also divided the church, or accentuated the divisions already implicit in the churches' household structure. There is no direct mention in Ignatius' letters of household meetings, but we do hear of people who refuse to meet with the rest of the church (Eph 5:2–3; Smyrn 7:1), whereas Ignatius is concerned to promote the claims of meetings under the leadership of the bishop or of those he appoints (Smyrn 8:1). Maier has persuasively argued that the social setting underlying these references is similar to that of the Johannine letters (2 John 10, 3 John 5–10). The church still meets in and consists of separate households, whose leaders are people of independence and importance, able to receive or refuse those who come as representatives of other churches and to hold their own meetings if they wish. There is a hint of a rival leader at Smyrna (Smyrn 6:1). The only Ignatian bishop about whom we have any personal details is Polycarp, and he appears to have been a person who owned slaves and farms (Mart Pol 6:1, cf Pol 4:3).[14]

It is in this context that the things Ignatius says about the bishop are to be understood. He is not arguing a case for episcopacy on theoretical grounds. True, he claims such a system of government obtains throughout the world (Eph 3:2), so that to be a church at all is to have a bishop, elders and deacons (Trall 3:1), but what matters is the unity of the church. This will best be secured by everybody being subject to the bishop and elders (Eph 2:2). In an orderly church, the elders are in tune with the bishop like the strings of a harp and the congregation sings in tune with it so as to render fitting praise to God (Eph 4:1–2). The possibility that the bishop might himself be captivated by the new teaching does not arise for Ignatius, because it is the authority of the bishop that he writes to uphold, and so he insists that even if the bishop is young (Mag 3;1), or silent, having little to say in argument perhaps (Eph 6:1, Philad 1:1),[15] as president he stands in the place of God (Mag

[14] Maier, *Social Setting*, pp. 147–56.

[15] Schoedel, *Ignatius*, p. 56. Michael Goulder has suggested to me in conversation that it is the household setting that explains why the church should have a young or inarticu-

6:1), so that it is nonsensical to profess devotion to God while separating oneself from his representative. Ignatius appeals to the universally prized virtue of unity as a way of legitimating the authority of the bishop.

We gain some idea of the work of a bishop from the letter of Ignatius to Polycarp. Here the accent is not so much on the power and authority of the bishop as on the cost of his leadership and the hard work and difficulty it will involve. Ignatius urges him to work hard (Pol 1:1–3). Not all his members will co-operate: some will be λοιμότεροι (2:1). There will be opposition and false teaching to be encountered, and Polycarp will need the qualities of the doctor and the athlete, gentleness, resourcefulness and steadfastness (2:1, 3:1). Like Solomon he should ask for wisdom (1:3), and rely not on his wits but on the *charisma* of spiritual insight (2:2). If we ask what it is that Polycarp is actually to do, as opposed to what he is to be, Ignatius tells us even less than the Pastorals, but the accent is clearly on teaching, πάντας παρακαλεῖν, ἵνα σώζωνται (1:2. Cf. 1 Tim 4:16), a phrase that aptly sums up most of what Ignatius says to him. Beside that he is to be leader of the community. He must see that the widows are not neglected (4;1), he is to hold meetings (more frequently), initiate business (7:2), and let nothing happen without his knowledge and approval, not even the marriages of believers (5:2). These instructions would suit a situation where Ignatius wants the bishops to centralize church activities around their own leadership, but where this is likely to encounter resistance from people who are used to enjoying their own independence.

Polycarp, then, and his fellow bishops are to be teachers and leaders of their communities. They are in fact pastors; are they also priests? If by a priest we mean someone who makes offerings on behalf of others, then the answer must be negative. In particular there is no evidence that Ignatius regarded the Eucharist as something that the bishop offered. From the numerous references to it, it is clear that Ignatius regarded the Eucharist as central to the life and

---

late bishop in the first place: the young man has succeeded his father as head of the house where the church meets, and as such is *ex officio* the leader, even though more powerful people are present in the meeting.

worship of the church, and he is insistent that it must not take place apart from the bishop or one whom he appoints, but that is because the bishop's presence guarantees unity, not because there is something about the Eucharist that only a bishop can effect, or some spiritual endowment that only the bishop has. What is wrong with a Eucharist or Agape when the bishop is absent is that it represents division in the church. It is noteworthy that Ignatius uses no word for the bishop's activity in the Eucharist, such as 'celebrating' or 'offering'.

ἐκείνη βεβαία εὐχαριστία ἡγείσθω, ἡ ὑπὸ ἐπίσκοπον οὖσα (let that Eucharist be considered valid which takes place under the presidency of the bishop) (Smyrn 8:1)

The Eucharist is 'under' the bishop, that is he presides, and all that matters is his legitimating presence rather than anything that he contributes to the proceedings.

A contrary view might seem to be suggested by Ignatius' use of the word θυσιαστήριον (Eph 5:2; Mag 7:2; Trall 7:2; Philad 4). It might be thought that the use of a word taken from the vocabulary of sacrificial worship shows that for Ignatius the Eucharist is seen as a sacrifice which the bishop offers. It is doubtful whether this idea is really present. In the Ephesian passage, Ignatius is arguing for the importance of unity expressed in meeting together, and he supports it with a fourfold appeal to Scripture and common knowledge. There is an allusion to Jesus' words about the power of the prayer of the one or two together, to the Old Testament maxim that God resists the proud and to the well-known principle that to accept or reject the servant is to accept or reject the master. In such a context, it is likely that the θυσιαστήριον is not a Christian altar but the Jewish altar. Ignatius is doing what Paul also does, using the analogy of the Jewish altar to draw not so much a liturgical as a common-sense conclusion (1 Cor 9:13, 10:18). The words, ἐὰν μή τις ᾖ ἐντὸς τοῦ θυσιαστηρίου, ὑστερεῖται τοῦ ἄρτου τοῦ θεοῦ, (if anyone is not within the altar, he lacks the bread of God) look like an appeal to a truth considered self-evident; those who separate themselves from the sacrifice do not partake in whatever material or spiritual blessing is deemed to flow from it. The same is true in Trall 7:2. A comparison is being drawn between a state of affairs known to hold in the world of Judaism ('He who is within the altar is pure ...'), and the situation in the church as Ignatius sees it ('He who acts without the bishop, eldership or deacons is not pure in his conscience').[16] Accordingly, it seems doubtful whether Ignatius sees the bishop as a priest. Rather he is using the well-known and respected model of the Old Testament cultus to argue for unity in submission to the bishop. What we *can* say is that here, as in 1 Clem 40:5, Old Testament language is being used which will quickly lead to such a view of the bishop's ministry.

The elders are frequently mentioned by Ignatius, always in close association with the bishop. In fact, Ignatius hardly ever calls for submission to the bishop without at the same time adding a reference to the elders and usually the deacons too. Yet while one or two deacons are mentioned by name in the letters, so that we get some idea of their activity as envoys of the churches and helpers of the bishop, the elders remain faceless and we get no idea from Ignatius of their duties. Ignatius speaks either of elders in the plural or of τὸ πρεσβυτέριον (Eph 2:2, 20:2). They are regularly compared to or associated with the apostles in those places where Ignatius calls for obedience to the bishop as to God himself (Mag 6:1; Trall 3:1; Smyrn 8:1), but this is more likely to be a compliment than any indication of their present responsibilities.[17] They apparently sit at the front together with the bishop (Mag 6:2), and the description of them as 'an aptly woven spiritual crown' also probably refers to their sitting with the bishop at the Table in the Eucharist, and is clearly intended to flatter them.

So, on the one hand, Ignatius pays the elders compliments and honours, and on the other gives them nothing to do. It is a reasonable conclusion that, while Ignatius' interest is all in promoting the office of the bishop, the elders are too important to be ignored.

[16] Only in *Philad* 4 is θυσιαστήριον closely connected with the Eucharist so as to suggest that Ignatius is thinking of a Christian altar, but Schoedel comments: 'This must remain doubtful in the light of the symbolic use of the word "altar" elsewhere in the letters.' (*Ignatius*, p. 199).

[17] Contra Jay who thinks it implies that they carried out apostolic tasks of evangelism, preaching and teaching ('Presbyter', p. 138).

This would fit well with our reconstruction of events. The elders are people of considerable prestige, senior men, well-to-do, leaders of house-churches of which each has been ὁ ἐπίσκοπος. Recently, the attempt has been made to gain greater order and coherence in the churches by appointing one of their number to be leader of the whole church in the town and to give him the title of ὁ ἐπίσκοπος. The relationship of this person to the other elders is bound to be difficult, for if he is to lead them, they must have a large hand in electing him. From the earliest times, it has been difficult to control the activities of such men and to monitor the teachers they receive, as we see from Paul's Corinthian correspondence, from the Pastorals and from the Johannine letters. Now Ignatius is seeking to curb their cherished independence and persuade them to give up a role that enjoys considerable status and the leading of the Eucharist in their own homes, in exchange for a seat on the platform and the possibility of leading a Eucharist when appointed to this by the bishop (Smyrn 8:1). It is for this reason, we may think, that he loses no opportunity to affirm the authority of the elders – to offset the fact that he is actually diminishing it!

It is for the same reason, we may think, that three writers of the period, all arguably bishops themselves, seek to disguise their superior position by merging themselves among the elders over whom they have been elevated. The writer of 1 Peter calls himself συμπρεσβύτερος when addressing the πρεσβύτεροι, even though he is clearly in a position to tell them what to do. Polycarp writes to the church in Philippi styling himself, 'Polycarp and the Elders with him' (Phil 1:1), which look like the words of a man anxious to minimize a difference which was nevertheless real, and, as we have seen, this may well be the best explanation of the way in which the author of 3 John calls himself 'The Elder'. Writing as the leader of the church, the Elder plays down his recently created office by using a word which associates him with other house-church leaders.

Hermas and the Didache

Two other early Christian texts deserve to be mentioned at this point, although they are difficult to use as evidence because, even more than is the case with Clement and Ignatius, their date is very uncertain and their references to leaders tantalizingly vague. Rather than claim that they provide additional evidence for our reconstruction, it will be sufficient to show how they can be fitted into it without straining credulity.

The *Shepherd of Hermas* is usually dated to the middle of the second century,[18] but Maier has recently argued that it is a good deal earlier.[19] In the first place it speaks of sending a copy to Clement (Vis 2.4.3), who was generally thought to be the same Clement as the author of 1 Clement, who wrote before the end of the first century. Secondly, as we shall see, the church order in *Hermas* appears to be very primitive with no trace of a *monepiskopos*. Thirdly, there is a reference to:

> apostles, and bishops and teachers and deacons who walked according to the majesty of God, and served the elect of God in holiness and reverence as bishops and teachers and deacons; some of them are fallen asleep and some are still alive (Vis 3.5.1).

The natural meaning of this is that *Hermas* was written when some representatives of the first Christian generation are still living.

The problem with inferring an early date for *Hermas* is the testimony of the Muratorian Canon, according to which Hermas wrote the Shepherd 'recently – *nuperrime*' in Rome while Pius was bishop there, that is to say, between 139 and 154 CE. The usual solution has been to accept the testimony of the Canon and to postulate for *Hermas* a long period of composition and/or multiple authors.[20] Maier by contrast has shown that *Hermas* makes sense as a unified document concerned with the problems of wealth and worldliness, and that it is the evidence of the Muratorian Canon that needs re-evaluation. He suggests that *nuperrime* may mean not 'recently' in the sense of 'not long before the author's time', but 'most recently'

---

[18] Brox, *Hirt*, p. 25f. not without hesitation.
[19] Maier, *Social Setting*, pp. 55–8.
[20] Metzger, *Canon*, p. 63–4.

THE ELDERS

in relation to the other Christian writings just described. *Hermas* is thus said to be later than the New Testament writings, not recently composed by a contemporary of Pius.

An earlier date certainly suits the primitive church order in *Hermas*. References to church leadership in this work are scattered and unsystematic, reflecting Hermas' concern, which is not church office but a proper attitude towards wealth. There are wealthy people in the church, and Hermas is concerned that their wealth does not lead to worldliness and to the loss of the church's purity.[21] These well-to-do people appear to include the church's leaders, variously called προηγούμενοι, πρεσβύτεροι, or ἐπίσκοποι, and Hermas addresses them as τοῖς προηγουμένοις καὶ τοῖς πρωτοκαθεδρίταις (the leaders and those who occupy the first seats) (Vis 3.9.7). Earlier, Hermas has spoken of οἱ πρεσβύτεροι οἱ προϊστάμενοι τῆς ἐκκλησίας (the elders at the head of the church) (Vis 2.4.3). The phrase closely recalls one of the most primitive Christian documents known to us (1 Thess 5:12). Later, Hermas speaks of ἐπίσκοποι καὶ φιλόξενοι, οἵτινες ἡδέως εἰς τοὺς οἴκους ἑαυτῶν πάντοτε ὑπεδέξαντο τοὺς δούλους τοῦ θεοῦ ἄτερ ὑποκρίσεως (hospitable overseers, who always gladly and without hypocrisy welcomed into their own houses the servants of God) (Sim 9.27.2). This exactly agrees with the conclusions we have reached earlier about ἐπίσκοποι being house-church leaders whose hospitality is extended not merely to travellers but to the church, here described as the servants of God. As in 1 Clement, there is no mention of a single overseer, and most people think this is because there was no such officer in the Roman church when Hermas wrote. If there is a chairman of the elders, it is possible that Clement holds this position and that it is as such that it falls to him to correspond with other churches (Vis 2.4.3), but there is no sign that he is exalted above the other leaders. This may have something to do with the nature of community and religious life in the city of Rome. We have seen that the Jewish community was fragmented, with no overall ethnarch, and the silence of the earliest Christian

[21] Maier, *Social Setting*, p. 58–65.

224

sources creates the suspicion that monepiscopacy arrived later in Rome than in the East. This, coupled with the fact that *Hermas* is probably later than the date I propose for the Pastorals is a reminder that the development of church order did not proceed everywhere at the same pace.

The other writing of which brief mention should be made here is the Didache. The interpretation of this document bristles with problems, which makes it hard to fit into anybody's understanding of the development of the early church. In the first place, its date has been hotly disputed, with widely differing dates being suggested, from 50 CE to the fourth century. Very late dates, however, seem largely to have been abandoned, and while Audet presents an impressive case for a date not later than 70 CE, his view has not generally been accepted, and scholars seem to have settled for a date at the end of the first century, somewhat by default.[22]

The Didache contains instructions on how travelling prophets and teachers, which it also calls apostles, are to be received in the churches (Did 11–13). It then adds:

> Therefore appoint for yourselves bishops and deacons worthy of the Lord, men who are humble and not avaricious and true and approved, for they too carry out for you the ministry of prophets and teachers. You must not, therefore, despise them, for they are your honoured men, along with the prophets and teachers. (Did 15:1–2)[23]

This, combined with Paul's reference to apostles, prophets and teachers (1 Cor 12:28), formed the basis of Harnack's famous theory of two kinds of ministry in the early church, a translocal charismatic

---

[22] Audet, *Didache*, pp. 187–206; Koester, *Introduction*, p. 158; Nierderwimmer, *Didache*, p. 79 (who suggests 110–120 CE), Rordorf, 'Didache', *EEC*, I, p. 234–5.

[23] Some scholars have suggested that this section, or the passage beginning 14:1, is a later addition, on the grounds that the church order envisaged differs from that of *Did* 11–13 (Kraft, *Fathers*, pp. 64, 174; Rordorf/Tuilier, *Doctrine*, pp. 49, 63ff.). De Halleux ('Ministères', pp. 20–1) shows that this is unnecessary and rests on a misunderstanding of what *Did.* 11–13 really say. Niederwimmer also argues for the unity of the text at this point (*Didache*, p. 241).

ministry, and a settled ministry of bishops and deacons. We have already discussed this in connection with Burtchaell's view that in the churches of the first century, the charismatics led but did not preside, while the officers (bishops and deacons) presided but did not lead.[24] As we noted, we would give much to know more of the context of these words: who is speaking, and to whom, where do they live,[25] and in what decade? Above all, what is this instruction written *for*, what is it directed *against*? Does the appointment of bishops and deacons represent a change, or is it a matter of routine? For lack of any assured answers to these questions, it is extremely difficult to relate these instructions to the development of the churches' ministry as we know it in the pages of the New Testament with any confidence.

In the light of the preceding discussion we may consider the following hypothesis. Although the Didache says quite a lot about travelling teachers of which the New Testament is largely silent (Paul's prophets and teachers are not itinerant![26]) and although the Didache says nothing about the house-church and its leaders as we meet them in the Pauline letters, it does not follow that the church context taken for granted by the Didache is different from anything we meet in the New Testament. That travelling prophets and teachers came to the New Testament churches also, I have no doubt, and Paul as little tells his churches how to receive them as he tells them how to baptize. At the same time, in the absence of any evidence to the contrary, it is natural to suppose that the churches of the Didache were meeting in houses, as did the churches of Acts and the letters. That being so, the leadership of the *paterfamilias* and of other socially influential people will not have been in dispute (which is why it is not mentioned). The Didache's bishops and deacons, then, will not have been the household ἐπίσκοποι, what I have called the

---

[24] Burtchaell, *Synagogue*, pp. 188, 310–12, 335–8, 348–51, discussed in chapter 4, pp. 114–120.

[25] Syria is still the most popular suggestion. See Streeter, *Primitive*, pp. 144ff.; Audet, *Didachè*, p. 206; Rordorf, *Doctrine*, pp. 97f.; Niederwimmer, *Didache*, p. 79f. Kraft, following Harnack, suggests Egypt, *Fathers*, p. 77.

[26] This point is acknowledged by von Campenhausen, *Authority*, p. 61, as also by Greeven, 'Propheten', p. 9.

leaders κατ' οἶκον. No church will have lacked leadership of this sort.[27] A. de Halleux, who agrees that bishops and deacons in that sense are nothing new for the Didachist, having co-existed with the prophets and teachers all along, thinks therefore that 15:1–2 simply concerns the routine appointment of such leaders, but it is hard to escape the impression that the command χειροτονήσατε implies that the situation is to be *changed* in some way.

May it not be that what we have here is an instruction very similar to that addressed in the Pastorals to Titus, who was to appoint elders κατὰ πόλιν (Tit 1:5ff.)? The house-churches of a locality and their leaders are to recognize one of their number as ἐπίσκοπος, and other men as his assistants, to provide the local church with some measure of unity and, perhaps, a remedy in the face of unsatisfactory visitors. The reason that the text speaks of bishops in the plural is that it is addressed to churches in several places, not that there are to be several such bishops in one place.[28]

This is clearly incapable of proof, for the reasons given, but it is put forward to show that the evidence of the Didache can fit very well within the overall picture being proposed. The Didache in that case stands at the same point in the process as do the Pastorals,[29] and the Didachist may even have been familiar with them. There are impressive similarities in thought and vocabulary between the Didache and the Pastorals at this point. The same words are used for the leaders to be appointed: ἐπισκόπους καὶ διακόνους (cf. 1 Tim 3:1–8), and the same concern about their character: πραεῖς καὶ ἀφιλαργύρους (cf. 1 Tim 3:1–7; Tit 1:5–9). Ἀφιλάργυρος

---

[27] To suggest, as does Campenhausen (*Authority*, p. 93), that the Didache addresses its commands to the congregation as a whole, rather than to the congregation at whose head stand the leaders, ignores Linton's point about 'eine beschlissende ungleichmassende Versammlung'. The command, 'Appoint for yourselves', is not addressed to a leaderless mob.

[28] The contrary is regularly asserted, as by de Halleux, p. 20; Niederwimmer, pp. 241–2, simply on the ground that the word here is plural. Yet the Didache was surely addressed to more than one church.

[29] Of course, that does not mean that it necessarily dates from the same period. The development of the churches may well have proceeded at different rates in different places, so that the emergence of a single church bishop did not happen at the same time everywhere.

in particular is a favourite Pastoral word (cf. 1 Tim 3:3, 6:10, 2 Tim 3:2). There is the same concern for testing: δεδοκιμασμένους (cf. Tim 3:10, καὶ οὗτοι δοκιμαζέσθωσαν πρῶτον). Finally, there is the same concern that those appointed should be duly honoured: τετιμημένοι (cf. 1 Tim 5:17, 'worthy of double honour', τιμή). The call to hold leaders in respect is common in the New Testament (1 Thess 5:12; Gal 6:6; 1 Cor 16:15ff.; Heb 13:17), and finds another echo in the Pastorals' concern that Timothy not be despised (1 Tim 4:12). All this suggests that the Didache, so far as its church order is concerned, fits very well into the period following the demise of the apostles, and shares the concerns and developments that arose elsewhere towards the close of the first century.

From Elders to Priests

At the start of the second century, the relationship of bishop and elders may, with some risk of oversimplification, be stated as follows.[30] The local churches met in houses and consisted of house-churches. 'The elders' had always been a natural way of referring collectively to the heads of these households who led such churches. In the interests of greater unity, the attempt was increasingly made to gather these household congregations into one, and one of their leaders was being recognized as the leader of the local church, the ἐπίσκοπος or overseer or bishop, not merely as chairman of the board of elders, but as president of the common eucharistic meeting. This change was not without its accompanying tensions, however, and Clement and Ignatius give us evidence of this from opposite points of view. Clement writes as one who upholds the traditional role of the household presbyter-bishops, while Ignatius writes as an advocate of the new order. 'The elders' now refers not to the house-church leaders viewed collectively, but to those household

---

[30] We cannot be sure that the same kinds of developments took place everywhere at the same time, but the writings we have examined do not suggest that there was wide variation.

leaders who are no longer to be called 'overseer'. But while 'overseer' had a precise denotation, 'elders' did not and so we find that later in the second century Irenaeus can refer to bishops as elders (Adv Haer III.ii.2), though the identification would not work the other way round. True to its history, the word 'elder' remains a title of honour rather than of office or function.

With whatever struggles and tensions, at different times in different places, (and we need always to remember how little hard evidence we have for the first part of the second century), the Ignatian pattern prevailed in the churches. As a result, *in terms of their liturgical functions*, the bishop increased while the elders/presbyters decreased. The bishops did not only preside at the Lord's Supper, they increasingly laid claim to liturgical roles that had originally been exercised by others, such as the leading of public prayer, and the ministry of the Word, although P. Bradshaw shows that there is evidence that the bishop's monopoly of preaching was neither immediate nor total.[31] The elders sat with the bishop at the Lord's Table and in this way shared in his leadership, and they joined with him in laying on hands in blessing and ordination. But Tertullian, for example, regards their participation in baptizing as something delegated by the bishop, and as perhaps exceptional (de Bapt 17).

The difference between the bishop and his elders can be seen clearly by a comparison of the ordination prayers for each as preserved by Hippolytus (early third century). The prayer for the bishop says that God has chosen him to,

> feed your holy flock, and to exercise the high-priesthood before you blamelessly, serving night and day; to propitiate your countenance unceasingly, and to offer to you the gifts of your holy Church; and by the spirit of high-priesthood to have the power to forgive sins according to your command, to confer orders according to your bidding, to loose every bond according to the power which you gave to the apostles, to please you in gentleness and a pure heart, offering you a sweet-smelling savour. (AT 3)

The prayer for the presbyter asks only that God will,

[31] Bradshaw, *Presidency*, p. 15.

impart the Spirit of grace and counsel of the presbyterate, that he may help and govern your people with a pure heart. (AT 7)

Unfortunately we have very little idea what it would mean for the presbyters at this time 'to help and govern your people', since the bishop apparently teaches (feeds the flock), presides, prays, pardons, ordains and exorcises (loose every bond?) Yet this is to view things from a purely liturgical point of view. There is evidence that in other respects the elders did not simply fade away.

For if the elders declined in terms of their liturgical functions, there is evidence to suggest that *they did not disappear as a social force* within the church. Nor would we expect them to. After all, we have seen that the elders had many things which gave them power within the churches: seniority of age and in Christian faith, social position and the ability to provide the churches with places to meet and other benefits of patronage. These things did not cease to be true simply because they were deprived of liturgical presidency. From the North African church of the fourth century comes evidence for the existence of people called variously *seniores plebis, seniores christiani populi*, or *seniores laici*. Although the evidence is much later than our period, W. H. C. Frend says they are,

> clearly a survival of lay control derived from a much earlier period. Their functions were administrative and disciplinary, and on occasion they exercised control even of the bishop.'[32]

Ambrosiaster (late fourth century) says that the church, like the synagogue, has *seniores ... quorum sine consilio nihil agebatur in Ecclesia*.[33] P. Caron believes this office to go back to the earliest times of the church and to arise from the impossibility of the bishop looking after everything himself.

> But the bishop will also have at his side lay colleagues, whom he will have chosen from among the 'notables' of the community, and in general from among those Christians who are most education, most honourable, and most experienced.[34]

[32] Frend, 'Seniores', p. 281.
[33] Ambrosiaster, *Comm in 1 Ep. ad Tim* 5:1, Migne. *PL* 17.475D.
[34] Caron, 'Seniores', p. 13.

From the elders in fact!

Although all our evidence comes from North Africa, there is no reason to suppose that such a necessary and sensible arrangement was confined to that region, and although the written sources are late for establishing what was the case in the second century, we may think that this is due to the scantiness of any second century material at all, and the preoccupation of most of what we have with other more theological matters. The *seniores* must surely be a survival rather than a fourth century innovation, so that what we need to ask is whether there is any good reason why they should first start to receive mention in fourth century sources — and we may think there is.

The increasing numbers and spread of the church must from early times have made it difficult for the bishop to be personally present for every celebration of the Eucharist, and in such circumstances he delegated his presidency to presbyters (Cyprian, Ep 5:2). Yet it appears to be only in the fourth century that the bishops delegated their presidency to the presbyters on a regular basis,[35] thus bringing about a change in the way presbyters were perceived. From being largely a council of honourables,[36] participating in baptisms on special occasions (Hippolytus, AT 21), some presbyters now acquired an individual ministry, presiding at the Lord's Table in their own right. It was from this development that the term *sacerdos* which had been applied to the bishop since at least the beginning of the third century, began to be used of presbyters individually.[37] This may explain the appearance of the word *laicus* to describe the other presbyters, those who were not in the process of becoming priests. The presbyters had always been in some sense laymen, and E. G. Jay suggests that many of them would have to earn their own living.[38] If some of them were in the fourth century 'turning professional', it would explain the need for a way of referring to those who remained what elders had always been.

---

[35] Bradshaw, *Presidency*, p. 27.
[36] See AT 8: the deacon 'does not share in the counsel of the presbyterate'.
[37] Bradshaw, *Presidency*, p. 27.
[38] Jay, 'Presbyter', p. 158.

That in the second century the elders, or τὸ πρεσβυτέριον, though denied the liturgical power they had previously enjoyed within their own house-churches, nevertheless exercised considerable power in the church, is suggested by the likelihood that at that time it was they who chose and ordained the bishop himself. As they stand, the instructions for the ordination of the bishop contained in Hippolytus direct that the ordination be carried out by one of the other bishops, as was later the case. The rubric, however, contains a number of anomalies that suggest that it has been altered to conform with later practice. The original text may have run as follows:

> Let him be ordained bishop who has been chosen from all the people as we appointed above; and when he has been named and accepted by all, let the people assemble together with the presbytery (and the deacons?) on the Lord's day. When all give consent, *the presbyters shall lay hands on him* and all keep silence, praying in their hearts for the descent of the Spirit, of whom one, having been asked by all, laying his hand on him who is to be ordained bishop, shall pray, saying thus: ... (emphasis mine).[39]

If this is correct, it shows that in the second century the elders continued to retain considerable power in the church, even after their liturgical freedom was curtailed. The later references to *seniores laici* suggest that this continued into the fourth century before being overtaken by the growing clericalism of the church.

It remains to say, finally, that the word 'elders' true to everything we have seen about it in earlier times, continues to be an imprecise term throughout the second century. Thus we find Irenaeus speaking of,

> that tradition which originates from the apostles, and which is preserved by means of the successions of *presbyters* in the Churches (*Adv Haer* III.ii.2).

In the next paragraph he says,

[39] This is discussed by Bradshaw, 'Ordination', p. 34.

we are in a position to reckon up those who were by the apostles instituted *bishops* in the Churches and to demonstrate the succession of these men down to our own times' (*Adv Haer* III.iii.1).

According to Jay,[40] this is no slip of the pen, since a little later Irenaeus can write;

> Wherefore it is incumbent to obey the *presbyters* who are in the Church – those who, as I have shown, possess succession from the apostles; those who, together with the succession of the *episcopate*, have received the certain gift of truth (*Adv Haer* IV.xxvi.2).

Jay concludes that Irenaeus understood the succession as basically presbyteral. I would rather say that the term 'presbyter' continued to be a flexible term for Irenaeus, capable of denoting bishops as the successors of the apostles. If πρεσβύτερος had by this time come to mean what it means for the text of Hippolytus in its final form, the member of the second tank of the hierarchy, Irenaeus could not have so used it. This receives support from the way in which, according to D. Powell, Irenaeus uses the phrase '*Ordo presbyterii*' to mean the seniority which true leaders display along with sound speech and blameless conduct.[41]

In the case of Tertullian (c. 160–c. 225 CE), distinctions between different ranks of minister are clearly more pronounced. He can call the bishop *summus sacerdos*; he can speak of presbyters and deacons as being in the next place and only able to baptize with the bishop's authority; and he can speak of laymen who baptize as (legitimately) exercising powers that belong to their superiors (*de Bapt* 17). Like Irenaeus he appeals to the succession of bishops as a guarantee of sound doctrine (*de Praescr* 32). Yet elsewhere he can say,

> The tried men of our elders preside over us, obtaining honour not by purchase, but by established character. (*Apol* 39)

---

[40] Jay, 'Presbyter', p. 153.
[41] Powell, 'Ordo', pp. 316–20.

Those who preside over the church in Tertullian's day can only be the bishops, and yet he calls them 'elders'. It is only fair to point out, however, that Tertullian is here writing for outsiders to interpret the Christian society to the outside world, so that the use of elders is really another example of how the word functioned in the Graeco-Roman background, rather than evidence of how Christians used the word among themselves.

Conclusions

At the start of the second century, the centralizing of the churches' life around the presidency of a single *episkopos* entailed a significant loss of authority by the elders of the churches, those who had hitherto been *episkopoi* in their own house-churches. This change was not achieved without considerable tensions, as we see from the letters of Clement and Ignatius, who represent opposite sides in the resulting disputes. Although the elders lost their liturgical power they retained their social influence and remained a real power in the churches of the second century. Tracing the development of the eldership is made more difficult, not only by the paucity of sources but by the way in which the term 'the elders' itself changes its referent. Thus we have seen that πρεσβύτεροι could be used,

(1) of those who sat with the bishop at the Table and as his Council;

(2) of the bishops themselves, considered as successors of the apostles;

(3) later, of individual ministers who, as deputies of the bishop, exercised his ministry of presidency in the churches.

Since that presidency had itself come to be seen as the action of a priest (*sacerdos*), it followed that in time the word πρεσβύτερος came to mean *sacerdos*.[42] It is for this reason that, when the Latin

---

[42] By 375 CE or earlier, OED (1933), Vol. VIII, p. 1352.

word 'presbyter' was taken into English, it was with the meaning 'priest', rather than 'elder'. But when, for example, the translators of the AV translated πρεσβύτερος by 'elder', and used 'priest' to translate ἱερεῦς, rather than πρεσβυτερος from which it had been derived, they were correctly reflecting the meaning of the word πρεσβύτερος for the New Testament writers. But that is another story.

Chapter Eight

Towards a New Consensus?

Strictly speaking, there is no such thing as a consensus view to be found on any subject within New Testament scholarship. In the first place, there is hardly ever a position so discredited that it completely lacks defenders; no finding of scholarship so self-evidently true that it lasts for long without assailants. In the second place, every consensus contains within itself a spectrum of views, the agreement of the consenting scholars being confined to broad outlines for the most part. This is clearly the case with the consensus view that is the target of the present study. It has never been held by all, and those who hold it do so with considerable variations among themselves as to details. Identifying a consensus, however, is a useful forensic gambit, serving either, in the case that one agrees with the consensus, to provide a cloud of witnesses in support of one's view, a platform from which to proceed to higher things, or, if one does not agree with it, to provide a convenient target to attack, and an imposing edifice for demolition.

Nevertheless, in the case of the origins of the church's ministry, and the place of the elders within it, we can fairly speak of a consensus, or at least a majority view, among New Testament scholars during most of this century, according to which the Jewish-Christian churches from very early on adopted a system of government by elders, along the lines of the synagogue, while the Pauline churches looked to the Spirit to direct the church through the operation of 'gifts' distributed to different members from time to time. In the latter, although in time certain administrative tasks necessitated the appointment of officers, for whom the Greek clubs and associations provide the closest antecedents, these in no way compromised the freedom of the Spirit to direct the church through the ministry of apostles, prophets and teachers. By contrast, the elders, like their synagogue counterparts, were guardians of tradition, albeit the tradition of the gospel, and represented the beginnings within the church of a pattern of government that would become legal and ecclesiastical. After Paul's death, the Pauline vision faded, and there took place an amalgamation of the two patterns, out of which Catholicism was born. Pauline overseers and deacons combined with Jewish-Christian elders to produce the threefold pattern of ministry, a nominal victory of the Pauline order of overseers and deacons, but in reality a retreat into religion that was scribal and clerical. The hands were the hands of Esau, but the voice was the voice of Jacob!

This, as we saw, is the view put forward by von Campenhausen and followed in this century by mainstream Protestant scholarship. It can be show to derive from the views of Rudolf Sohm at the end of the last century, although Sohm did not distinguish between Pauline- and Jewish-Christianity and did not see the elders as 'the first and decisive prerequisite for the elaboration of a narrowly 'official' and 'ecclesiastical' way of thinking.'[1] In recent years, as was mentioned earlier, this view has found favour with some Catholics, notably K. Kertelge and E. Schüssler-Fiorenza among New Testament scholars, and has been taken up in the cause of reform by the theologians H. Küng, E. Schillebeeckx.[2] Its claim to be a consensus view is thereby strengthened.

Overcoming a consensus, like conquering a mountain, can be attempted from different sides and by different routes, and climbers can learn from and encourage each other. We have seen that in recent years an assault has been mounted from the side of sociology, calling in question the adequacy of the consensus' understanding of *charisma*. A more traditional route has proceeded by way of questioning the consensus' exegesis of the Pauline letters, emphasizing their character as occasional documents containing rather more evi-

---

[1] von Campenhausen, *Authority*, p. 77.

[2] Kerelge, *Gemeinde und Amt im NT*; E. S. Fiorenza, *Memory*; Küng, *The Church* (1967); Schillebeeckx, *The Church with a Human Face* (1985). These contributions are discussed by Burtchaell, *Synagogue*, pp. 167–79.

dence of recognized leadership than the consensus is usually willing to admit. Climbers on these two routes have sometimes met up and joined forces, and both, we may think, have been successful in planting flags of common sense on top of the mountain of consensus thinking. The present study, which is indebted both to their methods and their achievements, has sought to approach the mountain from the side of social history by questioning the consensus' understanding of the *elders* and seeking from that starting point to mark out a new exegetical route over terrain where there are few fixed landmarks. It is time to sum up the argument and suggest what has been achieved.

The Argument Summarized

1. Although the earliest churches developed rapidly within a Graeco-Roman environment, their primary cultural heritage was, of course, Jewish. Accordingly, we began our survey of the New Testament background by looking at the elders in Ancient Israel. We saw that they constituted a form of leadership that was collective and representative, with an authority derived from their seniority relative to those they represented, whether household, clan, tribe or nation. 'The elders' was shown to be a term of honour for those whose power was based on relationships that already existed, rather than a precise office, entered through appointment, election or ordination.

Jewish writers of the Second Temple period (including New Testament writers when they refer to the Jewish leaders) display a notable lack of precision in the use of the term 'elders', usually linking it with other terms to reinforce the impression that the whole leadership was involved. Elders, we may say, are those who have πρεσβεῖον, rather than the holders of an office of eldership at either national or local level.

A particularly important question for the study of Christian origins is whether there was any office of elder in the synagogue, and we saw that it is possible to say that while the congregation gave precedence to persons of seniority, and used the term 'the elders' to refer to them, there does not seem to have been an office of elder as such to which a person might be appointed and with clearly defined functions. Those who in virtue of being the heads of well-to-do families were honoured as the elders of the community enjoyed that status also when the community assembled to read the Scriptures and pray, but an elder did not hold an office in the way that the ἀρχισυνάγωγος did. In cities with large Jewish populations, where there were many synagogues, it is these synagogues which form the closest parallel to the Christian churches, and there is no reason to think that each of them had a board of elders.

In the Qumran scrolls, 'the elders' appears as a title very rarely, and we saw that this is readily explicable in the context of a monastic community. As a term for those whose prestige was based on their family background it was hardly appropriate to a community dedicated to priestly purity and celibacy. Its very occasional appearance probably owes more to scriptural reminiscence than to constitutional actuality. The Essene communities appear to have gathered under the presidency of a single overseer, whereas 'the elders' is everywhere an imprecise collective term. As such it did not naturally suggest itself to those who wrote from within the sect, though we are not surprised to find it used by those like Josephus and Philo who wrote about the community from the outside.

In all Jewish contexts 'the elders', where they are mentioned, should be seen as a way of referring to those whose opinion counted for more than that of others, whether because of their age, or because they held some office, or because their family traditionally 'ran' things and they were senior within it. By comparison with the classical Greek sources, Jewish writers of all periods use the term 'the elders' rather often to refer to those in authority. Nevertheless, eldership is never an office as such, but more a matter of status enjoyed by those who in virtue of their seniority led and represented their families.

2. In turning our attention next to the Graeco-Roman world, we looked at the main outlines of its constitutional history, and the status of older men in public and private life. In constitutional terms, there are similarities as well as differences between the Graeco-Roman and Jewish worlds. Both emerge from an archaic period

whose government may be called aristocratic, in which the elders as local chieftains play a prominent part. In both worlds their peoples experienced, for much of the time, the autocratic rule of local kings and distant emperors. Democracy, whether of the Athenian or modern variety, was not often, or for long, the experience of the peoples of the Graeco-Roman world. In most places, at most times, power lay with those born to wealthy families, whose senior members were leaders in the state, city, or rural community. The leaders owed their position in society to the power of their family, and their position in the family to their relative seniority.

They were not often called οἱ πρεσβύτεροι. This was partly because the preferred term for the ruling oligarchy is οἱ γέροντες, or ἡ γερουσία. In this respect, Greek usage differed from Jewish, though we have seen that the terms came together in the γερουσίαι that flourished in the cities of the eastern Roman empire at the turn of the eras. οἱ πρεσβύτεροι connoted rather a class of person to whom respect was instinctively felt to be due, not so much the leaders of the state or town, but *one's own elders* within family, clan or acquaintance. Although the Greeks held this respect in tension with a fear of the aging process, and a willingness on occasion to lampoon the failings of the old and to strain against the leash of their authority, there is no reason to think that it ceased to be a cohesive force in the home and in the community.

The work of comparative anthropologists tends to show that respect for older people has been typical of most human societies, but that there is a tendency for this respect to be eroded in the face of rising living standards, increased literacy, social mobility, urbanization and the whole process that can be called 'modernization'. We would, therefore, expect to find within the ancient world a high respect for the old, but also a tendency for this to be challenged by increased urbanization.

Comparative studies of societies in the modern world also show, however, that the erosion of respect is arrested wherever people live in extended families that preserve a strong sense of belonging. The typical Graeco-Roman household, especially in the case of the well-to-do, can fairly be described as an extended family, and we should expect that the senior people within such families would continue to enjoy considerable respect. The writings of Plutarch show that this expectation is justified for the world of the first century.

So, although the *word* elders is much more frequently found in Jewish sources than in Greek, in the East than in the West, the way of thinking that it expresses was common to both. From the earliest times the elders' position was closely linked with their family, or household, and the ancient household continued to run according to strict notions of seniority.

3. In the light of this, it is of the highest importance that the earliest Christian congregations of which we have firsthand knowledge came to birth within households or extended families. If this is so, and if it is further true that it was the household that formed the basis of the respect accorded to the elderly in society, then it is extremely likely that the principle of seniority that was taken for granted in the household was taken for granted in the congregation also, and the *Haustafel* form of paraenesis in the later Pauline letters reinforces this belief.

For this reason, it would be a mistake to suppose that Paul does not mention elders in his (generally acknowledged) letters because he had some objection to them in principle. Such a view rests, as others have argued, on an incorrect understanding of the meaning and purpose of his *charisma* teaching. A better explanation lies ready to hand. The letters in question belong to the very early days of the Pauline congregations, when the church in a place may only have consisted of a single household congregation, or where, if there were several households, relations between them were very informal and overshadowed by the apostle's own pastoral oversight. Within his own household no κύριος would normally be known as 'the elder' (or even 'an elder'). 'The elders', on the other hand, would be a natural way to refer to the several κύριοι at the point where they started to meet together as the representative leadership of the church in a given place. However, this is not to suggest that an office of elder emerged later, simply that 'the elders' *as a way of referring to* the household leaders only began to be appropriate as the house-churches multiplied.

Furthermore, if Paul is silent about elders, preferring to use terms, like προϊστάμενοι or ἐπίσκοποι, which emphasize the functions

241

performed by the leaders within their own congregations rather than their relationship with one another *ad extra*; or if, more commonly, he speaks of διάκονοι or ἀδελφοί, that may be because he writes from the standpoint of his mission, and his letters reflect the terminology and practice of those who travelled and worked with Paul as part of his team. Within that team, we suggested, a greater degree of egalitarianism was practised than was natural within the household-based churches growing up within settled communities. If so, Luke is hardly guilty of anachronism in portraying Paul as sending for the elders of the church at Ephesus, whom he naturally addressed as 'brothers', not as 'elders', emphasizing their relationship to himself rather than to their communities.

4. At the same time, if the churches Paul founded had elders in all but name, the 'churches of Christ in Judea' (Gal 1:22) probably had 'overseers' from the start also, and for the same reason. Even if they did not use a Greek word to describe them, the evidence of Acts suggests that the Jerusalem church met in homes, and it is a natural conclusion that, if they met in homes, the well-to-do patron who placed his or her house at the disposal of the church exercised a leading role within it, including the leading of prayers as was the traditional role of the Jewish family head. We may think that it is this (admittedly conjectural) figure who stands between the Essene *mebaqqer* and the ἐπίσκοποι of Philippians 1:1 to form a single and unbroken line of development grounded in the household matrix of the congregations.

In this way, it is here maintained against the consensus that there were not two quite different patterns of church government, Jewish- and Pauline-Christian, waiting to be merged into one following the apostle's death. On the one hand, as others have argued, the 'charismatic' church order attributed to Paul by the heirs of Sohm is a myth born of wishful exegesis of the Pauline letters. On the other, as this study maintains, the evidence of the New Testament permits us to postulate for the Jewish-Christian churches a simple form of organization natural to household churches, and indistinguishable from the 'Pauline model'.

References to the elders in Acts, then, are not the proof we need that the Jewish-Christians organized themselves in a different way that betokens their imperfect emancipation from the synagogue, but represent a collective term for the household leaders of the Jerusalem church considered as a representative group. If the Twelve, as the ruling group within the Jerusalem church, are sometimes to be included among the elders and are sometimes named separately alongside them, that is entirely in accordance with the way the term 'the elders' has been shown to behave in Septuagintal Greek.

The two references in Acts to elders in the Pauline churches are not an anachronism, as if Luke were, as is commonly supposed, attributing to the Pauline churches the conditions of his own time. In the first place, careful attention to the language Luke uses to describe the 'appointment' of the elders in Lycaonia suggests that he is not so much thinking of the appointment of men to the office of elder as of Paul commending to God's grace those who were elders of their communities already. In the second place, the terms Luke uses may enable us to see that he distinguishes between two levels or stages of church organization — that in which the churches assemble κατ' οἶκον, and that in which the various household leaders can be considered κατ' ἐκκλησίαν. Talk of 'elders' naturally belongs to the second.

5. If in the early period represented by the Pauline letters the household leaders were coming to be known as ἐπίσκοποι, and if, in time, the several ἐπίσκοποι in a place could be seen collectively as οἱ πρεσβύτεροι, then the Pastorals do not reflect the merging of two distinct patterns of organization. Instead, the way in which they speak of elders in the plural, but of the overseer in the singular, makes sense if they were written precisely to commend and legitimate the recognition of a single ἐπίσκοπος from among those who, as ἐπίσκοποι in their own house-churches, have begun to be known as the elders of the church.

This is to agree with those who think that the Pastorals presuppose a 'monepiskopos', but differs from them in thinking that this is not a development already accomplished, but rather something that is in process. It is this which accounts for the ambiguities of the Pastorals, which would be very strange if they were taking for granted an arrangement that had been in place for one or more decades.

The Pastorals call for the appointment of elders in every city (Tit 1:5). In the light of what we know of the household basis of the

Pauline churches, who can these elders have been? They can hardly be the household leaders themselves, since these will have been in position from the start. Why, moreover, does the writer immediately switch to speaking of an overseer in the singular? Both puzzles are solved if we allow that the verse refers to the appointment of 'monepiskopoi', leaders over the churches in the various cities, the words κατα' πόλιν denoting the sphere or level of responsibility of the new overseers, in contrast to their more limited oversight hitherto (which Luke expresses by the phrase κατ' οἶκον). Those to be appointed are first called πρεσβύτεροι, either because that is the group from which they come, or because πρεσβύτεροι is a collective term of honour no less suitable for a number of leaders of town churches than of house churches. The writer then refers to the ἐπίσκοπος in the singular since it is the recognition of a single overseer with which he is concerned.

It is in favour of this reconstruction that in all three of the key passages we have studied a new state of affairs is explicitly or implicitly envisaged. In Titus 1:5 it is explicit that a new appointment is to be made. 1 Timothy 3 also has to do with appointment, both encouraging the prospective overseer to aspire to the job, and requiring that he be tested and display appropriate personal qualities. 1 Timothy 5:17 is concerned with a change in the way such leaders will be rewarded, now that they are giving all their time to preaching and teaching. Like Timothy and Titus before him, the overseer is to do the work previously done by the apostle, teaching the truth and safeguarding the church from false teaching. He will need to have a proven record as a household leader (1 Tim 3:1–7), and is doubly worthy of the church's honour, being both a senior believer and now a full-time shepherd of the church in his town (1 Tim 5:17).

6. It will be in favour of this understanding of the elders in the New Testament, if it not only agrees with, but also throws new light on the evidence of the earliest documents outside the New Testament itself — and this it can claim to do.

The elevation of one of their number to be overseer necessarily involved some diminution of the prestige of the overseers not appointed. For the sake of unity and good order, this was followed in due course by the requirement that Christians assemble for a single

Eucharist presided over by the overseer, the other ἐπίσκοποι being honoured with the title of 'the elders', and with the chief seats, but no longer exercising the same degree of responsibility. This cannot always have occurred without tension and resentment on the part of those household leaders who no longer had the liberty of celebrating the Eucharist in their own homes, as they had always done, and the letters of Clement and Ignatius can fruitfully be understood against this background.

Clement writes to champion the dispossessed elders against what he sees as the overweening claims of the 'monepiskopos', while Ignatius writes in the opposite sense. The church at Corinth is represented as having risen up against its elders, when in reality it has demoted most of the elders in favour of the 'monepiskopos'. Clement invokes the tradition of the apostles, not because he is concerned with a doctrine of apostolic succession, but as ammunition in his bid to have the *status quo* restored.

What matters for Ignatius is that the overseer be *present*, and that no meetings are held in other places or without his approval. The strength with which he is having to argue this, coupled with the way in which he flatters the elders while saying nothing of any active role for them, is the best indication that there was resistance to the centralizing policy Ignatius commends.

Yet the elders did not just fade away. They were senior Christians, possessed of considerable powers of patronage in the church. Nor, on the other hand, did they immediately join the ranks of what we would now call 'the clergy'. Evidence of this, as of the general correctness of these proposals, is provided by the references to *seniores laici* in the North African churches of the fourth century. Although quite detached in time from any of the other evidence we have been considering, these *seniores* may be compared to an island far out at sea which is in fact the tip of a mountain most of which lies beneath the water. It stands precisely in line with the hill-tops on the mainland, enabling us to see that the range continued beyond the point where it is now lost to sight, and showing where it ran. In this case, we may think, the practice of honouring the most influential members with the title of 'the elders' (πρεσβύτεροι/ *seniores*) continued until the term πρεσβύτερος was annexed by those who, as the bishop's deputies, joined the ranks of the clergy. The other *seniores* then came to be known as *laici*, which is what, as 'non-bishops', they had always been!

The Conclusion to be Drawn

Not every part of this reconstruction is of equal importance. Some of the positions taken up are little more than suggestions of what may possibly be the case if the main contentions of this thesis are accepted. For example, the connection of the Christian ἐπίσκοπος with the Essene *mebaqqer* may now seem more likely, but nothing in the overall argument depends on it. In the same way, these suggestions as to what is 'really going on' in the Pastorals and the letters of Clement and Ignatius are offered as plausible solutions to old problems, and as suggestions for further research, based on what we have shown about the development of the church's ministry in general and role of the elders in particular, but they serve to decorate the main thesis rather than underpin it.

The main contention of this thesis is that in the ancient world *the elders are those who bear a title of honour, not of office, a title that is imprecise, collective and representative, and rooted in the ancient family or household.* To put it another way, we do not know who is referred to by the term 'the elders' unless we know the context, and even then we do not know whom the term includes or excludes.

The ancient world was a world that honoured its older men. We saw that this was true of the Greeks no less than the Jews, and it was true of the Christians also. From the remotest antiquity known to us, but surviving strongly into the relatively modernized world of the first century, natural piety dictated that those who were older should be deferred to, and their counsel sought. Younger men might hold office and exercise political power, but the old did not simply retire, nor was their influence on events negligible.

Comparative anthropological study tends to suggest that there is a clear difference between the ancient and modern worlds in this regard. The patterns of ancient societies are to some extent preserved today in primitive societies which continue to accord their older men honour and influence, while even in modern societies the prestige of the elderly is preserved to the extent that extended families are the norm. Modernization diminishes the prestige of the elderly by breaking down the extended family within which the older person is honoured and on which his influence in the community depends.

This confirms what has long been known about the elders in the ancient world. The elders were recognized as the heads of their families in societies where families were seen as the constituent parts of the state itself. If kings and governors consulted councils of elders, this was not just because of the wisdom that older people were supposed to have, but also because of the power they represented and the people they spoke for. Elders are always representative. It would therefore be untrue to suggest that a person was an elder because of age alone; wealth also played its part. But wealth, being related for the most part to land, was closely tied up in families, and the headship of the family usually went according to age.

Nevertheless, 'eldership' was not usually an office to which people were appointed, but rather a way of referring comprehensively to the VIPs of the community. Among these the office-bearers can be specifically mentioned, either because it is from the ranks of the elders that the office-bearers have been chosen in the first place, or because it is among the elders that those who have held office will subsequently be ranked.

It makes no sense, then, to ask whether a particular community in the ancient world 'had elders'. One might as well ask whether a society today 'has' VIPs! All societies had elders, not just in the sense that they had older people, but in the sense that importance and age tended to go together. We should not suppose that the absence of the word 'elders' from literary or epigraphic sources indicates that older people were not so honoured. Nor, on the other hand, should we make the mistake of supposing that occurrence of the word 'elders' tells us anything about the functions performed by those to whom it refers.

Kings, high priests, governors, ἀρχισυνάγωγοι, *mebaqqerim*, overseers and deacons are office-holders. They can be referred to as οἱ ἄρχοντες. But οἱ ἄρχοντες are to be distinguished from οἱ

247

πρεσβύτρεροι, not as being two offices within a hierarchy, but as two different ways of thinking about those who exercise political power in the community. οἱ ἄρχοντες exercise power in virtue of the office to which they have been appointed, and English translations frequently render the term 'the magistrates'. οἱ πρεσβύτεροι is a wider term denoting all those who in virtue of their seniority within the leading families of the community help to form its opinions and direct its affairs.

In the first chapter, we saw Sohm maintaining that the elders are 'not an office but a rank'. They were not appointed to be elders; rather, the bishop was appointed from among them. Yet Sohm tended to idealize them, speaking of people being elders in virtue of their length of faithful service, endowed with 'the gift of love'.

The 'heirs' in effect moved the elders from the side of *charisma* to the side of Law. From being part of the church's golden age of freedom, elders come to be seen as the first sure sign of its degeneration, incipient embodiments of the Law and of the churches' transformation into Christian synagogues.

By stressing the household context of the earliest churches, we have seen that Sohm's view of the elders can be revived, but in a less idealized form. The elders are indeed the churches' 'honourables', but they are not honoured for their Christian character alone, but as leaders of families, hosts of the church, patrons of the weaker believers. They are not men of Law, nor yet men of Love; they are men of Leadership, that leadership which naturally falls to older men in the ancient world.

But what are we to say about Sohm's central contention that the church is a purely charismatic community, where leadership arises from the operation and recognition of spiritual gifts? It is this part of his legacy which has endured for over a century as Protestant scholarship's view of the primitive, and especially the Pauline church, and which continues to be so attractive in our own day. Are we saying that this insight is to be completely rejected? Were there really not *different* sources of authority in the New Testament churches, the household on the one hand and the *charismata* on the other, and may these two not have been in some tension?

248

In the first place, we need not doubt that the life of the earliest congregations witnessed extraordinary occurrences of many kinds. Miracles (Gal 3:4), signs and wonders (Rom 15:19), healings (Jas 5:14) — these things happened at least sometimes, however we may seek to account for them. Extraordinary things happened in the life of Jesus, and continued to happen in the experience of the earliest communities, as Acts makes plain.

Equally, we need not doubt that people 'spoke in tongues', in the sense of 'ecstatic utterance', though we have no means of knowing how common this was. Such utterance seems to have been evaluated by some as a form of prophecy (Acts 19:6), but prophecy seems also to have referred to Christian discourse, what we would call preaching and teaching inspired by the Holy Spirit (Acts 13:1). Probably there were many definitions of prophecy in the early church, and we should not forget that the word 'prophecy' may involve a claim as much as, or more than, a description.

It seems plain that in the earliest days of the movement many people were involved in all of this, but we do not know how many, how widespread, or for how long. Clearly at Corinth ecstatic utterance was highly valued, and enough people were engaged in this and other forms of expression to endanger the good order of the meeting, but what Paul says in 1 Corinthians 14:23, 26 should not be pressed to say that all members behaved like this, but only that all who did, did so at the same time and in a disorderly manner.

It is in response to the Corinthian situation that Paul first formulates his *charisma* teaching, and it is important to see that this is an attempt to interpret experience and direct behaviour, rather than to describe them. Spiritual manifestations (πνευμάτικα 1 Cor 12:1, 14:1) are evaluated as *charismata* (1 Cor 12:4, 31), that is as gifts of grace, to be received with humility, and evaluated according to the good they do (1 Cor 12:3, 14:12). Other less enthusiastic kinds of behaviour can also be evaluated as *charismata*,[3] so that *charismata* do

---

[3] We have argued on p. 108 that this applies to λόγος σοφίας, λόγος γνώσεως (1 Cor 12:8), and everyone would agree that it applies to ἀντιλήμψεις, κυβερνήσεις (1 Cor 12:28). Compare also Rom 12:6–8.

not refer simply to pneumatic manifestations, but any activity at all that contributes to the edification of the community, and only so far as it does so.

By contrast, 'charismatic' is regularly used by scholars, following Weber, to connote non-routine activity.[4] Travelling preachers, like the prophets in the Didache, are called 'charismatics'. They are then equated with the 'apostles, prophets and teachers' in 1 Corinthians 12:28, who are also called 'charismatics', and the conclusion is drawn that these people operated under the influence of the Spirit in an extraordinary way that excludes normal, planned, communication. But this is to use 'charismatic' in two different senses.

It is important to observe a distinction between *charisma* as a description of non-routine activity, and *charisma* as an evaluation of activity, whether routine or otherwise. We may express it as follows: let *charisma*^{G} refer to Christian activity and ability evaluated by Paul as a gift of grace, whether it is regular and normal, or spontaneous and abnormal; and let *charisma*^{P} refer to paranormal, or pneumatic, or spontaneous, activity, such as a sociologist of religion would describe as charismatic. Because Paul speaks of the life of the church in terms of *charisma*^{G}, this does not mean that everything that happened in his churches was a non-routine, extraordinary, spontaneous expression of *charisma*.^{P}

In 1 Corinthians, Paul is confronted by people who are placing excessive value on behaviour that could be called *charismatic*^{P}. He disapproves of their attitude, and evaluates their activities by a different scale. He wants them to see all such activity as *charisma*^{G} — and not pneumatic activity only, but routine activity as well, always provided that it builds up the church. The activity of apostles, prophets and teachers contributes more to this end than anything else, and more particularly than ecstatic utterance. Accordingly, they are to be placed first, and other things subordinated to them. This does not mean that Paul is subordinating the church to *charismatics*^{P}, but rather subordinating all such extraordinary activity to the church's leaders, evaluated as *charismata*^{G}. There is no reason why the proph-

---

[4] In Weber's phrase, activity characterized by *Ausseralltäglichkeit.*

ets and teachers should not have included Stephanas and others mentioned in 1 Corinthians 16:15ff., and every reason why they should have done. Paul calls for the church to recognize them (εἰδέναι) in exactly the same way as he asks the Thessalonians to do (1 Thess 5:12 οἴδατε) and for the same reason, because they work for the church (κοπιάω). This work, according to 1 Thess. 5:12, includes leading and instructing (νουθετοῦντας). These people are not *charismatics*[P], but they are certainly evaluated by Paul as *charismata*[G]. It is misleading to speak of apostles, prophets and teachers as necessarily charismatics. Paul may have been a *charismatic*[P], as indeed he testifies, but it was not *qua* apostle that he was charismatic, nor yet because he was charismatic that he was an apostle.

This is not to say that only household heads spoke or taught in the churches. Certainly there were others in the congregation who did so, whether on the basis of education, experience, fluency, Bible knowledge, or prayerful intuition, some from within the congregation, others as visitors. Some no doubt claimed to be prophets; others were so evaluated by the congregation. Some might have been labelled by a sociologist *charismatic*[P]; others would have been seen by Paul as *charismatic*[G], and the two groups might overlap, of course. But neither should we think that the early churches recognized two kinds of minister, those who governed in virtue of natural, institutional authority, and those who ministered out of charismatic endowment. Paul evaluated his leaders as *charismata*[G], and placed the *charismata*[P] under their control.

Finally, except where there was a militant strain of pneumatics challenging the apostle and his leaders, all kinds of *charismata*[G] probably got along together pretty well, natural leadership being accorded appropriate respect and more extraordinary manifestations of the Spirit being gratefully received. With the passage of time, there would be a tendency to appoint the gifted to office, and to expect office-holders to display gifts. Opposition between *charisma* and office might then arise from two causes: those who were unwilling to accept the teaching of the leader might claim personal inspiration for their views, or the leader might claim a monopoly of inspiration, provoking others to protest that they too were bearers of the Spirit.

The Question this Raises

Our study of the elders has inevitably involved us in the story of the development of the church's ministry in the first century at many points, and in the light of this, I pose this question. *When the identity of the elders, and their relationship to* charisma *and* Amt*, is rightly understood, may we not think that twentieth century scholars have greatly exaggerated the diversity of the early churches' patterns of ministry?*

Partly, no doubt, this has been a hangover from the days when it was customary among Protestant scholars to oppose the freedom of 'good' Pauline Christianity to the bondage of 'bad' Jewish Christianity. Partly it may be seen as a response to the ecumenical concerns of the twentieth century, the way to promote the unity of the churches being to dethrone all their proud claims to represent the one original and true pattern of church order. Finding diversity in the early church has thus been as fashionable as it once was to go to the New Testament to find one's own church's form of government set forth. We may sympathize with the aim, but disagree with the method. Claims to have preserved the original pattern of ministry are best undermined by showing the *strangeness* of the church's past rather than its diversity.

The basic error of the consensus view on this matter has been that it has operated with too static a concept both of *charisma* and of the elders, as if these terms describe relatively fixed and distinct entities. So that, if a person is called a prophet, then he is not also or in other contexts a teacher, a priest, an elder or a bishop. To question this is not just to say that being a prophet is not a full-time job; it is to say that 'prophet', like 'poet', is not simply a descriptive term, but also in part an evaluative term as well. In the same way, as we have seen, eldership is an expression of honour, and 'the elders' is a term that can be applied to people who can also and at other times be referred to by a wide range of other titles.

The household matrix of the early congregations has been extensively studied, and forms an agreed result of modern scholarship, but the implications of this for our present subject have not been drawn out. In particular, unquestioned (and therefore unrecorded) assumptions about seniority will have shaped the development of the church's leadership within the home and influenced the conduct of its meetings, and the co-operation of several household heads will have provided a natural context in which to speak of 'the elders'.

When we take seriously the household context of the earliest congregations, attested to us both for Pauline- and Jewish-Christianity, a rather uniform pattern of church organization becomes evident. The household has its head, who functions towards the believers as an overseer, presiding at the Table, offering prayer, inviting one or another to speak, handling monies perhaps, because it is natural that as a person of seniority, means and education he should do so. As the little congregation grows, others assist him, whether in teaching or in 'serving tables'. It will be natural to call such people 'helpers', *diakonoi*. As the house-churches multiply, the leaders need to confer, perhaps a Paul or a James needs to address them. These are the elders of the Christian community, owing their prestige to their leadership of their households, as the elders have always done. At some point, as when the Twelve cease to be a force in Jerusalem, or Paul's personal supervision is removed from his churches, the need for a local overseer is felt, to safeguard the unity of the churches in the face of threats from inside or outside, and the congregations come together in one place under one overseer, with a consequent loss of status by the elders who no longer lead their own meetings.

There is no need to suppose that this process of development happened at the same pace everywhere. Certainly it did not. The New Testament itself suggests that it proceeded more quickly in Jerusalem than in Ephesus, for example, but this is probably no more than a function of the rate of growth of the churches, rather than any theological resistance to centralized leadership. We must also constantly remember that our knowledge is fragmentary and only extends to the arc that runs round from Jerusalem to Rome. But with these caveats, it may reasonably be claimed that this is the pattern of development for which we have evidence, and it is remarkably uniform and intrinsically likely.

This question is closely related to the proper subject of this study, since the elders have been one of the main supports for the idea of opposed forms of organization in the first-century church. They have been made to encapsulate a supposed difference of outlook between Paul and Jerusalem. When, however, we see that there is nothing distinctively Jewish about deferring to seniority, and moreover that there was not within Judaism a defined office of elder waiting to be either taken over or rejected by the churches. And when we see that nothing in Paul's *charisma* teaching implies a hostility to honour, order or office, does not the case for diversity in the church's ministry largely collapse, opening the way for a detailed reconsideration of many aspects of what J. D. G. Dunn called 'the character of earliest Christianity'?[6]

Implications for the Ministry Today

This study has not been undertaken for the purpose of endorsing any particular pattern of church order for today, nor in the conviction that if we can only know what the first Christians did, then we are somehow bound to model our own structures on theirs. The writer belongs to a branch of the Christian church, but it is not a branch that has traditionally looked to elders for direction, nor called its leaders 'elders'. Even if we wanted to do so, it is difficult to imagine how the conclusions of this study could be straightforwardly translated into contemporary practice. The role of the elders in early Christianity was of a piece with their role in society as a whole. We cannot reconstruct the first-century house-church unless we first reconstruct the Graeco-Roman world of which it was a part. Countryman writes:

> There is no clear value in transposing one or another fragment of early Christian teaching directly into our world without taking account of the original social context in which that teaching came to life.[7]

[6] His book *Unity and Diversity* was subtitled, 'An Enquiry into the Character of Earliest Christianity'.
[7] Countryman, 'Equality', p. 138.

254

If the study of Christian social origins opens our eyes to the 'foreignness' of the New Testament world and warns us against too easily claiming that we are doing what the first Christians were doing without first entering their world, then it is not without a certain purgative value. But we do not need to rest content with that! Granted that we cannot recreate the conditions or the structures of first-century Christianity in our time, we may still ask what contribution the study of them makes to the questions currently exercising the church. One such question is that of women's ordination. Another is the search for a common understanding of ministry, as exemplified by the Lima report of the World Council of Churches. We shall take these in order.

1. *The elders and the role of women — then and now.* The role played by women in the earliest churches has been exhaustively studied in recent years, and this is not the place to rehearse the arguments or the evidence on which they are based. A clear picture is made difficult by the fact that, as we noted earlier,[8] there was no one attitude to women in the societies of the ancient world, and attitudes in the earliest churches were probably equally varied. Moreover, our evidence for first-century Christianity is largely confined to the churches that grew up between Antioch and Rome, especially those established through the work of Paul and his colleagues. However, in this part of the first-century church, two facts seem fairly well established. First, well-to-do women played a prominent role in the Pauline mission and in the early days of the churches that grew from it. In particular, they were among those who opened their homes to the first house-churches, both in Greece and Asia Minor, something for which we have the word of both Paul and Acts, and evidence from Jerusalem and Joppa also.[9] Secondly, however, in the generation after Paul's death this role was effectively extinguished, as the Pastoral Epistles testify, never to be rekindled by the dominant stream of the church in the Ante-Nicene period.

If we relate these two facts to our overall thesis, it would appear that women were to be found among those who came to be called

8 See p. 127.
9 Acts 9:36ff., 12:12, 16:15; Rom 16:1; Col 4:15.

the elders, the house-church leaders of the early days who were known by a variety of titles including ἐπίκοποι. *But the same process that led to these leaders being called the elders, led also in time to women being excluded from their number.*

'The elders', we have argued, was a collective way of referring to a group of leaders acting representatively, and did not appear in the churches (because it was not appropriate) until the household congregations began to multiply and consolidate their position in a town. As the households multiplied, they will have done so by preference in households where men presided, in accordance with the dominant ideas of the time. It was one thing for women to be given titles in socially acceptable cults and societies, and quite another for them to be leaders in religious associations already under suspicion of being subversive of the social order. What happened to the women who were already leading churches, we have no means of knowing, but we may guess that their number was not added to, so that before long there were few, if any, left in charge.

In any case, we have suggested, the elders themselves lost ground to the emerging 'monepiskopos'. It is possible that women were among those who sat with the bishop at the Table, but power and authority were increasingly concentrated in his hands, not theirs. When today we ask whether the New Testament church provides us with a precedent for ordaining women, we are effectively asking whether women enjoyed positions of *oversight* in the New Testament churches. The answer seems to be that they did in the early days when oversight meant oversight of a household church, but they did not (so far as we know) become 'monepiskopoi'. Nor in the second century did they become presbyters, when presbyter came to mean the bishop's deputy. Whether they were numbered among the *seniores laici* we do not know, but the question is hardly relevant.

What conclusions for today should be drawn from these facts, or probabilities, as we hold them to be, is of course quite another question, depending for its answer on prior hermeneutical convictions. At the end of her fresh look at Lightfoot's classic, *The Christian Ministry*, Christina Baxter says something that applies to all attempts to find the relevance of New Testament patterns for today:

We may need to ask not, 'Does this pattern conform to the order we have received?', but, 'Does this pattern serve the coming Kingdom, the good news of which we have heard from our predecessors?'[10]

Rather than striving to show that women played a more prominent part than our evidence suggests, or that the prohibitions of the Pastorals do not mean what they appear to say, it would be more honest to admit the facts and then, if so minded, set them aside. Again, rather than using the New Testament to establish a primitive, egalitarian innocence for the church, while discarding much of the New Testament in the process, those for whom the New Testament documents speak with authority would do better to take them as a whole and ask what we learn from the disciples of the apostles and the fact that they in their generation closed the door to women in leadership after Jesus and Paul had seemed to open it. They would say to us, I think: We did what we thought was right in our situation for the sake of the spread of the gospel (1 Cor 9:20–23). The spread of the gospel is still paramount, but your day is not ours. We refused to bring discredit on the gospel by an untimely and intemperate rush for freedom. See that you do not bring discredit on the same gospel by denying a freedom whose time has long come!

2. *The elders and current ecumenical discussion.* In seeking to relate our conclusions to the current ecumenical debate about the ministry, as set out in the Lima document of the WCC, *Baptism, Eucharist and Ministry* (*BEM*), it will be helpful briefly to summarize that statement. It begins by speaking of the Calling of the Whole People of God, and then seeks to define the role of the Ordained Ministry within that calling. The third section speaks of the Forms of the Ordained Ministry. The concluding sections of the statement speak about Succession in the Apostolic Tradition, Ordination, and the way towards the Mutual Recognition of Ministries.

---

[10] Baxter, 'Lightfoot', p. 51.

It is with the third section on the forms of the Ordained Ministry
that we are here most concerned. It begins by stating:

> The New Testament does not describe a single pattern of minis-
> try which might serve as a blueprint or continuing norm for all
> future ministry in the church (/// 19).

It traces the establishment of the threefold pattern of bishop, presbyter and deacon to the second and third centuries, and shows how
this changed over time. Despite this, it nevertheless says that,

> the threefold ministry of bishop, presbyter and deacon may serve
> today as an expression of the unity we seek and also as a means
> for achieving it (/// 22)

and concludes by suggesting that it has a powerful claim to be
accepted by all (/// 25). It goes on to speak of the way in which this
ministry should be exercised, personally, collegially and communally, and of the functions of each of the ministers (/// 26).

While everyone would agree that the New Testament offers no
blueprint for church order, the conclusion to which this study has
led us is that the diversity of patterns of ministry even in the New
Testament period has been considerably exaggerated. *BEM* is right
to say that the church has never been without persons holding
specific authority and responsibility (/// 9), and this is to say that
the church has never lacked ἐπισκοπή. The sphere over which the
ἐπίσκοπος had oversight in the first and second centuries steadily
increased, but the care and leadership by one person on behalf of
many people can be traced back to the very beginning in the personage of the household leader, who like the *mebaqqer* at Qumran
shepherded the flock of God. By whatever title he or she is known
— Priest, Presbyter, Minister or Pastor — today's congregational
leader exercises a ministry of oversight that was first performed by
this figure.

BEM is also right to say that a threefold order can in no way be
traced back to Jesus or his apostles, being a creation of the second
and third centuries. Insofar as any order can be found in the literature of the first century, we should have to speak of a *twofold* order,
overseers and deacons, to whom 'the elders' generally refers. Our

study has shown that 'the elders', πρεσβύτεροι, was originally no more than a way of referring collectively, in accordance with the manners of the time, to the leadership of the household churches, to whom we suggested the title of Overseer first belonged.

Although the needs of the growing church and the pressures upon it led to the terms Overseer, Presbyter and Deacon becoming the titles of separate offices with separate functions, we should remember that originally all three words could refer to the same people. Thus, while ἐπίσκοπος connoted the leaders' *function*, διάκονος, we may say, connoted their *style*. Representatives of God (1 Cor 3:5), they were servants of the church (2 Cor 4:5). *BEM* recognizes this. When it says that ordained ministers are not to be autocratic or impersonal functionaries (/// 16), it is effectively reminding us of the *diaconal* style of Christian leadership.

Πρεσβύτερος, on the other hand, connoted the *character* of those who thus served as overseers. Since 'the elders' was a title of respect for those who were the fathers of the community, calling the overseers 'the elders' spoke of the respect they enjoyed as fathers (and perhaps mothers) in the church, the household of God (1 Tim 3:15). To speak of the overseers as the elders of the community also spoke of the qualities such persons were expected to display, both before and after they were appointed. Overseers should be elders: mature, wise, able to teach and 'parent' the church.

This is still true, when *BEM* sets out the functions of presbyters, these functions could be summarized by the one word 'oversight', ἐπισκοπή (/// 30). Bishops and presbyters differ only in the area over which they are called to exercise responsibility. So although Presbyter became for historical reasons the title of an office of congregational oversight, reflection on the original connotation of the word πρεσβύτεροι can help us to see to what kind of person the function of congregational oversight should be entrusted. When 1 Tim 3:1–7 lists the qualities necessary in a bishop, it speaks of his maturity and wholesomeness of life and paints a portrait of an elder of the community. It thus roots the leader in the congregation, and provides a reminder that a person's fitness to lead the church comes first from their being a good member of it. The overseer never ceases to be such a member, *primus inter pares* not only with other leaders but with every member of the church.

The fact that 'the elders' is a collective term serves as a reminder that the Christian ministry of oversight is not to be exercised in isolation or without consultation. The original overseers were called 'the elders' when they began to consult together; even when a single overseer emerged from among their ranks to lead them, the other overseers were not thereby made redundant. They sat with him, and he presided with them. This fully supports *BEM's* saying that ordained ministry needs to be exercised collegially, as well as personally and communally (*/// 26*).

To sum up, we may say that our investigation into the meaning of the term 'the elders' in earliest Christianity, and its relationship to other titles in the church, serves to remind us of two things. While there is no office of Elder/Presbyter in the New Testament distinguishable from that of Overseer, calling overseers 'the elders' points by implication to the personal qualities required of those who serve as overseers. They must be those to whom respect can be given. The fact that it is always a collective title points to the collegial character of Christian oversight. While every overseer has his or her particular responsibility, be it household, congregation, parish or diocese, in which they are the leader, none should exercise that oversight without consulting other leaders, as well as the people under their care, since no community of God's people is 'an island entire unto itself'.

Works Cited

Except for those listed below, the abbreviations used for journals and standard works of reference are those recommended in the *Handbook of the Society of Biblical Literature*, (1991), pp. 201–10.

The following abbreviations do not appear there:

BAB	Bullétin de la Classe des Lettres et des Sciences Morales et Politiques, Bruxelles
LEC	Les Études Classiques
REG	Revue des Études Grecques
SEG	Supplementum Epigraphicum Graecum

Achtemeier, P. J
Quest

The Quest for Unity in the New Testament Church
Philadelphia: Fortress, 1987

Allo, E. B.
Corinthiens

Saint Paul: Premiére Épître aux Corinthiens
Paris: Gabalda, 1956

Amoss, P. T. & Harrell, S.
Other Ways

Other Ways of Growing Old
Stanford, Cal.: University Press, 1981

Anderson, H.

'3 Maccabees. A New Translation and Introduction'

OT Pseudepigrapha   *The Old Testament Pseudepigrapha,* Vol. 2,
J.H. Charlesworth, (ed.)
London: Darton, Longman & Todd,
1985, pp. 509–529

Arnheim, M. T. W.   *Aristocracy in Ancient Greece*
Aristocracy   London: Thames & Hudson, 1977

Audet, J.-P.   *La Didachè*
Didachè   Paris: Gabalda, 1958

Banks, R. J.   *Paul's Idea of Community*
Community   Exeter: Paternoster, 1980.

Barrett, C. K.   *Church, Ministry and Sacraments in the*
Church   *New Testament*
Exeter: Paternoster, 1985

Barrett, C. K.   'Paul's Address to the Ephesian Elders',
'Address'   *God's Christ and his People*
Jervell, J. & Meeks, W. A. (eds)
Oslo: Universitetsforlaget, 1977, pp. 107–21.

Barrett, C. K.   'Pauline Controversies in the Post-Pauline
'Controversies'   Period'
NTS 20, 1973–4, pp. 229–45.

Barth, M.   *Ephesians,* (AB), 2 Vols.
Ephesians   New York: Doubleday, 1974.

Barton, S. C. &   'A Hellenistic Cult Group and the New
Horsley, G. H. R.   Testament Churches'
'Cult'   *JAC* 24, 1981, pp. 7–41.

Bauckham, R.   *Jude and the Relatives of Jesus in the Early Church*
Relatives   Edinburgh: T&T Clark, 1990.

Bauckham, R.　　　　　'Pseudo-apostolic Letters'
'Letters'　　　　　　　*JBL*, 107, 1988, 469–94.

Baxter, C.　　　　　　'Classics Revisited: The Christian Ministry,
'Lightfoot'　　　　　　　J. B. Lightfoot'
　　　　　　　　　　　Anvil, 7, 1990, pp. 247–51.

Beall, T. S.　　　　　　*Josephus' Description of the Essenes*
Essenes　　　　　　　　*Illustrated by the Dead Sea Scrolls*
　　　　　　　　　　　Cambridge: CUP, 1988.

Beasley-Murray, G. R.　*The Book of Revelation*
Revelation　　　　　　London: Marshalls, 1974.

Beauvoir, S. de　　　　*Old Age*
Old Age　　　　　　　Harmondsworth: Penguin, 1977.

Berger, P. L.　　　　　*The Social Reality of Religion*
Religion　　　　　　　Harmondsworth: Penguin, 1973.

Berger, P. L. &　　　　*The Social Construction of Reality*
Luckmann, T.　　　　　Harmondsworth: Penguin, 1967.
Reality

Best, E.　　　　　　　'Paul's Apostolic Authority?'
'Authority'　　　　　　*JSNT*, 27, 196, pp. 3–25.

Best, E.　　　　　　　*Paul and his Converts*
Converts　　　　　　　Edinburgh: T&T Clark, 1988.

Beyer, H. W.　　　　　διακονέω, διακονία, διάκονος
διακονέω　　　　　　　*TDNT*, II, 1935, pp. 81–93.

Beyer, H. W. &　　　　'Bischof'
Kapp, H.　　　　　　　*RAC*, Vol. II, pp. 394–407.
'Bischof'

Bornkamm, G. / πρέσβυς — πρέσβυς, *TDNT*, Vol. 6, pp. 651–83.

Bourke, M. M. / 'Order' — 'Church Order in the New Testament' *CBQ*, 30, 1968, pp. 493–511.

Bowe, B. E. / Crisis — *A Church in Crisis: Ecclesiology and Paraenesis in Clement of Rome* Minneapolis: Fortress, 1988

Bradshaw, P. / Presidency — *Liturgical Presidency in the early Church* Bramcote: Grove, 1983

Bradshaw, P. / 'Ordination' — 'Ordination', *Essays on Hippolytus* Cuming, G. J. (ed) Bramcote: Grove, 1978, pp. 33–8

Braun, H. / Qumran — *Qumran und das New Testament*, (2 Vols) Tübingen, 1966

Brockhaus, U. / Charisma — *Charisma und Amt* Wuppertal: Brockhaus, 1972

Brooten, B. J. / Women Leaders — *Women Leaders in the Ancient Synagogue* Atlanta: Scholars Press, 1982

Brown, R. E. / 'Episkope' — 'Episkope and Episkopos *TS*, 41, 1980, pp. 322–38

Brown, R. E. / Epistles — *The Epistles of John* New York: Doubleday, 1982

Brown, R. E. / Priest — *Priest and Bishop* New York: Chapman, 1970

Brox, N.
Hirt

Der Hirt des Hermas, KAV 7,
Göttingen: Vandenhoeck & Ruprecht,
1991

Bruce, F. F.
Acts (1988)

The Book of the Acts
Grand Rapids: Eerdmans, (1st ed.)
1954, (2nd ed.) 1988

Bruce, F. F.
Acts (1990)

The Acts of the Apostles: the Greek Text
with Introduction and Commentary
Grand Rapids: Eerdmans, (3rd ed.) 1990

Bruce, F. F.
'Jerusalem'

'The Church of Jerusalem in Acts'
BJRL, 67, 1984, pp. 641–61

Bultmann, R.
Theology

Theology of the New Testament,
(2 Vols), London: SCM, 1955

Burtchaell, J. T.
Synagogue

From Synagogue to Church,
Cambridge: CUP, 1992

Byl, S.
'Plutarche'

'Plutarche et la Vieillesse'
LEC 45, 1977, pp. 107–23

Caird, G. B.
'Descent'

'The Descent of Christ in Eph. 4:7–11',
SE 2, Tu 87, Berlin: Akademie, 1964,
pp. 535–45

Caird, G. B.
Revelation

Commentary on the Revelation of St
John the Divine
London: Black, 1966

Campbell, R. A.
'Divisions'

'Does Paul Acquiesce in Divisions at the
Lord's Supper?'
NovT, 33, 1991, pp. 61–70

Campbell, R. A.   'The Elders of the Jerusalem Church'
'Elders'   *JTS*, 44, 1993, pp. 511–28

Campbell, R. A.   'Do the Work of An Evangelist'
'Evangelist'   *EvQ*, 64, 1992, pp. 117–29

Campbell, R. A.   'Identifying the Faithful Sayings
'Sayings'   in the Pastoral Epistles'
                         JSNT 54, 1994, pp. 73–86

Campenhausen, H. von   *Ecclesiastical Authority and Spiritual*
Authority   *Power in the Church of the First Three*
                              Centuries
                         London: Black, 1969

Caron, P.   'Les *Seniores Laici* de l'Église Africaine'
Seniores   *RIDA*, 6, 1951, pp. 7–22

Cartledge, P. &   *Hellenistic and Roman Sparta: a Tale of*
Spawforth, A.   *two Cities*
Sparta   London: Routledge, 1989

Chapple, A. L.   'Local Leadership in Pauline Churches'
'Local Leadership'   (unpub.) PhD Thesis, Durham, 1984

Clarke, A. D.   *Secular and Christian Leadership in Corinth*
Leadership   Leiden: Brill, 1993

Cohen, S. J. D.   *From the Maccabees to the Mishnah*
Maccabees   Philadelphia: Westminster, 1987

Collange, J-F.   *The Epistle of St Paul to the Philippians*
Philippians   London: Epworth, 1977

Collins, J. N.   *Diakonia*
Diakonia   Oxford: OUP, 1990

Congar, Y. 'Sohm'	'Rudolf Sohm Nous Interroge Encore' *RSPT*, 57, 1973, pp. 263–94
Conrad, J. זקן	זקן *TDOT*, Vol. VI, pp. 122–31
Conzelmann, H. *Acts*	*Acts of the Apostles* Philadelphia: Fortress, 1987
Cook, M. J. *Leaders*	*Mark's Treatment of the Jewish Leaders* Leiden: Brill, 1978
Countryman, L. W. 'Equality'	'Christian Equality and the Early Catholic Episcopate' *ATR*, 63, 1981, pp. 115–38
Countryman, L. W. 'Patrons'	'Patrons and Officers in Club and Church' *SBL, Seminar Papers*, 1977, pp. 135–43
Countryman, L. W. *Rich Christian*	*The Rich Christian in the Church of the Early Empire* New York: Edwin Mellen, 1980
Cowgill, D. O. & Holmes, L. D. *Aging*	*Aging and Modernization* New York: Meredith, 1972
Cranfield, C. E. B. 'Diakonia'	'Diakonia in the New Testament'. *The Bible and the Christian Life,* Edinburgh: T&T Clark, 1985, pp. 69–87
Cranfield, C. E. B. *Romans*	*A Critical and Exegetical Commentary on the Epistle to the Romans,* (ICC) (2 Vols) Edinburgh: T&T Clark, 1975, 1979
Dassmann, E. 'Hausgemmeinde'	'Hausgemeinde und Bischofsamt' *JAC*, 11, 1984, pp. 82–97

Davids, P. H.
1 Peter

The First Epistle of Peter
Grand Rapids: Eerdmans, 1990

Deissman, A.
Bible Studies²

Bible Studies, (2nd Ed)
Edinburgh: T&T Clark, 1901

Deissmann, A.
Light⁴

Light from the Ancient East, (4th Ed)
London: Hodders, 1922

Delcor, M.
Daniel

Le Livre de Daniel
Paris: Gabalda, 1971

Dibelius, M. &
Conzelmann, H.
Pastorals

The Pastoral Epistles
Philadelphia: Fortress, 1972

Dix, G.
'Ministry'

'The Ministry in the Early Church',
The Apostolic Ministry
Kirk, K. E. (ed.)
London: Hodder, 1946, pp. 183–303

Draper, J. A.
'Apostles'

'The Twelve Apostles as Foundation Stones of the Heavenly Jerusalem and the Foundation of the Qumran Community'
Neot, 22, 1988, pp. 41–63

Dunn, J. D. G.
Romans

Romans (WBC 38, A and B)
Dallas: Word, 1988

Dunn, J. D. G.
Spirit

Jesus and the Spirit
London: SCM, 1975

Dunn, J. D. G.

Unity²

Unity and Diversity in the New Testament, (2nd Ed)
London: SCM, 1990

Duverger, M. *Introduction*	*Introduction to the Social Sciences* London: Allen & Unwin, 1964
Ehrenberg, V. *Greek State*	*The Greek State* Oxford: Blackwell, 1960
Elliott, J. H. *Home*	*Home for the Homeless* Philadelphia: Fortress, 1981
Elliott, J. H. 'Ministry'	'Ministry and Church Order in the New Testament' *CBQ*, 32, 1970, pp. 366–91
Ellis, E. E. 'Co-workers'	'Paul and his Co-workers' *NTS*, 17, 1970–1, pp. 437–52
Ellis, E. E. 'Traditions'	'Traditions in the PE' *Early Jewish and Christian Exegesis* (ed) Evans, C. A. & Stinespring, W. F. Atlanta: Scholars, 1987, pp. 237–53
Engel, H. *Susannah*	*Die Susannah-Erzählung* Freiburg, Schweiz, 1985
Eph 'al, I., 'Political'	'Political and Social Organisation of the Jews in the Babylonian Exile' *ZDMG*, Supp. V., XXI. Deutscher Orientalistentag 1980, Steppat, F. (Hrsgbn.) Wiesbaden, 1983, pp. 106–12
Farrer, A. M. 'Ministry'	'The Ministry in the New Testament' *The Apostolic Ministry* Kirk, K. E. (ed.) London: Hodder, 1946, pp. 115–82

Fee, G. D.
Corinthians

First Epistle to the Corinthians
Grand Rapids: Eerdmans, 1987

Fee, G. D.
Pastorals

1 and 2 Timothy and Titus, NIBC 13
Peabody, Mass.: Hendrickson, 1988

Ferguson, E.
'Ordain'

'Ordain, Ordination'
ABD, (1992), Vol. 5, pp. 37–40

Ferguson, E.
'Ordination'

'Jewish and Christian Ordination'
HTR, 56, 1963, pp. 13–20

Ferguson, E.
'Laying'

'Laying on of Hands: its Significance in
    Ordination'
JTS, n.s. 26, 1974, pp. 1–12

Filson, F. V.
'Significance'

'The Significance of the Early House Churches'
JBL, 58, 1939, pp. 105–12

Fiorenza, E. S.
Memory

In Memory of Her
London: SCM, 1983

Fitzmyer, J. A.
'Jewish Christianity'

'Jewish Christianity in Acts in the Light
    of the Qumran Scrolls'
*Essays on the Semitic Background of the
    New Testament*
London: Chapman, 1971, pp. 271–303

Fitzmyer, J. A.
Luke

The Gospel according to Luke, (2 Vols),
New York: Doubleday, 1981

Frankfort, H.,
Intellectual

The Intellectual Adventure of Ancient Man
Chicago: 1946, pp. 343–54

Frend, W. H. C.
'Seniores'

'The Seniores Laici and the Origins of
    the Church in North Africa'
JTS 12, 1961, pp. 280–4

Frey, J. B. *CIJ*	*Corpus Inscriptionum Judaicarum* Rome: Pont. Inst. Arch. Crist, 1936 & 1952
Gardner, J. F. & Wiedemann, T. *Household*	*The Roman Household, a Sourcebook* London: Routledge, 1991
Georgi, D. *Opponents*	*The Opponents of Paul in 2 Corinthians* Edinburgh: T&T Clark, 1987
Gielen, M. 'Formel'	'Zur Interpretation der Formel ἡ κατ᾽ οἶκον ἐκκλησία' *ZNW,* 77, 1986, pp. 107–25
Giles, K. ΕΚΚΛΗΣΙΑ'	'Luke's Use of the term ΕΚΚΛΗΣΙΑ with special reference to Acts 20:28 and 9:31' *NTS,* 31, 1985, pp. 135–42
Giles, K. *Patterns*	*Patterns of Ministry among the First Christians* Melbourne: Dove Collins, 1989
Giles, K. 'Protestantism'	'Is Luke an Exponent of Early Protestantism?' *EvQ* 55, 1983, pp. 3–20
Gnika, J. 'Amt'	'Geistliches Amt und Gemeinde nach Paulus' *Kairos,* 11, 1969, pp. 95–104
Gnilka, J. *Philemon*	*Der Philemonbrief,* HThKNT X/4, Freiburg: Herder, 1982
Gnilka, J. *Philipper*	*Der Philipperbrief,* HThKNT 10/3, Freiburg: Herder, 1968

271

Goetz, K. G.
נבקר

'Ist der נבקר der Genizafragmente
wirklich das Vorbild des christlichen
Episkopats?'
ZNW, 30, 1931, pp. 89–93

Goldstein, J. A.
1 Maccabees

1 Maccabees (AB 41)
New York: Doubleday, 1976

Goodman, M.,
Ruling

The Ruling Class of Judaea
Cambridge: CUP, 1987

Goppelt, L.
Apostolic

Apostolic and Post-Apostolic Times
London: Black, 1970

Goppelt, L.
Petrusbrief

Der Erste Petrusbrief
Göttingen: Vandenhoeck & Ruprecht,
1978

Goulder, M. D.
Luke

Luke, A New Paradigm, (2 Vols),
Sheffield: JSOT, 1989

Goulder, M. D.
'Visionaries'

'The Visionaries of Laodicea'
JSNT 43, 1991, pp. 15–39

Grant, R. M.
Fathers

The Apostolic Fathers, Vol. 1,
New York: Nelson, 1964

Grayson, K. &
Herdan, G.
'Authorship'

'The Authorship of the Pastoral Epistles
in the light of Statistical Linguistics'
NTS 6, 1959–60, pp. 129ff.

Greeven, H.
'Propheten'

'Propheten, Lehrer, Vorsteher bei Paulus'
ZNW, 44, 1952, pp. 1–43

Grudem, W. A.
Prophecy

The Gift of Prophecy in 1 Corinthians
Washington: UPA, 1982

Günther, W.
ἀδελφός

ἀδελφός
NIDNTT, I, pp. 254–8

Hadas, M.
Aristeas

Aristeas to Philocrates
New York: Harper, 1951

Haenchen, E.
Acts

The Acts of the Apostles
Oxford: Blackwell, 1971

Hainz, J.
'Anfänge'

'Die Anfänge des Biscofs — und
    Diakonenmates'
Die Kirche im Werden
Münich: Schöningh, 1976

Haley, P.
'Charisma'

'Rudolph Sohm on Charisma'
JR, 60, 1980, pp. 185–97

Halleux, A. de
'Ministères'

'Les Ministères dans la Didachè
Irenikon, 53, 1980, pp. 5–29

Hanson, A. T.
Pastorals

The Pastoral Epistles
London: SCM, 1961

Harnack, A. von
Constitution

The Constitution and Law of the Church
London: Willians & Northgate, 1910

Harrison, P. N.
Problem

The Problem of the Pastoral Epistles
Oxford: OUP, 1921

Harvey, A. E.
'Elders'

'Elders'
JTS, 25, 1974, pp. 318–31

Hatch, E.
Organization

*The Organization of the Early Christian
    Churches*
London: Revingtons, 1881

Hawthorne, G.
Philippians

Philippians, WBC 43
Waco, Texas: Word, 1983

Heard, R. G.
'Prologues'

'The Old Gospel Prologues'
JTS 6, 1955, pp. 1–16

Hemer, C. J.
Acts

*The Book of Acts in the Setting of Hel-
lenistic History*
Tübingen: Mohr, 1989

Hengel, M.
Acts

*The Book of Acts in the Setting of Hel-
lenistic History*
London: SCM, 1979

Hengel, M.
'Proseuche'

'Proseuche und Synagogue: Jüdische
Gemeinde, Gotteshaus und
Gottesdienst in der Diaspora und in
Palästina',
Tradition und Glaube
Jeremias, G. et al.
Gottingen, 1971, pp. 157–84

Hoenig, S. B.
'City Square'

'The Ancient City Square: the Forerunner
to the Synagogue'
ANRW II.19.1. 1979, pp. 448–76

Holmberg, B.
Power

Paul and Power
Lund: CWK Gleerug, 1978

Holmberg, B.
'Order'

'Sociological Analysis versus Theological
Analysis in the Question concerning
a Pauline Church Order', *Die
Paulinische Literatur und Theologie*
Pedersen, S. (ed.), Göttingen:
Vandenhoeck & Ruprecht, 1980, pp.
187–200

Hooker, M. D. 'False Teachers'	'Were there False Teachers in Colossae?' *Christ and Spirit in the New Testament* Lindars, B. & Smalley, S. S. (eds) Cambridge: CUP, 1973, pp. 315–31
Horsley, G. (ed) *Documents*	*New Documents Illustrating Early Christianity*, Vols 1–5 Sydney: Macquarrie U.P., 1981–9
Jackson, F. & Lake, K. *Beginnings*	*The Beginnings of Christianity,* Vols 4 and 5 London: Macmillan, 1933
Jay, E. G. 'Presbyter'	'From Presbyter-Bishops to Bishops and Presbyters' *SecCent,* 1, 1981, pp. 125–62
Jeremias, J. *Jerusalem*	*Jerusalem in the Time of Jesus,* (3rd Ed) London: SCM, 1969
Jeremias, J. *Pastoral*	*Die Briefe an Timotheus und Titus* (NTD 9^{12}) Göttingen: Vandenhoeck & Ruprecht, 1981 (originally 1936)
Johnson, L. T. *Acts*	*The Acts of the Apostles (Sac. Pag. 5)* Collegeville, MN: Liturgical Press/ Michael Glazier, 1992
Johnson, L. T. *Writings*	*The Writings of the New Testament* London: SCM, 1986
Jones, A. H. M. *Athenian Democracy*	*Athesian Democracy* Oxford: Blackwell, 1957

Jones, A. H. M.
City

The Greek City
Oxford: Clarendon, 1966

Karrer, M.
'Ältestenamt'

'Das urchristliche Ältestenamt'
NovT 32, 1990, pp. 152–88

Käsemann, E.
'Ministry'

'Ministry and Community'
Essays in New Testament Themes
London: SCM, 1964

Kee, H. C.
Good News

Good News to the Ends of the Earth
London: SCM, 1990

Kee, H. C.
'Transformation'

'Transformation of the Synagogue after
    70 AD'
NTS, 36, 1989, pp. 1–24

Kelly, J. N. D.
Pastorals

A Commentary on the Pastoral Epistles
London: A. & C. Black, 1963

Kertelge, K.
Amt

Das kirchliche Amt im New Testament
Darmstadt: Wissenschaftliche
Buchgesellschaft, 1977

Kertelge, K.
Gemeinde

Gemeinde und Amt im New Testament
München: Kösel, 1972

Kirk, J. A.
'Salary'

'Did Officials in the New Testament
    Church receive a Salary?'
ExpTim 84, 1972/3, pp. 105–8

Klauck, H-J.
Hausgemeinde

*Hausgemeinde und Hauskirche im früen
    Christentu* SBS 103
Stuttgart: Verlag Katholisches
Bibelwerk, 1981

Knibb, M. A.   *The Qumran Community*
Qumran   Cambridge: CUP, 1987

Knight, G. W. III   *The Pastoral Epistles* (NICGT)
Pastorals   Grand Rapids: Eerdmans, 1992.

Koester, H.   *Introduction to the New Testament,* (2 Vols)
Introduction   Philadelphia: Fortress, 1982

Kraft, R. A.   *Apostolic Fathers,* Vol. 3
Fathers   New York: Nelson, 1965

Krauss, S.,   *Synagogale Altertümer,*
Synagogale   Berlin: Harz, 1922

Küng   *The Church*
The Church   London: Burns & Oates, 1968

Lacey, W. K.   *The Family in Classical Greece*
Family   London: Thames and Hudson, 1968

Lacey, W. K.   'Patria Potestas'
'Potestas'   *The Family in Ancient Rome*
                    Rawson, B. (ed.)
                    London: Croom Helm, 1986

Lampe, G. W. H.   *A Patristic Greek Lexicon*
PGL   Oxford: Clarendon, 1961

Leon, H. J.   *The Jews of Ancient Rome*
Jews   Philadelphia: JPSA, 1960

Levine, L. I. (ed) *The Synagogue in Late Antiquity*
Synagogue   Philadelphia: ASOR, 1987

Lévy, I. 'Études'	'Études sur la Vie Municipale de l'Asie Mineure' *REG*, 8, 1895, pp. 203–50
Lieu, J. *Letters*	*The Second and Third Epistles of John* Edinburgh: T&T Clark, 1986
Lightfoot, J. B. *AF*	*The Apostolic Fathers* (5 Vols) London: Macmillan, 1889
Lightfoot, J. B. *Philippians*	*Epistle of St Paul to the Philippians* London: Macmillan, 1902
Lincoln, A. T. *Ephesians*	*Ephesians* (WBC 42) Dallas: Word, 1990
Lindsay, T. M. *Church*	*Church and Ministry in the Early Centuries* London: Hodders, 1902
Linton, O. *Problem*	*Das Problem der Urkirche in der neueren Forschung* Uppsala: University Press, 1932
Lips, H. von *Glaube*	*Glaube, Gemeinde, Amt* Gottingen: Vandenhoeck & Ruprecht, 1979
Lohfink, G. *Community*	*Jesus and Community* Philadelphia: Fortress, 1984
Lohse, E. 'Entstehung'	'Entstehung des Bischosamts in der früen Christenheit' *ZNW* 71, 1980, pp. 58–73
Lohse, E. 'Ordination'	'Ordination im *AT* und im Judentum, und im New Testament' *RGG*³, Vol. IV, pp. 1671ff.

Lohse, E.
Ordination

Die Ordination im Spätjudentum und im New Testament
Göttingen: V & R, 1951

Lohse, E. (ed.)
Qumran

Die Texte aus Qumran Hebräisch und Deutsch²
Munich, 1971

Lowrie, W.
Church

The Church and its Organisation: The Primitive Age
New York: Longmans, 1904

Lüdemann, G.
Early

Early Christianity according to the Traditions in Acts
London: SCM, 1989

MacDonald, M. Y.
Pauline Churches

The Pauline Churches
Cambridge: CUP, 1988

McKenzie, J. L.
'Elders'

'Elders in the Old Testament'
Bib 40, 1959, pp. 522–40

McLaren, J. S.
Power

Power and Politics in Palestine
Sheffield: JSOT, 1991

MacMullen, R.
Social Relations

Roman Social Relations
New Haven: Yale, 1974

Macro, A. D.
'Cities'

'The Cities of Asia Minor under the Roman Imperium'
ANRW, II, 7.2, 1980, pp. 658–697

Maier, H. O.
Social Setting

The Social Setting of the Ministry as reflected in the Writings of Hermas, Clement and Ignatius
Ontario: Wilfred Laurier, 1991

Malamat, A.
'Kingship'

'Kingship and Council in Israel and
Sumer'
JNES 22, 1963, pp. 247–53

Malherbe, A.
Social

Social Aspects of Early Christianity
Philadelphia: Fortress, 1983

Malherbe, A.
Thessalonians

Paul and the Thessalonians
Philadelphia: Fortress, 1987

Marshall, I. H.
Acts

Acts
Leicester, IVP, 1980

Marshall, I. H.
'Early Catholicism'

'"Early Catholicism" in the New Testament'
New Directions in New Testament Study
Longenecker, R. & Tenney, M. (eds)
Grand Rapids: Zondervan, 1974, pp. 217–31

Marshall, I. H.
'Resurrection'

'The Resurrection in the Acts of the Apostles'
Apostolic History and the Gospel
Gasque, W. and Martin, R. P. (eds)
Exeter: Paternoster, 1970

Martin, Dale B.
Slavery

Slavery as Salvation
New Haven: Yale, 1990

Meade, D. G.
Pseudonymity

Pseudonymity and Canon
Grand Rapids: Eerdmans, 1987

Meecham, H. G.
Oldest

The Oldest Version of the Bible
London: Holborn, 1932

Meeks, W. A.
Urban

The First Urban Christians
Yale: University Press, 1983

Merkel, H. *Pastoral*	*Die Pastoralbriefe*, NTD 9/1, Göttingen: Vandenhoeck & Ruprecht, 1991
Merklein, H. *Amt*	*Das Kirchliche Amt nach dem Epheserbrief* München: Kösel, 1973
Metzger, B. *Canon*	*The Canon of the New Testament* Oxford: Clarendon, 1987
Metzger, W. *Letzte Reise*	*Die Letzte Reise des Apostels Paulus* Stuttgart: Calwer, 1976
Meyer, B. F. *Aims*	*The Aims of Jesus* London: SCM, 1979
Michaelis, W. *Ältestenamt*	*Das Ältestenamt* Bern, 1953
Michaels, J. R. *1 Peter*	*1 Peter*, (WBC 49) Waco: Word, 1988
Michel, O. *Römer*	*Der Römerbrief* Göttingen: V'hoeck & Ruprecht, 1978
Minois, G. *History*	*A History of Old Age* Cambridge: Polity, 1989
Moore, C. A. *Additions*	*Daniel, Esther and Jeremiah: the Additions* (AB 44) New York: Doubleday, 1977
Moule, C. F. D. 'Problem'	'The Problem of the Pastoral Epistles' *BJRL* 47, 1965, pp. 430–52
Murphy-O'Connor, J. *Corinth*	*St Paul's Corinth* Wilmington, Delaware: Glazier, 1983

Nauck, W.
'Probleme'

'Probleme des fründchristlichen
Amtsverstandnisses'
ZNW 48, 1957, pp. 200–20

Neill, S. & Wright, N. T.
Interpretation

*The Interpretation of the New Testament,
1861–1986*
Oxford: OUP, 1988

Niederwimmer, K.
Didache

Die Didache
Göttingen: Vandenhoeck & Ruprecht, 1989

O'Brien, P. T.
Philippians

*Epistle to the Philippians: a Commentary
on the Greek Text*
Grand Rapids: Eerdmans, 1991

Oster, R. E.
'Anachronism'

'Supposed Anachronism in Luke-Acts use
of συναγωγή: A Rejoinder to H. C.
Kee' *NTS*, 39, 1993, pp. 178–208

Pesch, R.
Apostelgeschichte

Die Apostelgeschichte, EKK V/1
Zürich/Neukirchen-Vluyn: Benziger/
Neukirchener, 1986

Plescia, J.
'Potestas'

'Patria Potestas and the Roman Revolution;
*The Conflict of the Generations in Ancient
Greece and Rome*
Bertman, S. (ed.)
Amsterdam. Grüner, 1976

Ploeg, J. van der
'Anciens'

Les Anciens de l'Ancien Testament'
Lex Tua Veritas: Festschift. H. Junker
Trier: Paulinus, 1961, pp. 175–91

Ploeg, J. van der
'Chefs'

'Les Chefs due Peuple d'Israel et leurs Titres'
RB 57, 1950, pp. 40–61

Poland, F.
Vereinswesens

Geschichte des griechischen Vereinswesens
Leipzig: Teubner, 1909

Powell, D.
'Ordo'

'Ordo Prebyterii'
JTS 26, 1975, pp. 290–328

Prast, F.
Presbyter

*Presbyter und Evangelium in nach-
 apostolicher Zeit*
Stuttgart: VKB, 1979

Prigent, P.
L'Apocalypse

L'Apocalypse de Saint Jean
Geneva: Labor et Fides, 1988

Prior, M.
Paul

Paul the Letter Writer
Sheffield: JSOT, 1989

Quinn, J. D.
'Last Volume'

'The Last Volume of Luke'
    Perspective on Luke-Acts
Talbert, C. (ed)
Macon, Ga: Mercer, 1978, pp. 62–75

Quinn, J. D.
Titus

The Letter to Titus, AB 35
New York: Doubleday, 1990

Ramsay, W. M.
Cities

Cities and Bishoprics of Phrygia
Oxford: Clarendon Press, 1895

Rawson, B. (ed.)
Family

The Family in Ancient Rome
London: Croom Helm, 1986

Reicke, B.
'Chronologie'

'Die Chronologie der Pastoralbriefe'
ThL, 101, 1976, pp. 81–94

Reicke, B.
'Constitution'

'The Constitution of the Church in the
    Light of Jewish Documents'
The Scrolls and the New Testament

Stendahl, K. (ed)
London: SCM, 1958, pp. 143ff.

Reinach, T. 'Inscription juive des environs de Con-
'Inscription'   stantinople'
REJ, 26, 1893, pp. 167–71.

Reinhold, M. 'The Generation Gap in Antiquity'
'Generation Gap' *The Conflict of the Generations in Ancient
    Greece and Rome*
Bertman, S. (ed.)
Amsterdam: Grüner, 1976, pp. 15–54

Reviv, H., *The Elders in Ancient Israel*
Elders   Jerusalem: Magnes Press, 1989

Roberts, C. H. 'Note on Elders'
'Elders'   *JTS* 26, 1975, pp. 403–5

Rogerson, J. *Anthropology and the Old Testament*
Anthropology   Oxford: Blackwell, 1978

Roloff, J. 'Amt, Ämter, Amtsverstandnis im neuen
'Amt'   Testament'
TRE, Vol. II, pp. 509–33

Roloff, J. *Apostelgeschichte*
Apostelgeschichte   Göttingen: Vandenhoeck & Rupecht, 1981

Roloff, J. *Der Erste brief an Timotheus*, EKK XV
Timotheus   Zürich: Benziger, 1988

Rordorf, W. 'Didache'
'Didache'   *Encyclopedia of the Early Church* (2 Vols)
Berardino, A. (Ed)
Cambridge : J. Clarke, 1992

Rordorf, W.
'Göttesdiensträume

'Was wissen wir über die christlichen
Gottesdiensträume der
vorkonstantinischen Zeit?'
ZNW, 65, 1964, pp. 110–28

Rordorf, W. & Tuilier, A.
Doctrine

La Doctrine des Douze Apôtres
Paris: Cerf, 1978

Safrai, S.
'Synagogue'

'The Synagogue'
The Jewish People in the First Century, Vol. 2,
Safrai, S. and Stern, M. (eds),
Assen/Amsterdam: van Gorcum, 1976,
pp. 908–44

Sanders, E. P.
Jesus

Jesus and Judaism
London: SCM, 1985

Sanders, E. P.
Judaism

Judaism: Practice and Belief
63 BCE — 66 CE
London: SCM, 1992

Sanders, E. P.
Law

Jewish Law from Jesus to the Mishnah
London: SCM, 1990

Schiffman, L. H.
Community

*The Eschatological Community of the Dead
Sea Scrolls*
Atlanta, GA: Scholars, 1989

Schiffman, L. H.
Sectarian

Sectarian Law in the Dead Sea Scrolls
Chico, CA: Scholars, 1983

Schillebeeckx, E.
Church

The Church with a Human Face
London: SCM, 1985

Schnackenburg, R.
Ephesians

The Epistle to the Ephesians
Edinburgh: T&T Clark, 1991

Schnackenburg, R.
'Ephesus'
'Ephesus: Entwicklung einer gemeinde
    von Paulus zu Johannes'
BZ, 35, 1991, pp. 41–64

Schnackenburg, R.
Church
The Church in the New Testament
London: Burns & Oates, 1974

Schneider, G.
Apostelgeschichte
Apostelgeschichte HThKNT V 1/2
Freiburg: Herder, 1982

Schneider, G.
'Zwölf'
'Die Zwölf aks Zeugen'
Lukas, Theologe der Heilsgeschichte
Bonn: Hanstein, 1985, pp. 61–85

Schoedel, W. R.
Ignatius
Ignatius of Antioch
Philadelphia: Fortress, 1985

Schrage, W.
συναγωγή
συναγωγή,
TDNT, VII, pp. 798–839.

Schürer, E.
History
*History of the Jewish people in the Time
    of Jesus Christ*
Edinburgh: T&T Clark, 1885–1924

Schürer, E.
History²
*History of the Jewish people in the Time of
    Jesus Christ*, 2nd Edition
Vermes, G., Millar, F., Black, M. (eds)
Edinburgh: T&T Clark, 1973–87

Schwartz, D.
'Priests'
'The Priests in *Ep. Aristeas* 310'
JBL, 97, 1978, pp. 567–71

Schweizer, E.
Order
Church Order in the New Testament
London: SCM, 1961

Scullard, H. H.
Gracchi
From the Gracchi to Nero
London: Methuen, 1963

Shepherd, M. H. 'Development'	'The Development of the Early Ministry' *ATR* 26, 1944, pp. 135–51
Shepherd, M. H. 'Elder'	'Elder in the New Testament' *IDB* Vol. II, E-J, 1962, pp. 73–5
Sherwin-White, A. N. *Roman Society*	*Roman Society and Roman Law in the New Testament* Oxford: Clarendon, 1963
Shils, E. 'Charisma'	'Charisma, Order, Status' *ASR*, 30, 1965, pp. 199–213
Shutt, R.J.H. *OT Pseudepigrapha*	'Letter of Aristeas. A New Translation and Introduction' *The Old Testament Pseudepigrapha,* Vol. 2, J. H. Charlesworth (ed.), London: Darton, Longman & Todd, 1985, pp. 7–34
Skeat, T. C. 'Parchments'	'Especially the Parchments: a Note on 2 Tim 4:13' *JTS*, 30, 1979, p. 173–7
Sobosan, J. G. 'Role'	'The Role of the Presbyter' *SJT* 27, 1974, pp. 129–46
Soden, H. von ἀδελφός	ἀδελφός *TDNT*, I, pp. 144–6
Sohm, R. *Kirchenrecht*	*Kirchenrecht*, I, Leipzig: Duncker und Humbolt, 1892
Spicq, C. *Pastorals*	*Les Épîtres Pastorales* (4th ed.) Paris: Gabalda, 1969

Stählin, G.
Apostelgeschichte

Apostelgeschichte
Göttingen: Vandenhoeck and Ruprecht,
1962

Stanton, G. N.
Gospel

A Gospel for a New People
Edinburgh: T&T Clark, 1992

Streeter, B. H.
Primitive

The Primitive Church
London: Macmillan, 1929

Stuhlmacher, P.
Philemon

Der Brief on Philemon, EKK,
Zürich: Benziger, 1975.

Talbert, C. H.
Reading John

Reading John
London: SPCK, 1992

Taubenschlag, R.
Law²

*The Law of Graeco-Roman Egypt in the
light of the Papyri* (2nd ed.)
Warsaw, 1955

Taylor, N.
Paul

Paul, Antioch and Jerusalem
Sheffield: JSOT, 1992

Tcherikover, V.
Hellenistic

Hellenistic Civilization and the Jews
New York: Ktav, 1985

Tcherikover, V. &
Fuks, A.
CPJ

Corpus Papyrorum Judaicarum, Vol. 1
Cambridge, MA: 1957

Theissen, G.
Social Setting

The Social Setting of Pauline Christianity
Edinburgh: T&T Clark, 1982

Thiering, B. E.
'Mebaqqer'

'Mebaqqer and Episkopos in the light of
the Temple Scroll'
JBL, 100, 1981, pp. 59–74

Thurston, B. B.
ὑπερῷον

'τὸ ὑπερῷον in Acts 1:13'
ExpTim, 80, 1968, pp. 21–2

Tomsin, A.
'Étude'

'Étude sur les πρεσβύτεροι des Villages
de la χώρα égyptienne'
BAB, XXXVIII, 1952, pp. 95–130, 467–
532.

Trebilco, P. R.
Communities

Jewish Communities in Asia Minor
Cambridge: CUP, 1991

Trummer, P.
Paulustradition

Die Paulustradition in der Pastoralbriefe
Frankfurt: Lang, 1978

Van Tilborg, S.
Leaders

The Jewish Leaders in Matthew
Leiden: Brill, 1972

Vaux, R. de,
Israel

Ancient Israel
London: DLT, 1961, pp. 69–70.

Vermes, G.
DSSE

The Dead Sea Scrolls in English (3rd ed.)
Harmondsworth: Penguin, 1987

Vermas, G.
Jesus²

Jesus the Jew (2nd ed.)
London: SCM, 1983

Verner, D. C.
Household

*The Household of God: the Social World
of the Pastoral Epistles*
Chico, California: Scholars Press, 1983

Vielhauer, P.
'Paulinism'

'On the "Paulinism" of Acts'
Studies in Luke-Acts
Keck, L. E. & Martin, J. L. (eds)
New York: Abingdon, 1966, pp. 33–50

Wace, A. J. B. &
Stubbings, F. H.
Companion

A Companion to Homer
London: Macmillan, 1962

Wachege, P. N.
Ideal

Jesus Christ Our Muthamaki (Ideal Elder)
Nairobi: Phoenix, 1992

Walbank, F. W.
'Monarchies'

'Monarchies and Monarchic Ideas in the
    Hellenistic World'
CAH², VII. 1, 1984, pp. 62–100

Watson, F. B.
Paul

Paul, Judaism and the Gentiles
Cambridge: CUP, 1986

Weber, M.,
Judaism

Ancient Judaism,
Glencoe, Illinois: Free Press, 1952

Weber, M.
Sociology

Sociology of Religion
Boston, Mass: Beacon, 1963

Weber, M.
Theory

*The Theory of Social and Economic Or-
    ganisation*
New York: Glencoe, 1947

Wegner, J. R.
Chattel

Chattel or Person?
Oxford: OUP, 1988

Welborn, L. L.
'Date'

'On the Date of First Clement'
BR, 29, 1984, pp. 35–54

White, L. M.
God's House

Building God's House in the Roman World
Baltimore: John Hopkins U.P., 1990

White, L. M.
'Social Authority'

'Social Authority in the House Church
    Setting and Eph 4:1–16'
ResQ, 29, 1987, pp. 209–28

Wilckens, U.
Römer

Der Brief an die Römer
Köln: Benziger, 1982

Wilson, B. R.
Religion

Religion in Sociological Perspective
Oxford: OUP, 1982

Wilson, B. R.
'Sect'

'An Analysis of Sect Development'
Patterns of Sectarianism
London: Heinemann, 1967, pp. 22–45

Wilson, S. G.
Gentiles

*The Gentiles and the Gentile Mission in
Luke-Acts*
Cambridge: CUP, 1973

Wilson, S. G.
Luke and PE

Luke and the Pastoral Epistles
London: SPCK, 1979

Witherington, B.
Earliest

Women in the Earliest Churches
Cambridge: CUP, 1988

Wolf, C.U.
'Traces'

'Traces of Primitive Democracy in Ancient Israel'
JNES 6, 1947, pp. 98–108

World Council of
Churches
BEM

Baptism, Eucharist and Ministry
Geneva: WCC, 1982

Wright, N. T.
NTPG

*The New Testament and the People of
God*
London: SPCK, 1992

Ziesler, J. A.
Romans

The Letter to the Romans
London: SCM, 1989

Index of Modern Authors

Index of Texts

Hypothetica
7:13   47, 49, 53

Josephus
Antiquities (AJ)
4:223   66
6:312   167
7:27.6   41
8:216.5   41
10:51.1   41
10:91.1   41
11:81.1   41
11:105.4   41
12:108   40
13:45   167
14:7.2   51
19:299-305   48
19:300   46

War (BJ)
1:169   66
2:146   63
2:285, 289   46, 48
2:293-405   29
2:570-1   41
7:44   46, 48

Apion
2:175   47

Life (Vita)
276-303   47-48

DEAD SEA SCROLLS

Damascus Document (CD)
3:21-4:4   55

4:2-3   60, 64
10:4-10   62
13:7-10   58-59, 125, 155
14:6-9   59-60
14:13   59

Community Rule (1QS)
2:19   60
2:20   57
3:13   58
5:2-3   55, 59, 63-64
5:20-23   57
6:3-6   60, 64
6:4   57
6:8   60
6:11-12   58-59
6:14   58
6:19-20   59
8:1   62
9:14   58

Messianic Rule (1QSa)
1:13-15   58
1:23-25   61

War Rule (1QM)
2:1   61
13:1   61

NEW TESTAMENT

Matthew
16:16-9   7
16:21   42

5-10	218	5:2-3	218, 220
		6:1	218
Revelation		12:2	179
4:4	208	20:2	221

Magnesians

OTHER EARLY CHRISTIAN
LITERATURE

3:1	218
6:1	97, 221
7:2	220
8-10	217

1 Clement

1:3	97, 211-212
3:3	211
5:6	178
21:6	97, 211-212
40:2	213
40:5	221
41:2	213
42:4	174, 185, 212
43:1	186, 214
44:2	186, 192
44:3	212
44:4	214
44:5	97, 183, 192, 212
47:6	97, 214, 216
53:4	213
54:1-2	214
54:2	9, 186, 212
57:2	212
63:3	211

Philadelphians

1:1	218
4	220-221
5-9	217
8:2	218
10:1	134, 167

Trallians

3:1	97, 218, 221
7:2	220-221

Smyrneans

6:1	218
7:1	218
8:1	97, 220-222
11:2	167

Letter to Polycarp

1-8	219
7:2	167

Ignatius
Ephesians

2:2	97, 218, 221
3:2	218
4:1-2	218

Polycarp
Philippians

1:1	222

Subject Index